T0367855

Defending the Bible against "Christians"

A study of how the Bible in English came to be and the unlikely sources who challenge its authenticity and translation even today.

MARTIN ROBERTS

WESTBOW
PRESS
A DIVISION OF THOMAS NELSON
& ZONDERVAN

WestBow Press books may be ordered through booksellers or by contacting:

WestBow Press
A Division of Thomas Nelson & Zondervan
1663 Liberty Drive
Bloomington, IN 47403
www.westbowpress.com
1 (866) 928-1240

ISBN: 978-1-4908-2408-6 (sc)
ISBN: 978-1-4908-2410-9 (hc)
ISBN: 978-1-4908-2409-3 (e)

Library of Congress Control Number: 2014901452

Printed in the United States of America.

WestBow Press rev. date: 02/18/2014

Dedication

To my Beloved Wife and Friend Deborah

Your my ever-glowing source of encouragement and
Help in our journey of serving our
Lord Jesus Christ
Together.

Contents

Introduction

Many of you, I hope, reading this publication, if you are a Christian already, will enjoy learning how the word of God that you have in your possession came to be. For those of you who are either still searching for God or are, perhaps, even more skeptical of whether the Bible is truly a divine work, I hope you will quickly come to the realization by the end of our discussion that the Bible is a reliable and trustworthy source to learn about God and how you can gain salvation through Jesus Christ.

I confess, I struggled with the title of this book for some time. I was also concerned if I should inadvertently offend those who are, in fact, true and faithful servants of God, i.e. Christians. But as I discovered from looking at different titles of books I began to realize two things.

One, if I wanted the book to stand out and invite the person to pick it up, versus the hundreds of books in a bookstore or the thousands online, then the title had to be one that wasn't necessarily controversial, but did in fact make a person wonder why I had decided to choose such a title.

The second reason [which I offer no apology for] was to specifically challenge those who may profess to be a Christian but, by their comments or actions, can be seen or indeed are, opposite to how a true Christian conducts themselves.

Then I considered this. I wasn't questioning the comments of an unbeliever for, by default, by their unbelief in God, they cannot surely believe the Bible is the word of God. By this process of elimination and indeed consideration, I finally was at peace with the choice of the title of this book. By the very nature of my inserting the word "Christians" within quotation marks for the title of this work I am suggesting that their speech, teaching, actions or beliefs are, at best, questionable as to being a true follower of Christ. Note, I question but do not judge. I personally felt a deep burning desire far within me to attempt, at the very least, to personally defend the word of God as being truly the authenticated word of Almighty God. As a faithful follower of Jesus Christ I believe God deserves that we should hold His sacred word as the GOLD STANDARD for a Christian to follow and be prepared to defend even on a subject that will perhaps never receive full recognition or agreement. I believe it is incumbent on a Christian to stand firm if they truly believe God wrote the Bible. Any other stance, comment or contradiction of His Holy word is nothing short of suggesting that His word is erroneous but the true Christian knows it is not. Many books have been written about the Bible. This book was not meant to be just another study of the Bible and its origins but rather it became a direct result of an email "conversation" I had with a person who claimed to be a watchman of God. We find the reference of God's watchmen in Ezekiel 33:7-9 which reads, *"So you, son of man, I have made a watchman for the house of Israel. Whenever you hear a word from my mouth, you shall give them warning from me. If I say to the wicked, O wicked one, you shall surely die, and you do not speak to warn the wicked to turn from his way, that wicked person shall die in his iniquity, but his blood I will require at your hand. But if you warn the wicked to turn from his way, and he does not turn from his way, that person shall die in his iniquity, but you will have delivered your soul" (ESV).* The watchmen were charged to keep watch over the house of Israel. Whether this individual's claim is genuine or not is not the subject of this book, nor is it relevant.

My original thought before I wrote this book was to challenge, quite directly, this person's comments, which I will point out later in the book. Suffice to say, this person professes to represent God. Yet, at the same time, they say or promote derisory comments regarding the Bible, or a particular translation. This is surely contrary to being a Christian. It became apparent from this person's comments that if a Christian is not using the same version or translation of the Bible that this person insists upon (and this appeared to be the King James Version), then in this person's view a Christian is not following God's word correctly. How absurd!

My personal comments for these so-called Christians are not for these pages, but I do hold strong opinions and believe wholly on the words of Jesus in Matthew 18:6-7 which reads, *"If anyone causes one of these little ones—those who believe in me—to stumble, it would be better for them to have a large millstone hung around their neck and to be drowned in the depths of the sea. Woe to the world because of the things that cause people to stumble! Such things must come, but woe to the person through whom they come!" (NIV).*

Jesus went on to say in Matthew 18:8-9 what one should do with such things that cause a person to stumble.

Neither am I targeting the King James Version as a version or translation that does not hold merit, for I believe it does. To those who question translations other than the King James Version (which many Christians use in their teaching and ministry) I would suggest they carefully research how the King James Version came to be. This, in itself, would or should dispel any arguments that this version alone should be regarded as the ultimate authority over other versions or translations.

No attempt is made to suggest or promote any one version or translation but rather to establish that whatever version or translation a Christian uses to quote, preach, study or reference, is first, and always will be, the word of God, and second, is the readers personal choice and conviction.

Neither is it my right to judge why so-called Christians would say such a thing, but it is every Christian's right to defend the word of God and this publication sets out to do just that.

We are reminded in scripture that **"God breathed His word"** and the culmination of that was a collection of 66 books written by over 40 people.

The Christian should expect unbelievers to question the validity of God's word due to the blindness that Satan the devil has placed upon those who do not believe. But it is a totally different view and perspective hearing those who supposedly worship God Almighty but outwardly vilify good Christians who use a variety of Bible versions and translations in their teachings or private study.

Jesus warned of false prophets and those who would say they represent Him but by their actions or words they do not. He also prophesied what would be their end. Therefore, we should not be surprised when we are faced with challenges from a direction we would least expect.

The devil will stop at nothing to attempt to confuse and deride the true workings of God.

We have numerous examples in the Bible in the Old and New Testament of men and women of faith who believed in God and His promises yet faced many challenges which were written for our instruction today. This was so we may see the workings of God and remain faithful servants of our Lord Jesus Christ.

I hope you will continue to make it your goal to read God's word daily for its instruction and teachings to assist you in staying on the straight and narrow path to eternal life. I hope you will find enjoyment as I have, in consulting several Bible versions and translations in order to get the full meat of God's word. By reading from several translations, the word of God can expand our understanding of the scripture.

As you read this book you will come across many instances of persecution, murder, intrigue, spies, skullduggery and the like. All of these things we must separate from the word of God. It was sinful man, not God, that attempted to block access and alter scripture. This was for their own means or that of the denomination they supported. They will ultimately pay the price for their wrongdoing. I must also warn you, that you will read many atrocities, ordered in the name of religion, that can easily color a person's judgment as to those who ordered such. Some reading may be hard for you to accept, especially if you share the same faith as those who committed such things. While it is easy to fall into judging such actions and be offended by such, I would suggest we should free ourselves of such thoughts. It would be easy for the reader to condemn or alternatively defend such actions based on one's own doctrine or faith, affiliation or denomination. That is not my intention of either thought or action. In fact I do not suggest any such demand of the reader to choose sides, for the only side a person should find themselves on is God's. Rather, I hope you will see the unbiased position I have at least attempted to present in this book with regard to the terrible actions conducted by both Catholic and Protestant Reformers. Neither is guiltless and neither can defend their actions in what has occurred. But occur they did, which only proves that the devil will stop at nothing, including the influence of men, to alter what God has spoken. We can rest assured that the devil, and all those he has used, have and continue to fail. God will not allow his word to be altered or tarnished.

This book evolved into a work far removed from what caused me to embark on this journey in the first place. The information it contains was not even in my original thoughts for its content but as one piece of research led to another it became for me at least, a fascination and love of how God has ensured His word has remained intact over 3450 years. Even more interesting is that many people argue that if the Bible was copied over all this time it must surely have errors. I would point out that if we consider the year zero [0] as being the start of mankind then consider when Moses was born [sometime between 1500 – 1391 BCE as some suggest] then logically many of the events that happened in Genesis occurred well before Moses was born. Therefore, as he is identified as the writer of the first five books of the Old Testament [the Pentateuch] then he would most certainly have had to rely upon testimony from Adam and Eve or their direct offspring to record the events. This generally is neither thought of nor questioned. But there is a preponderance of argument in our present day of challenging the Bible and its authenticity.

These, and many arguments the unbelievers (the so called scholars, and false teachers) will continue to maintain as reasons not to trust the word of God as authentic. I dare say that when you conclude the reading of this book you will at least be more equipped with information, both with reasoning and facts, as well as historical, documentation. That, along with a Christians unseen faith, provides the light of God's word to shine forth through the Holy Spirit to those who choose God and the salvation He has provided through His precious son Jesus Christ.

We who remain faithful to God's word, no matter what choice of version or translation, epitomize the words of Paul in 2 Timothy 3:16-17 where he wrote, ***"There's nothing like the written Word of God for showing you the way to salvation through faith in Christ Jesus. Every part of Scripture is God-breathed and useful one way or another—showing us truth, exposing our rebellion, correcting our mistakes, training us to live God's way. Through the Word we are put together and shaped up for the tasks God has for us"*** *(The Message Bible)*.

Martin Roberts 2014

"If God spare my life, ere many yeares I wyl cause a boy that driveth the plough to know more of the Scripture, than he doust"

William Tyndale (c. 1494-1536)

~~~~~~

THE BIBLE

"This book had to be written by one of three people: good men, bad men or God. It couldn't have been written by good men because they said it was inspired by the revelation of God. Good men don't lie and deceive. It couldn't have been written by bad men because bad men would not write something that would condemn themselves. It leaves only one conclusion. It was given by divine inspiration of God."

John Wesley (1703-1791)

"The BIBLE -- banned, burned, beloved. More widely read, more frequently attacked than any other book in history. Generations of intellectuals have attempted to discredit it, dictators of every age have outlawed it and executed those who read it. Yet soldiers carry it into battle believing it more powerful than their weapons. Fragments of it smuggled into solitary prison cells have transformed ruthless killers into gentle saints"

Charles "Chuck" Wendell Colson (1931-2012)

CHAPTER 1

The History of Translation of the Bible

Erasmus, Wycliffe, Luther, Tyndale and many more are instantly recognizable names of men who blazed a trail in translating the Bible into the language of the people.

For centuries, the 'common people' were told, even commanded, that they could not own, let alone read, the Bible, which for the majority was something that was out of their reach for several reasons.

Some of those reasons were simply they could not read or write. Another was until the Bible was able to be mass produced by printing, the cost of owning a handwritten Bible was something that the majority of folk could not afford. But without question the predominant reason a person did not, nor could not, own a Bible, was simply the spiritual and secular authorities of the day insisted that the Bible was to be read only by Bishops, Priests etc. and then, only in Latin.

Under penalty of death (generally burning at the stake) brave men and women decided to make a stand for God and His word. A reading of John Foxe's Christian Martyr's will leave an indelible mark on anyone's memory of the terror and sheer illegal acts carried out by clergy who claimed to follow God but who were only interested in looking after their own positions of power and authority, or worse, the wage they received from their religious order. How they will explain their atrocities in front of the Almighty on the Day of Judgment can only be imagined but not understood.

But with regard to these brave martyrs, what compelled them to give up their lives if necessary to ensure the Bible was read by all in their common language?

How were those who could not read or write (and literally had to rely upon the priests) impacted by their reliance?

Many of the so-called spiritual leaders were not versed that well in scripture themselves and only held office to receive payment for a position they were ill equipped for, or worse, not capable of performing.

When John Hooper (1495-1555) became Bishop of Gloucester in 1551 he discovered that half of the 331 of his clergy within the diocese could not repeat the Ten Commandments. Forty of these so-called leaders of the people could not even recite the Lord's Prayer in English. [1]

Despite this lack of scriptural knowledge, unquestioning obedience to the church was demanded with excommunication being threatened to anyone who refused.

Many of our ancestors would have been ordered to attend church under threat of arrest and also ordered to tithe to the church irrespective of their financial ability.

I contemplated this very thought of my own ancestors whom I have so far traced back to living in a tiny hamlet on the English/Welsh border and who likely faced such demands. I found myself wondering if they faced demands from the local priest and if he perhaps commanded my family members to attend church and to tithe, irrespective whether or not they had the means to either get to church, or the finances to fund their contributions. In my particular ancestors case I fear they may have been challenged by both, for there are no records of any of them being of stable means. The thoughts of the head of the house telling his wife and children they were to be at church and scraping the few coins they had together, whether they were spare or needed for food, were irrelevant to these priests. For they were not ordering tithes based on the commandments of God or for the benefit of the church nor to support the town folk. Rather they lined their pockets with the money and lived very comfortable lives. Their lives in fact were contrary to scripture, some giving of themselves to every lawless act and debauchery. One of the most hypocritical acts by many of the priests [these also certainly included Monks, Friars, Deacons and Bishops] was concerning celibacy. They outwardly and unashamedly took women for themselves for sexual gratification without any promise of marriage, but rather as 'concubines' as if by some magic using the ancient Biblical term meant they were somehow justified.

This then was the "norm" for our ancestors. To do or say anything contrary was considered a sin against church and God, and the only way to save one's soul was to give the priests money to pay for 'indulgences'. Indulgences were a particularly nasty and disgusting form of offering which the priest would suggest should be given for forgiveness of sins. They claimed the more money a person paid them, the more sins would be forgiven, including the sins of their dead loved ones. This was a particularly evil way to extract money out of the people in their care. Believing they could save their dead loved ones from purgatory or worse, hellfire, people willingly paid for indulgences and were oblivious to the evil wrongdoing of the priests. One cannot begin to imagine the horror these workers of Satan put upon the lives of people. For their part, many could not read or write, which the priests knew only too well. The people were easy prey. In researching for the contents of this book this [and many other lies] haunted my thoughts as to how many good people feared for their souls, only to be told to pay more money to gain salvation. They neither had the means nor the intellect to know any better. All of this in the name of religion. It wasn't based on any scripture. It never has been based on any scripture. These vipers of Satan went on their daily course of falsehood knowing full well it was all about how much money they could extract from their poor itinerant flock.

This, and many other false teachings, continued on for several centuries while those claiming they were the true teachers of scriptures hid God's written word away from the masses. Like an innocent man locked away for his entire life, generations of families lived and died not knowing or being aware of what the Bible contained.

It should be noted at this point that in the early church to the Middle Ages there was perhaps three occupations that led one to financial security. One was to be a fine scholar. Another was to study the law. And the final one was that of a theologian. All of these for the majority of the populace were beyond their means, but for those who had the good fortune of being born into a family that had some kind of wealth or public station it meant a life of secure financial means and status, as long as you did as you were told by those above you. One immediately knew who belonged to the elite group of educated men. They dressed well, and spoke a language that few knew or could recognize but for a few words. Latin was that language that had flowed from the times of the Roman Empire through, to, and including the early church and eventually what would become Roman Catholicism.

Erasmus admitted that he followed the Pope and the Emperor when they did well because it was the safest thing to do. He even suggested that bearing or accepting the bad decisions both rulers made was also something he accepted, in order to remain out of the limelight.

To question the religious authorities of the day was something many probably wanted to do, but were likely afraid of doing or simply could not, due to their intellect or position in life.

God put in the hearts of the martyrs mentioned in this and many other works, the light that grew ever stronger in order to bring out into the open the word of God so that the common people could be fed by His word.

Today, the Bible is accessible to virtually everyone. It is the world's most widely translated book, available in over 1000 languages and dialects.

In the era known as the Dark Ages or Medieval Times, the situation was far different. The Bible was in fact not available anywhere in Western Europe.

The Old Testament was for the most part only available in Hebrew, in a Greek translation [known as the Septuagint], and in a Latin translation [called the Latin Vulgate].

As far as the New Testament was concerned, this was only available in Greek and in the Latin Vulgate.

As a result only scholars and educated clergy, along with a few others, had any direct personal access to God's Word.

Translations in the second to fifth centuries were written in Armenian, Coptic, Ethiopic, Georgian, Gothic, and Syriac, but these languages for the most part were not known nor understood by the majority of Europeans.

In order for us to establish credibility that the Word of God is inspired, we have to go back as far as one is allowed. We have to consult actual records, to establish what, if any, variation could question the validity of God's authorship. It's a road that can seem rocky at times but the reader is encouraged to read with an open mind. We should pay close attention to what the Almighty God tells each and every one of us in Isaiah 55:8-11 that, *"I don't think the way you think. The way you work isn't the way I work." God's Decree. "For as the sky soars high above earth, so the way I work surpasses the way you work, and the way I think is beyond the way you think. Just as rain and snow descend from the skies and don't go back until they've watered the earth, Doing their work of making things grow and blossom, producing seed for farmers and food for the hungry, So will the words that come out of my mouth not come back empty-handed. They'll do the work I sent them to do, they'll complete the assignment I gave them"* (MSG).

Again, I have chosen to use the Message Bible translation for this scripture in Isaiah and I offer no apology to those who choose to believe that a person should quote a certain Bible. I will certainly make mention later in this book of translations that could be questionable and the reasons I can confidently say this is because in certain translations there has been attempts to twist or worse, omit, scripture. But this isn't some new phenomenon. This happened as early as the 3rd century with regard to the Latin Vulgate by Jerome. Rather we should do like the Jews in Berea did which Paul writes about in Acts 17:10-11. It reads, ***"Then the brethren immediately sent Paul and Silas away by night to Berea. When they arrived, they went into the synagogue of the Jews. These were more fair-minded than those in Thessalonica, in that they received the word with all readiness, and searched the Scriptures daily to find out whether these things were so" (NKJV).***

If you read further to verse 15 you will see that other so called believers from Thessalonica came to Berea to stir up trouble and cause derision in the church. Therefore, we should not be troubled by what people may say about the Bible for it is the irrefutable word of God. God does not change. God cannot change. Neither can His word, for they are His words that He has spoken.

The Christian accepts and believes that the Bible available today is indeed the inspired word of God without question. This, in fact, is a huge statement. The acceptance of a Christian's faith is that what they know as the Bible today is what God determined to be written. They believe, however many times copied or translated, the Bible is what God said, as if He were talking directly to them.

Sadly, there are many more that reject the Bible as God's inspired word. Rather than believe in a Divine Creator many reject any content of the Bible. A continual argument is that the Bible we have today is not the original transcript and mere men wrote it, so it must have changed over time.

Here I must state the obvious. The Bible IS the inspired word of God. To put it more plainly, what God inspired the writers of the 66 books (that make up the Bible as we know it today) was dictated by God to those writers as testified by 2 Timothy 3:16.

Translations are not inspired by God. If they were, then human errors (that have been discovered) would not have been in the said translation. Translations that are created to support a denominational sect, or based only on one gender, clearly are not the work of inspiration of God.

God warned us of such corruption in many scriptures. Let us consult several now to illustrate this point. In the 31st chapter of Deuteronomy Moses was nearing the end of his life and he gave several warnings of corruption. In Deuteronomy 31:24-29 it reads, ***"After Moses finished writing in a book the words of this law from beginning to end, he gave this command to the Levites who carried the ark of the covenant of the Lord: "Take this Book of the Law and place it beside the ark of the covenant of the Lord your God. There it will remain as a witness against you. For I know how rebellious and stiff-necked you are. If you have been rebellious against the Lord while I am still alive and with you, how much more will you rebel after I die! Assemble before me all the elders of your tribes and all your officials, so that I can speak these words in their hearing and call the heavens and the earth to testify against them. For I know that after my death you are sure to become utterly corrupt and to turn from the way I have commanded you. In days to come, disaster will fall on you because you will do evil in the sight of the Lord and arouse his anger by what your hands have made" (NIV).***

Jeremiah declared God's condemnation of the Israelite nation and warned them to change from their wicked ways to no avail. In Jeremiah 8:8 we see the corruption of scribes where we read, ***"How can you say, We are wise, and we have the written law of the Lord [and are learned in its language and teachings]? Behold, the truth is, the lying pen of the scribes has made of the law a falsehood (a mere code of ceremonial observances)" (AMP).***

The Apostle Paul wrote extensively on the subject of false teaching and corruption. In Galatians 1:6-9 he makes his point clear, ***"I can't believe your fickleness—how easily you have turned traitor to him who called you by the grace of Christ by embracing a variant message! It is not a minor variation, you know; it is completely other, an alien message, a no-message, a lie about God. Those who are provoking this agitation among you are turning the Message of Christ on its head. Let me be blunt: If one of us—even if an angel from heaven!—were to preach something other than what we preached originally, let him be cursed. I said it once; I'll say it again: If anyone, regardless of reputation or credentials, preaches something other than what you received originally, let him be cursed" (MSG).***

Paul was clear why we would see such falsehood and where it came from. He also warns what would happen to those supporting it. In 2 Corinthians 11:12-15 he wrote, ***"And what I am doing I will continue to do, in order to undermine the claim of those who would like to claim that in their boasted mission they work on the same terms as we do. For such men are false apostles, deceitful workmen, disguising themselves as apostles of Christ. And no wonder, for*** *even Satan disguises himself as an angel of light. So it is no surprise if his servants, also, disguise themselves as servants of righteousness. Their end will correspond to their deeds"* (ESV).

Notice how Paul gives us guidance in 1 Thessalonians 5:19-22, *"Don't suppress the Spirit, and don't stifle those who have a word from the Master. On the other hand, don't be gullible. Check out everything, and keep only what's good. Throw out anything tainted with evil. May God himself, the God who makes everything holy and whole, make you holy and whole, put you together—spirit, soul, and body—and keep you fit for the coming of our Master, Jesus Christ. The One who called you is completely dependable. If he said it, he'll do it!"* (MSG).

The Apostle Peter was not silent on this subject either. Like Paul he warned Christians in 2 Peter 2:1-3 saying, *"But false prophets also arose among the people, just as there will also be false teachers among you, who will secretly introduce destructive heresies, even denying the Master who bought them, bringing swift destruction upon themselves. Many will follow their sensuality, and because of them the way of the truth will be maligned; and in their greed they will exploit you with false words; their judgment from long ago is not idle, and their destruction is not asleep"* (NASB).

I shared these scriptures not to suggest the scriptures are corrupted for we know they are not. Rather, I make mention of them from both the Old and the New Testament that corruption did occur. Paul and Peter confirmed such falsehood will continue because Satan will stop at nothing in order to deceive man. As the Bible is God's book of direction for our lives, we should not be surprised that Satan will directly attack it and attempt to either falsify or discredit it.

But let me suggest this point as a standing statement in defense of God's inspired word. The scrolls [that made up the Bible canon] within the temple were not to be altered. Any alteration meant a person was to be put to death.

So why, centuries later, did the papal authorities hide it from the majority of the people and not allow them to see or read it?

What would those same authorities have had to fear if what was said in the Bible could change a person's life and bring them into a relationship with God?

It never had to be hidden, unless of course these same authorities knew they themselves had corrupted it.

On the contrary, the fact that the papal authorities lied, twisted, and did alter many words in order to fulfill their sinful, corrupted acts meant they were working not for God, but for the devil.

But shining lights, some of which were of their own faith, soon recognized the errors and many paid with their earthly lives by speaking out and translating the pure scriptures so that the people could feed on God's word, the Bible, as intended.

You see, when we read this, we should not be shocked. The Bible records for us the fall and sin of man and who has always been behind it. The despot Satan will continue to attempt to influence men right up to the very last second he can until Christ finally chains him in the abyss, and eventually throws him into the fire of eternal punishment.

We could think it folly on his part [and it was] that Satan's pride even extended to him believing he could tempt Jesus. He failed miserably. But have you ever thought this? The man Jesus was proving that we as men and women have that same capacity to cause Satan to fail. In fact God promises as much. He told us in 1 Corinthians 10:13 saying, *"**For no temptation (no trial regarded as enticing to sin), [no matter how it comes or where it leads] has overtaken you and laid hold on you that is not common to man [that is, no temptation or trial has come to you that is beyond human resistance and that is not adjusted and adapted and belonging to human experience, and such as man can bear]. But God is faithful [to His Word and to His compassionate nature], and He [can be trusted] not to let you be tempted and tried and assayed beyond your ability and strength of resistance and power to endure, but with the temptation He will [always] also provide the way out (the means of escape to a landing place), that you may be capable and strong and powerful to bear up under it patiently"** (AMP).*

I purposely chose the Amplified Bible for this scripture we just read because of the explanation it gives of how protected we are under God if we obey his commands.

The most tragic comment (and a core reason for the origin of this book) that I personally have read and heard is for those who profess to be "Christian" call a Bible translation "corrupted".

Some of these "Christians" are church leaders, so-called watchmen, who have the audacity to say God's written word is corrupted because they personally hold a viewpoint as to the use of a specific Bible translation.

They remind me of the same men who were quick to burn true Christians at the stake who simply wanted to provide God's word in a language the common people could understand.

To be fair to these critics of new versions and translations of the Bible I will address many of their points and let the reader decide for themselves where they stand on such issues. Whether critics or others make the determination if the comments found in these pages should be accepted or rejected is of no consequence as far as I am concerned, for God will be their judge and mine also. I do believe when a true Christian reads or hears someone who claims to follow Christ say a certain Bible is corrupted, then they should not stand by and allow [or accept] that comment to go without defense or answer. That said, everyone must act upon their own conscience. I will concede, we will discuss some translations that are certainly dubious, to say the least, and I would personally recommend a person avoid such translations. In fact these translations [that I will cover] are not true translations but fabricated to induce false teachings to support a person's denomination or social beliefs. More of that later.

The intention of this book is not to suggest any one Bible should be considered as 'the' Bible to use in our ministry or worship, but rather to investigate and clarify that whatever the Bible version or translation used, it is still, and remains, the infallible word of God.

It is a fact that the original Bible text is no longer available or in existence. All we have are copies of the original text with many of those created centuries later.

So, how far can we go back to see the Bible's accuracy?

Until the discovery of the Qumran Scrolls better known as the Dead Sea Scrolls, the earliest Hebrew biblical manuscripts were from the ninth century AD.

The Qumran manuscripts have been dated to various ranges between 408 BCE and 318 AD. Additional timelines consist of bronze coins found on the site that contained series beginning with John Hyrcanus (135-104 BCE) and continuing until the First Jewish-Roman War (66–73 CE).

The find was formidable for Bible scholars as no fewer than 972 texts were found.

Before the Dead Sea Scrolls were discovered Bible scholars had to rely on the extant manuscripts of the Masoretic Text which only represented the Old Testament in Hebrew. Very few [complete] documents dating from the 9th century AD were found. Documents dating from the 10th – 11th century AD do however, contain complete texts.

There are those who would criticize this work with regard to the accuracy of the Hebrew texts. I will address this now before we go on.

There are some who will say that the Masoretic Text was written by Jews who rejected Jesus, and that Jesus was teaching from the Greek Septuagint. Some comments are correct as to the Jews rejecting Jesus but they omit that Jesus and His family were devout Jews and as such, He would have been brought up to learn the Old Testament, which was in Hebrew. We know the Hebrew language and text of the 1st century AD differed to that of the Hebrew language and text of the 9th – 11th centuries AD. However, to suggest that the Masoretic Text was corrupted by Jews who wanted to eradicate the teachings of Christians is somewhat mute by the fact that Jesus lived in a multicultural/multilingual society. He conversed with a Centurion and also Pontius Pilate neither are likely to have spoken Hebrew but most likely spoke Greek. We can therefore conclude that Jesus was likely to have spoken Hebrew and Greek and possibly Latin, as well as knowing Aramaic. On a faith based point, would it be hard for the Son of God to have read, spoken or written any language of His choosing when he created all in the first place? Of course not.

The account in Luke 2:39-47 tells us that the 12 year old Jesus was sitting in the Temple discussing the teachings of God. This for a devout Jewish boy would have no doubt been the Torah [God's law] and the texts in the Bible [Old Testament] which would have been in Hebrew. Therefore Jesus would have been conversing in Hebrew. Further evidence of this is Luke 4:16-17a where we read, **"So He came to Nazareth, where He had been brought up. And as His custom was, He went into the synagogue on the Sabbath day, and stood up to read. And He was handed the book of the prophet Isaiah" (NKJV).**

Furthermore, we read in the 26th chapter of Acts the account of Paul on the road to Damascus. Paul meets Jesus who questions him and charges him to become His apostle to the Gentiles. But notice what Acts 26:14 says, **"And when we all had fallen to the ground, I heard a voice speaking to me and saying in the <u>Hebrew</u> language, 'Saul, Saul, why are you persecuting Me?" (NKJV)** [Underline mine].

Isn't it amazing that so called scholars choose to issue their rhetoric against the accuracy of translation when if they only read scripture the answer is there all the time!

Moving on, the Masoretic Text is the authoritative Hebrew text of the Jewish Bible. It is also widely used as the basis for translation of the Old Testament in Protestant Bibles and some Catholic Bibles.

Of note, is that the Masoretic Text has shown to be near identical to the Tanakh (Hebrew Bible) as shown by the Dead Sea Scrolls.

The Talmud confirms that a standard copy of the Hebrew Bible was to remain in the court of the Temple in Jerusalem in order for copyists to review. These copyists were paid correctors of the Biblical books. We have independent references to these copies from at least three historical writings.

Primarily the Masoretic Text was written by a group of Jews called the Masoretes between the 7th – 10th centuries CE.

The Aleppo Codex (once the oldest complete copy of the Masoretic Text) dates from the 10th century. We will discuss several Codex manuscripts in chapter 3 and their significance as to Bible translation for us today.

Very few manuscripts are said to have survived during the destruction of Jerusalem in 70 AD. This means that the number of variants in circulation was drastically reduced, but it also created an urgency to preserve those that were. New Greek translations were also made. However, unlike the Septuagint, large scale deviations in sense [in this case by reason or direction], between the Greek and what we now know of the Masoretic Text were minimal. There are variations between different Hebrew texts but most of these variations are limited to things such as particular vowel sound as to whether it should or should not be used at a particular point. Despite any disagreement on this, one fact remains. There is NO difference in meaning.

The Masoretes School of scribes achieved prominence through their reputation of their work being highly accurate and employing error control during and through their editing techniques. This allowed them to establish their authority beyond all others with regard to accurate recordings of text.

Considerable influence was exercised on the development and spread of Masoretic literature from the 11th – 13th centuries.

Copyists for the Masoretic Text were paid for their work according to the number of stichs [lines of verse]. Because the prose books of the Bible were not, or hardly ever, written in stichs, in order to estimate the amount of work done the copyist had to count the letters.

For the Masoretic Text this proved statistically significant, ensuring accuracy in the transmission of the text with additional copies done by hand. But beyond just counting letters there were word-use statistics also employed and similar documentation relating to expressions, phraseology etc.

These observations all made up for the Masoretic Text to be the result of a passionate zeal to safeguard the accurate transmission of the sacred text.

In what is called the rabbinic period, if a single letter deviated from the Torah scroll it immediately made the writing of the copyist invalid. This was how strict and accurate the work of the copyists were and the Masoretes were known and recognized as the masters of copying the manuscripts to create a pure translation. They were the authoritive body beyond any other group during this time period.

It is true there were some differences. But the differences were local differences in terms of pronunciation. Different Masoretic schools had differing geographical locations and they would prepare their codices following one school or another, each examining each other's text for variation and noting any differences. This reminds me of the scene you will read in the chapter, 'The King James Version' later in this book. The scene is of the appointment of theologians/scholars by King James I of England in preparation for the translation of the King James Bible (KJV). Six committees of scholars were appointed and when the work of translation was finished each committee would inspect the other's work for accuracy etc.

As we noted earlier, the Torah scroll was so sacred it could only contain the Hebrew consonant text. Nothing was to be added and nothing could be removed. What could and did occur with reference to the Masoretic codices was the ability or permission if you will, for works that were perhaps considered for personal study which could include additional material. These became known as the Masorah magna [large] and the Masorah parva [smaller]. Here, the copyist could show correct pronunciation and cantillation [to chant or recite] as well as to protect scribes errors and even suggest potential variants. As a result, the manuscripts eventually included varying degrees of accents with regard to the text, marks for pronunciation, brief annotations in the margins and vowel points. Larger annotations were subject to being written at the end of each book.

What did all this mean if the Torah could not be altered?

Remember we are discussing the document that was considered a personal copy for private study rather than the ritualistic form of a Torah scroll being altered or marked in any way. But the fact we have these documents which have differences tells us two things.

1. It confirms that scribes were actively translating the scriptures in such a way as to provide better understanding of the text.
2. The differences were made up primarily of pronunciation, phraseology and observations of word-use statistics.

All the time, these copyists were passionately safeguarding the accurate transmission of the sacred text. All they were guilty of [if indeed we should even use the word guilty] was their desire to ensure the reader understood the word of God fully. They were, in effect, the early versions of the proof reader we know of today.

Any comments or corrections made by the scribe were to be collated or written at the end of the Biblical books. They contained statistical information with regard to word count as well as the aforementioned improvements for understanding the text. One should remember these scribes were living in a time period of great differences and emerging languages. This evidently made them fully aware that it was important that their work be an accurate rendering of the scriptures, but one that the common people could read and understand in their own tongue. This fact should not be lost to modern translators today and it most certainly should have been clear to translators in centuries past.

One significant point regarding the Masoretic notes we have just mentioned is the detail of the Kethiv-Qere (Kethiv "[what is] written") (Qere "[what is] read") is part of the Masorah parva. Given the fact that the Masoretes would in no way alter the sacred text, the Kethiv-Qere provided a way of commenting and/or correcting the text for a variety of reasons that were considered sufficiently important for the copyist to make mention of.

Ultimately, the Masoretes were passionate and insistent of not altering the meaning of the sacred text. Their emendations [the process of making a revision or correction to a text] can be categorize into four main types.

1. They removed expressions that were not appropriate in reference to God.
2. They ensured the safety of the Tetragrammaton. [The tetragrammaton (from Greek τετραγράμματον, meaning "four letters") is the Hebrew theonym יהוה, commonly transliterated into Latin letters as YHWH. It is one of the names of the God of Israel used in the Hebrew Bible. While YHWH is the most common transliteration of the tetragrammaton in English academic studies, the alternatives YHVH, JHVH and JHWH are also used].
3. They removed the application in reference to pagan gods.
4. They ensured the unity and safety of the divine worship at Jerusalem.

If you will notice, all four points are in reference to protection, not alteration.

Much of these early works of translations have filtered through to the translations many of us own today. Jacob ben Hayyim ben Isaac ibn Adonijah (c.1470-c.1538) was one such Masoretic scholar of textual notes on the Hebrew Bible, and a printer. Eventually settling in Venice he worked as a corrector of the Hebrew press of Daniel Bomberg (died 1549). Jacob later embraced Christianity and he is remembered primarily for his edition of the Rabbinical Bible (1524–25). This edition was in fact one of the source texts used by the translators of the King

James Version of 1611 as well as the New King James Version in 1982.

We will delve into more manuscripts in other chapters that will attempt to cross reference why so many of these documents were written and what significance they play in regard to the Bible's accuracy and proof of being the word of God.

We will also discuss why we need new translations (chapter 10) and the historical records of writings of almost 500 years ago and why, through the movement of time it was felt necessary to continue writing more versions and translations right up to this day.

At the core of our discussion a person needs to ask the following question:

Do I believe the Bible to be the inspired word of God?

If we answer yes to this question then we accept without question that the Bible is God's word and that He is the author of all its contents.

To believe this we must have a living faith, for Satan will try and put doubt into a believer's mind and will use an array of ways in which to fulfill his purpose, which is to stumble mankind. He is a liar and the father of the lie and he will fabricate evidence to try and make it look as though he can prove what he says.

The following chapters do recognize that of the vast array of manuscripts available, many do have differences between them. Some of those differences appear to be startling but by study and research we will show that any differences mentioned were not of content but of style, grammar and punctuation. Meaning of scriptures remained intact.

I'm reminded that we all believe in the Constitution of the United States signed by congress in 1776. Many of us will defend this document with the utmost vigor and strength. Another document of high importance, similar to the Constitution of the United States is the Magna Carta (Latin for Great Charter) which was originally issued in 1215. The Magna Carta was forced upon King John of England by a group of his subjects, the feudal barons, in an attempt to limit his powers by law and protect their privileges. The Magna Carta had no signatories but rather the King's seal. Like the Constitution of the United States, the Magna Carta likewise has remained the law of the land ever since. Both of these documents were written centuries before anyone of us were born but we accept the content that is in them. In fact both the US and the British government respectfully accept and adhere to both documents as being the rule of law for their respective countries.

I find myself asking the question, if entire government's rule of law is based on a few pages written by mere mortals, then why is it so hard to accept and believe that God wrote the Bible?

The weight of real evidence (not fabricated) is abundant. Paul wrote in Hebrews 4:12, ***"For the Word that God speaks is alive and full of power [making it active, operative, energizing, and effective]; it is sharper than any two-edged sword, penetrating to the dividing line of the breath of life (soul) and [the immortal] spirit, and of joints and marrow [of the deepest parts of our nature], exposing and sifting and analyzing and judging the very thoughts and purposes of the heart" (AMP).***

I mention this scripture for several reasons but one specific reason. The Bible, God's word, is alive and active. How do I know this? One answer is belief, but for those who don't believe, let me just base my reasoning on fact.

There are approximately 26 other religious books that people of faith believe have divine inspiration. I am not going to name them here so as to avoid offense to another person's faith. Suffice to say that of the aforementioned number, not one of them contain any specific fulfillment of prophecy.

In contrast, the Bible is filled with hundreds of detailed and specific prophecies many of which were written centuries before their fulfillment.

One significant Old Testament passage that identifies Jesus as the Messiah and that he died for our sins is mentioned in one of my previous books, "Front and Center". That book is Psalms and the twenty second chapter. When the reader inspects this chapter of Psalm and compares it with the Gospel account in Matthew chapter 27 there is undisputable proof of prophecy being fulfilled regarding Jesus, 1000 years before he was born and several hundred years before crucifixion was even invented! Read both passages and you will be amazed that it is actually word for word scripture [specifically Psalm 22:1 – Matthew 27:46].

I know of no book that does this and I would submit, neither do you!

I would encourage you to do this little exercise. If you have access to the New King James Version Bible (NKJV) giant print, center column reference edition by Thomas Nelson Bibles, in the front of the publication it mentions the use of Messianic stars. Here is what it says regarding these symbols.

"Throughout the Bible the use of a star has been used next to the verse to denote Messianic prophecy. An Outline Star "☆" indicates that the text contains a prophecy that at the time of the action had yet to be fulfilled. A Solid Star "★" indicates that the text contains the fulfillment of a prophecy".

Amazingly, many of these "stars" you will find dotted all over the Old Testament as well as the New Testament, revealing prophecies that were foretold centuries, sometime millennia beforehand.

The writers did not predict vague things as in the examples of Nostradamus, but they foretold prophecies with pinpoint accuracy not because they knew, but because God told them what to write through inspiration.

While archaeological evidence does not prove divine inspiration, it can prove the truthfulness of the Bible.

Professor Donald Wiseman (1918-2010) was a Biblical scholar, archaeologist and Assyriologist who devoted his life to ancient discoveries. In 1958 he wrote a paper entitled "Archaeological Confirmation of the Old Testament". At the time of this paper Professor Wiseman estimated that there were more than 25,000 discoveries that confirmed the truthfulness of the Bible. [2]

But let us go further than anything we have mentioned so far.

Let us assume we did not have the more than 25,000 fragments or intact handwritten manuscripts, or the copies of the Old Testament, some of which pre-date the time of Christ.

Can we still prove divine inspiration while not having the 'evidence' of actual manuscripts?

Indeed we can.

The early church leaders or 'fathers' and scholars as we may call them during the first three centuries, following the original disciples of Christ, wrote extensively.

Men such as Eusebius, Martyr, Polycarp and Tertullian, to name a few, wrote and corresponded with each other and sent letters to their respective churches similar to what the Apostle Paul did.

Interestingly, in these letters both the Old and the New Testament are quoted. In fact, with regard to the New Testament, it is said that no fewer than 85,000 times scriptures are quoted collectively between them all. [3]

So much is recorded for us by these early writers that if all we had to rely on for scripture was what was contained in their letters scholars could reconstruct most of the New Testament from these writings.

Jesus said in Matthew 24:35 that, ***"Heaven and earth will pass away, but my words will never pass away" (NIV).***

The Message Bible puts it this way, ***"Sky and earth will wear out; my words won't wear out" (MSG).***

No. We can be confident that what the prophet Isaiah was instructed by God to write in Isaiah 55:10-11 was proof of His divine word. We quoted it earlier, but it is certainly worth reminding us of His word again.

"For as the rain comes down, and the snow from heaven, And do not return there, But water the earth, And make it bring forth and bud, That it may give seed to the sower And bread to the eater, So shall My word be that goes forth from My mouth; It shall not return to Me void, But it shall accomplish

what I please, And it shall prosper in the thing for which I sent it" (NKJV).

As you continue reading I hope you will prosper in the knowledge that the Bible [whatever translation or version] you possess or prefer, is the Divine Word of God.

"To what greater inspiration and counsel can we turn than to the imperishable truth to be found in this Treasure House, the BIBLE?"

Queen Elizabeth I (1533-1603)

CHAPTER 2

The Dead Sea Scrolls

The Dead Sea Scrolls were discovered in caves at Khirbet Qumran in the West Bank, Israel between the years of 1946 – 1956. The location of the Dead Sea spans both Israel and Jordan and is approximately 15 miles east of Jerusalem. The sea itself is very deep with an average depth of around 1000 feet and is extremely salty. It already sits in a low elevation and therefore with its deep basin this gives the Dead Sea an unusual climate. It produces a very high evaporation which in turn produces a haze, but humidity is low. The position and climatic conditions may play somewhat of a role in the area around the Dead Sea being very arid and favorable for preservation. One could consider if indeed God directed the positioning of the Dead Sea Scrolls so they would be preserved for future generations to study for proof and corroboration.

Not only were the manuscripts preserved [some of which were wrapped in cloths and/or buried as was the custom] but hundreds of everyday items and utensils were discovered that gave the archaeological team insight as to how the people occupying the area lived. Vessels [or jars] were brimming to the top with all types of coins that were in use during the period. Some of the coins were identified as being minted in

Tyre and included tetradrachms [ancient Greek silver coins] of Antiochus VII Sidetes and Demetrius II Nicator dating from around 136-126 BCE. They also found six Roman Republican denarii from around the mid-first century BCE.

The Dead Sea Scrolls contained 972 texts which are of great historical, religious and linguistic significance, due to the fact that included in these texts are the earliest known surviving manuscripts of works that were included in the Hebrew canon of the scriptures [Old Testament].

Four languages are noted in the manuscripts, namely; Hebrew; Aramaic; Greek; and Nabataean. The majority of the manuscripts are written on parchment but some are written on papyrus and bronze.

One of the most significant things for Biblical scholars is the manuscripts have been dated to several ranges between the 2nd century BCE and 2nd century CE. This point is significant, as it pushes the date back for Biblical manuscripts, albeit copies, close to 1000 years. The availability to compare all previously known extant manuscripts could now be compared to the Dead Sea Scrolls that pre-dated all of them! They could immediately search for accuracy and content in confirming God's word remained true, which it did.

Arguments still continue as to who were the scribes of these manuscripts, with tradition stating it was an ancient Jewish sect called the Essenes, but others argue that others are responsible for the writings.

Of the total number of manuscripts located, approximately 40% comprised of texts from the Hebrew Bible, with the remaining 60% divided equally between two other groups of writings of Jewish history not related to the Biblical canon.

The series of caves that lie approximately a mile inland from the northwest shore of the Dead Sea were recorded by number. In cave 4, ninety percent of the scrolls were found. The original discovery was made by three young men of the Ta'amirah tribe of Bedouin. Muhammad Ahmed el-Hamed [nicknamed Edh-Dhib 'the Wolf'], Jum'a Muhammad Khalil and Khalil Musa discovered the manuscripts by accident sometime between November and December 1946.

They initially discovered 7 scrolls which were in jars and took them to their camp to show other family members. There the scrolls remained, hanging on tent poles while they decided what to do with them.

Eventually they took the scrolls to Ibrahim 'Ijha who was a dealer in Bethlehem who told them the scrolls were worthless. Undaunted, they continued to seek a buyer and went to another market nearby where a Syrian Christian offered to buy them. It was during this conversation that a sheikh joined in the conversation and suggested they take the scrolls to a cobbler and part-time antique dealer by the name of Khalil Eskander Shahin [known as Kando].

The Bedouin eventually left one scroll with Kando and sold three others to a dealer for £7.00 [about $11]. The scrolls continued to change hands several times until sales could be arranged, and in 1947 they caught the attention of Dr. John C. Trever (1916-2006) of the American Schools of Oriental Research (ASOR), who compared them to the Nash Papyrus which was then the oldest Biblical manuscript and noticed similarities with each of them. Due to the Arab-Israeli war in March 1948 the scrolls were moved to Lebanon for safe keeping and in April of that year the ASOR released a press release announcing the discovery.

Almost two years after the original discovery search teams had not located the original cave and in the midst of war and unrest no large scale search could be undertaken. However, cave 1 was rediscovered by a Belgian UN observer in January 1949 and this prompted excavation of the initial site during February and March of 1949 by the Jordanian Department of Antinquities, who discovered additional scroll fragments and other artifacts.

Further discoveries of more scrolls and fragments followed at the close of 1951 with a team from the ASOR and the Bedouin people who collectively located caves 2,3,4,5, and 6 by December 1952.

By this time, the monetary value for the scrolls had increased due to their historical significance becoming public which forced the ASOR and Bedouin people to search separately but more diligently than before.

The ASOR conducted four more expeditions sometime between 1953-1956 and discovered the last cave in the latter year.

As mentioned earlier, the dominant theory still exists that the scrolls were the product of Essenes Jews living near Qumran but some modern scholars have challenged this theory.

Qumran–Essene Theory

It was universally believed until the 1990's that the scrolls were written by the Essene sect or possibly another Jewish sect. The thought was the scrolls were hidden in the nearby caves during the Jewish revolt between 66-68 CE. With the Qumran site being destroyed, the scrolls were never recovered by those who had placed them there for safe keeping.

One of the strongest arguments to support the Essene theory is due to one of the scrolls found known as the 'Community Rule'. In this scroll it describes the initiation ceremony of new members. These same descriptions bear striking similarities to the same ceremony mentioned in the works of Flavius Josephus (37-c.100 AD). Josephus mentions Essenes sharing property within the community which is confirmed also by the Community Rule scroll.

Gaius Plinius Secundus (23-79 AD), better known as Pliny the Elder also describes a group called Essenes living in a desert community in almost the same spot as the Qumran caves location.

Christian Origin Theory

The Spanish Jesuit José O'Callaghan Martínez (1922-2001) argued that a portion of New Testament text supported a Christian Origin theory and others since have suggested that some of the scrolls describe a Christian community. Supporters also tried to connect the Apostles James and Paul to some of the documents found.

Jerusalem Origin Theory

Certain scholars have suggested that the scrolls were actually written by Jews living in Jerusalem and that it was this group that hid the scrolls in the Qumran caves as they fled Jerusalem during the siege and destruction of their city by the Romans in 70 AD.

These scholars suggest that the diversity of the handwriting found in the scrolls are a valid argument that the scrolls did not originate from the area from where they were found.

Qumran–Sectarian Theory

The basis of this theory is that there is a hesitation to link Qumran with Essene. Proponents of this theory are reluctant to agree that the Jews who wrote the scrolls may have been from the Qumran area but were not Essenes.

Qumran–Sadducean Theory

Yet another theory which has gained popularity is that a group of Zadokite priests led the community based on purity laws which reflected those of the rabbinic writings to the Sadducees.

What theory a person decides to follow I believe is irrelevant, especially to the Christian as the base of a Christian's belief is 2 Timothy 3:16-17 which reads, ***All Scripture is breathed out by God and profitable for teaching, for reproof, for correction, and for training in righteousness, that the man of God may be complete, equipped for every good work"*** ***(ESV).***

A Christian undeniably believes the Bible to be the true word of God, irrespective of who God directed to write it. Copyists were not part of the original forty or so inspired writers.

One exciting process that occurred in 1950 was to perform tests that could 'carbon date' a document. This process took place with regard to the Dead Sea Scrolls in the hope to date the time as to when they were written with some accuracy.

An initial test was performed using carbon dating on a piece of linen found along with the scrolls in the caves. The test indicated a date of 33AD (+/- 200 years).

This date eliminated several ideas that the scrolls originated from mediaeval times. Both VanderKam and Flint said the tests provided "strong reason for thinking that most of the Qumran manuscripts belong to the last two centuries BCE and the first century CE".[1]

Paleography is the study of ancient writing which includes the discipline and practice of deciphering, reading and dating historical manuscripts.

This technique was also used to attempt to date the scrolls. The findings by experts in this field was that the scrolls were thought to be written from 225 BCE to 50 CE which was uncannily similar to the carbon dating time periods.

The determination of dating during the paleographic process was by examining the size, style and variability of the text. The fragments used in this process were also subjected to radiocarbon date testing and the dates suggested were 385 BCE to 82 CE with a 68% accuracy rate.

At the University of California another test was performed using cyclotron which is a type of particle accelerator that can measure (in this case) ink. The test found two types of black ink had been used, namely; iron-gall nut and carbon soot. A third ink that was red was also found, which was made from cinnabar. There were only four uses of this red ink found in the entire collection of scrolls.

With regard to the black ink, the carbon soot came from olive lamps. The gall nuts from oak trees that were in some of the inks were added to make the ink more resilient to smudging which is common with pure carbon ink. Additionally, mixtures of honey, oil, water and vinegar were added to the inks to form a consistent level of writing. It was also shown that reed pens had been used for writing the documents.

Of the three types of material used for writing of the scrolls between 85 – 90% were made from vellum which is a parchment made from animal skin that employs a painstaking process to provide a smooth writing surface. There are many examples of historical documents made by this process.

Between 8 – 13% of the scrolls were written on papyrus. This type of material resembles a thick paper-like material and is derived from the pith [soft spongy tissue] of the papyrus plant.

Only between 1 - 2% of the scrolls were written on bronze which was composed almost exclusively of copper with some tin.

The Dead Sea Scrolls appeared to be preserved by the dry, arid and low humidity conditions that were present in the Qumran area. Due to a lack of tanning material and the low airflow of the caves it is also thought that this contributed to the preservation process as well. Not only that, but some of the scrolls were found in clay jars which likely provided further protection.

Sadly, mishandling of the scrolls by archaeologists and scholars was inappropriate and careless for preservation of the scrolls. Together with them being stored in an uncontrolled environment upon their discovery, the mishandling accelerated the process of deterioration much faster than that of their environment in the caves. Fragments were taped together using adhesive tape which also caused significant damage to the documents.

The Jordanian government recognized the urgency to protect the scrolls but did not have sufficient funds to buy all the scrolls so some were moved to the Palestine Archaeological Museum in East Jerusalem, where further deterioration occurred during transportation and storage. This museum lacked funds and scrolls were left lying between simple window glass which trapped moisture and caused additional deterioration.

During the Arab-Israeli war in 1956 the scrolls were sent to a bank in Jordan to be stored in the bank's vault where they were exposed to dampness. Then, between 1956-1957 additional damage occurred, so much so that some of the fragments developed mildew, while others were destroyed by glue and paper from the envelopes that the scrolls had been placed in while in the vault. By 1958 up to 5% of the scrolls had been lost to deterioration.

This deterioration sadly continued until the 1970s because of uncontrolled storage usage from a variety of elements. In the late 1960s, the deterioration was becoming a major concern with scholars and museum officials alike. Many voices strongly advocated for better preservation techniques.

It wasn't until 1991 that the Israeli Antiquities Authority established a laboratory that provided the scrolls a temperature controlled environment to store and preserve them.

Since 1948 the Dead Sea Scrolls have been extensively photographed. It would be remiss of me not to include some of those stories.

In February 1948, Biblical scholar and archaeologist Dr. John C. Trever photographed three of the scrolls found in cave number 1. The pictures were in black and white and standard color. Despite the fact that Trever was an amateur photographer, the quality of his photographs exceeded the visibility of the scrolls themselves due to the inks of the texts deteriorating after the scrolls had been removed from their linen wrappings.

The Palestine Archeological Museum had acquired the majority of the collection from the caves and between 1952 – 1967 their Master photographer, Najib Anton Albina (1901-1983), photographed and documented the scrolls which was a five stage process of arrangement and assembly of the scrolls using broadband, fluorescence infrared photography [a process known as reflected NIR photography]. Using this process Albina and a team at the museum created over 1750 photographic plates of the scrolls and fragments. Using large format film and placing the scrolls on top of animal skin caused the text to stand out making it very useful for the team to collate the fragments. Because these are the earliest photographs by the museum, which at the time was also the most complete in the world, they are often considered to be the best recorded copies of the scrolls.

In 1993 NASA staff in their Jet Propulsion Laboratory used digital infrared imaging technology to produce photographs. While using this technology they were able to read a previously unreadable fragment which they noted read, "he wrote the words of Noah".

NASA then joined with both the Ancient Biblical Manuscript Center and West Semitic Research to expand their earlier findings using infrared photography adding the range of spectra at which images are photographed. Using this technology which had originally been developed for its remote sensing planetary probes they revealed previously illegible text. To accomplish this they used a crystal tunable filter that photographed the scrolls at specified wavelengths of light which diminished image distortion. The camera and digital imaging assembly was developed by Dr. Gregory Bearman, a scientist with NASA's Jet Propulsion Laboratory who worked for NASA for almost 30 years (1979-2008). This technology was utilized to photograph illegible ancient texts and resulted in 1000 new images being taken with this advancement.

Believe it or not DNA was also employed by taking DNA from parchments to match the fragments together in order to reassemble the scrolls. This process enables scientists to determine if certain scrolls held a greater significance depending on what animal hide was used.

In partnership with Google, the Museum of Jerusalem is working to photograph the Dead Sea Scrolls and make them available to the public digitally. Lead photographer of the project, Ardon Bar-Hama, and his team are utilizing the Alpa 12 MAX camera accompanied with a Leaf Aptus-II back in order to produce ultra-high resolution digital images of the scrolls and fragments. By taking photographs at 1,200 megapixels, the results are digital images that can be used to distinguish details that are invisible to the naked eye. To minimize damage to the scrolls and fragments, photographers are using a mind boggling 1/4000th of a second exposure time and UV-protected flash tubes. This project, estimated in 2011 to cost approximately 3.5 million U.S. dollars, is expected to be completed by 2016.

As stated earlier, when the scrolls were at the Palestine Archaeological Museum in 1953 decomposing due to the poor care by their charges, they were assembled and logged for translation and study in a room that was known as the "Scrollery".

The scrolls are written in four languages; Hebrew, Aramaic, Greek, and Nabataean. By far the greatest percentage of script is in Hebrew called the Assyrian block script (approx. 76-79%) dating from the 3rd century BCE. Aramaic square script represents approx. 18% with the rest in single digit percentages, including what is known as Biblical Hebrew [Classical Hebrew] or Paleo-Hebrew scribal script (less than 1.5%).

There has been much controversy during the past several decades regarding the publication of the scrolls. John Strugnell (1930-2007) led a small team that controlled who had access to the scrolls with many scholars not even being allowed to view them let alone photograph them. Strugnell came under increasing controversy for his slow progress in publishing the scrolls, and his refusal to give scholars free access to the unpublished scrolls. After his removal from his editorial post which ended more than a thirty year blockade that he and others had maintained to keep other scholars from accessing the scrolls, the controversy finally ended in 1991 when the Biblical Archaeology Society was able to publish the "Facsimile Edition of the Dead Sea Scrolls", after an intervention by the Israeli government and the Israeli Antiquities Authority.

Scholar Hershel Shanks (b.1930), the founder of the Biblical Archaeology Society, had personally waged a 15 year campaign to allow researchers access to the scrolls.

Emanuel Tov (b.1941) who was appointed Editor-in-Chief of the Dead Seas Scrolls Publication Project was responsible for the publication of 32 volumes of the Discoveries in the Judean Desert series.

Between 1955 and 2009 Oxford University Press published a 40 volume series known as the 'Discoveries in the Judean Desert'.

Also in 1991 researchers Ben Zion Wacholder (1924-2011) and Martin Abegg (b. 1950) at the Hebrew Union

College in Cincinnati, Ohio developed a computer program that used previously published scrolls [500] to reconstruct the unpublished texts.

Officials at the Huntington Library in San Marino, California, led by Head Librarian William Andrew Moffett (1933-1995), also announced that they would allow researchers unrestricted access to the library's complete set of photographs of the scrolls.

Not long after, officials of the Israel Antiquities Authority agreed to lift their long-standing restrictions on the use of the scrolls.

Despite all of the foregoing freedom of viewing and reading of the scrolls, that one would assume would be available to learned scholars, several court actions were made against differing entities, arguing trivial points such as who owned what etc. I find it somewhat ironic that both men and governments alike claimed ownership when in fact the true owner was, is and always has been God as the author. He alone owns divine 'Copyright' to His work.

At the time of writing there are several online versions available to see the Dead Sea Scrolls, with a complete facsimile set being offered for over $60,000. The facsimiles have since been exhibited in Qumrân, the Bibliothèque Nationale, Paris, France in 2010 and the at the Vatican, Rome, Italy (2012) as well as Google.

As previously mentioned, the Israel Antiquities Authority and Google digitization project started in 2010 is set to be completed by 2016. On 25 September 2011 the Israel Museum Digital Dead Sea Scrolls site went online. Google and the Israel Museum teamed up on this project, allowing users to examine and explore these most ancient manuscripts from Second Temple times at a level of detail never before possible. The new website gives users access to searchable, high-resolution images of the scrolls, as well as short videos and background information on the texts and their history. Scrolls can be magnified so that users may examine texts in detail.

As we have already noted, prior to the discovery of the Dead Sea Scrolls the oldest manuscripts known were Masoretic texts, an old Hebrew language dating to the 10th century CE. An example of this is the Aleppo Codex.

The biblical manuscripts found at the Dead Sea caves push the date back over 1000 years to the 2nd century BCE. This is significant for Bible scholars for a number of reasons.

Before the Dead Sea Scrolls were found the earliest extant manuscripts of the Old Testament were the Codex Vaticanus and the Codex Sinaiticus both dating from the 4th century CE. We will discuss these two along with the Codex Alexandrinus in a separate chapter.

The collection of Dead Sea Scrolls include, at the very least, fragments of every book of the Old Testament with the exception of Esther. It is believed by some, because Esther was a Jew who married the Persian King Ahasuerus that some scribes may have not wanted to copy the record or may have even refused despite the fact that Esther actually saved the Jews from being destroyed by the evil schemes of Haman.

The Dead Sea Scrolls are specifically a set of three groups, divided by their specific works. One group contains texts of the Hebrew Bible. A second group consists of texts that were not considered inspired and were not canonized into the Hebrew Bible [many of these became known as the Apocrypha]. And the third group are known as sectarian documents detailing certain rules and beliefs. Examples of these are the War Scroll and the Community Rule Scroll.

Of the 11 caves we previously mentioned, some caves gave up far more Biblical and historical treasure than others. For example, cave 4 which was, in fact, two hand cut caves, was by far the most productive in content. It produced 90% of the Dead Sea Scrolls which amounted to approximately 15,000 fragments from 500 different texts. Cave 5 had 25 manuscripts while cave 6 had 31. Twenty fragments of Greek documents were found in cave 7 but cave 8 only had five. Cave 11 contained 21 texts including what is known as the Temple Scroll which details the construction of the Temple of Jerusalem.

It should be noted that the Bedouins discovered scrolls in 5 caves and the archaeologists in 6. We should give acknowledgement where due to both parties' efforts in securing these important documents for posterity.

The discovery of these scrolls, along with archaeological artifacts, establishes both provenance and proof of the authenticity of the scrolls, along with the dates they were written. In fact, among scholars today, the Dead Sea Scrolls time span and background is firmly established by historical, linguistic and paleographic evidence and collaborated by carbon dating techniques.

While Josephus mentions in his writings of the divisions of the Jews into three specific groups, namely the Sadducees, Pharisees and the Essenes, scholars still argue as to the third group [Essenes] as being the scribes that wrote the Dead Sea Scrolls. In fact the word Essenes is not found in any of the scrolls. While I do not suggest one way or another who the copyists were of the Dead Sea Scrolls, it is known the Essenes referred to themselves as Judea.

The Roman historian, Pliny the Elder, referred to the Essenes sect as being geographically located at the Dead Sea also. Many scholars remain vehemently opposed to the Essenes as being the copyists and it is my belief the Christian should not lose any time on this subject. As historical and Biblical proof has already been shown as to the scrolls' authenticity, I find the argument as to who the scribes were specifically, irrelevant as to their merit.

The fact that the Dead Sea Scrolls survived for over 20 centuries, thanks to both the arid climate conditions, and the way in which they were faithfully stored, make them a truly remarkable find. For scholars they provide an incredible wealth of information and source for exploration of post Bible times.

Even though many of the scrolls are not of scriptural content, they should not be ignored as to their content. These scrolls provide us with an historical window that we can open and peer through to see first-hand as it were, the critical and turbulent times of the Jews. The Dead Sea Scrolls have indeed added to our understanding of the Jewish background of Christianity.

The scrolls provide a much older cross section of Scriptural tradition for scholars than what was available prior to the scrolls discovery.

Many of the scrolls containing the Biblical text are almost identical to the Masoretic, or traditional, Hebrew text of the Old Testament. There are dramatic differences however to the books of Exodus and Samuel that are in the scrolls that were located in cave 4, both relating to content and language. A possible reason for this may be the fact that at the time of the writing of the scrolls the area was undergoing several political changes. For example, the Greek Macedonian Empire and Roman dominance [in particular Roman Judea] were experiencing transitions of governmental changes. Jewish society had some measure of autonomy after the death of Alexander the Great which had fractured the empire he had built among his successors.

The particular area where the scrolls were located had long been called Ιουδαία or Judæa [Judea] and had been named so for the Hebrews that had returned to dwell there.

Biblical texts.

Over 200+ Biblical text were found in the Dead Sea Scrolls which represented approximately 22% of the total content.

Non-Biblical texts.

The majority of the texts found among the Dead Sea Scrolls are non-Biblical in nature and were thought to be insignificant for understanding the composition or canonization of the Biblical books.

The Majority of the Dead Sea Scrolls collection at the time of writing is under the ownership of the Government of the state of Israel. The scrolls are housed in the Shrine of the Book on the grounds of the Israel Museum. The Israeli claim of ownership is contested by both Jordan and Palestine. The debate over the Dead Sea Scrolls stems from a more general Israeli-Palestinian conflict over land and state recognition.

So what can we glean from the Dead Sea Scrolls?

For one thing they have allowed Biblical and archeological scholars alike to view records over 1000 years prior to what they originally had access to. The fact that there were some changes in consistency and language can easily be argued that political and religious transitions were occurring, but as many have mentioned before, separate to this publication, the Jewish scribes were fanatically protective of ensuring the accuracy of God's word to be handed down and were operating under the Mosaic Law to faithfully record the information for future generations.

As we take our journey further into the history of the Bible's writings we will learn that God will never allow His word to be distorted or changed.

The Message Bible in 2 Peter 1:19-21 says of God's word, **"We couldn't be more sure of what we saw and heard—God's glory, God's voice. The prophetic Word was confirmed to us. You'll do well to keep focusing on it. It's the one light you have in a dark time as you wait for daybreak and the rising of the Morning Star in your hearts. The main thing to keep in mind here is that no prophecy of Scripture is a matter of private opinion. And why? Because it's not something concocted in the human heart. Prophecy resulted when the Holy Spirit prompted men and women to speak God's Word" (MSG).**

The same verses in the Amplified Bible read, **"And we have the prophetic word [made] firmer still. You will do well to pay close attention to it as to a lamp shining in a dismal (squalid and dark) place, until the day breaks through [the gloom] and the Morning Star rises (comes into being) in your hearts. [Yet] first [you must] understand this, that no prophecy of Scripture is [a matter] of any personal or private** *or special interpretation (loosening, solving). For no prophecy ever originated because some man willed it [to do so—it never came by human impulse], but men spoke from God who were borne along (moved and impelled) by the Holy Spirit" (AMP).*

When we recognize that God's thoughts are higher than our thoughts and that whatever He wishes to be accomplished will come to pass, then we can faithfully believe in the accuracy in the word of God that we hold in our hands.

As Christians, we are used to the naysayers, atheists', evolutionists, and many more who readily try and denounce God's word. We know where their intentions are contrived and grounded. 2 Corinthians 4:3-4 identifies whose side these people are on, *"If the Good News we preach is hidden behind a veil, it is hidden only from people who are perishing. Satan, who is the god of this world, has blinded the minds of those who don't believe. They are unable to see the glorious light of the Good News. They don't understand this message about the glory of Christ, who is the exact likeness of God" (NLT).*

I encourage you to keep an open mind all the time when you hear someone challenging the word of God or, more likely how it came to be the Bible we have now. This book is designed to help you navigate, in simple terms, through the challenges that Satan will put in front of you. In some cases such challenges may even appear from those who actually purport to be a follower of Christ.

I promise you, if you stay the course in reading this publication you will be able to ward off these challenges and it will help you to identify those who you may have first thought had good intentions but have somehow caused you or another to doubt. Jesus identified these as false prophets and gave specific warnings and utterances of condemnation to those who would distract or affect a person's faith or belief structure in God.

God cannot err. He cannot and does not make any mistakes. In the Bible His words "breathed" through divine inspiration to those He chose to be His writers. Any thought contrary to this puts us in a dangerous place which we need to quickly flee from and seek God's word for direction and understanding.

The Dead Sea Scrolls are just one example of the many sets of documents that proves the authenticity and divineness of the word of God. Through His divine plan He has ensured we hear the words, "He Breathed".

"We all therefore have to face this ultimate and final question: Do we accept the BIBLE as the Word of God, as the sole authority in all matters of faith and practice, or do we not? Is the whole of my thinking governed by Scripture, or do I come with my reason and pick and choose out of Scripture and sit in judgment upon it, putting myself and modern knowledge forward as the ultimate standard and authority? The issue is crystal clear. Do I accept Scripture as a revelation from God, or do I trust to speculation, human knowledge, human learning, human understanding and human reasons. Or, putting it still more simply, do I pin my faith to, and subject all my thinking to, what I read in the BIBLE? Or do I defer to modern knowledge, to modern learning, to what people think today, to what we know at this present time which was not known in the past? It is inevitable that we occupy one or the other of those two positions."

D. Martyn Lloyd-Jones (1899-1981)

CHAPTER 3

Codices and Uncials

The word codices is plural for codex. A codex (or sets of codices) are manuscript pages that were generally held together by stitching to form a rudimentary book and replaced scrolls and wax tablets from earlier times.

The word is generally assigned to a manuscript volume, usually of an ancient classic or the scriptures.

It can also be termed a book of statutes.

Uncials relate to a style of writing which is characterized by rounded capital letters and is found especially in Greek and Latin manuscripts of the fourth to the eighth century AD.

Uncials provided the model from which most of the capital letters in the modern Latin alphabet are derived.

In relation to the subject matter of this book, codices are identified as those manuscripts that are identified as being related to the Old Testament and could also be considered or called a Hebrew Bible manuscript.

A Hebrew Bible manuscript is a portion of text of the Hebrew Bible (Tanakh) which is handwritten on either papyrus, parchment or paper and in the language of Hebrew.

The Old Testament was written between 1450-450 BCE. The original manuscripts, written by the writers whom God chose by inspiration for the original Bible text disappeared over time, due to wars and also intentional acts of destruction by enemies. Because of these factors the time between original manuscripts and any surviving copies is much longer than that of the New Testament manuscripts.

Later manuscripts written after the 9th century use the Masoretic Text.

Since the 16th century the lists of manuscripts have continued to grow giving the Biblical scholar a wealth of information and resources confirming the accuracy of the Bible.

Benjamin Kennicott (1718-1783) was an English churchman and Hebrew scholar. In 1760 he proposed to collate all Hebrew manuscripts to date. In the course of this work he listed 615 Hebrew manuscripts and 52 printed editions of the Bible either wholly or partially collated.

Between 1784-1788 the Italian Christian Hebraist Giovanni Bernardo De Rossi (1742-1831) published a list of 731 manuscripts.

In 1896 the Cairo Geniza discovery collected approximately 300,000 Jewish religious and secular manuscript fragments. These were found in the genizah [sacred storeroom] of the Ben Ezra Synagogue in Fustat or Old Cairo, Egypt.

These manuscripts outline a 1,000-year continuum (870-1880 CE) of Jewish Middle-Eastern and North African history and comprise the largest and most diverse collection of medieval manuscripts in the world.

As the Jews considered Hebrew to be the language of God, and the Hebrew script to be the literal writing of God, the texts could not be destroyed even long after they had served their purpose. The normal practice was to remove the contents periodically and bury them. The Jews who wrote the materials in the Geniza were familiar with the culture and language of their contemporary society.

We read in the last chapter, the Dead Sea scrolls were discovered in 1947 adding over 200 Biblical manuscripts for Biblical scholars to research and study. Further, between the years 1963-1965 parts of 14 Biblical, apocryphal and sectarian scrolls were discovered at Masada, Israel. The Biblical scrolls are mostly identical with Masoretic texts but some show slight variations. One important find was a sectarian document identical with one found in Qumran, and using a 364-day calendar used also by a Dead Sea Sect. This was additional proof that the Dead Sea Scrolls were dated correctly. Another important scroll was the original manuscript of "The wisdom of Ben-Sira", an apocryph of the 2nd century; its Greek translation was knows as "Ecclesiasticus". Since this text was not included in the Tanakh, the original Hebrew text was lost; excerpts from it were found only in 1896 in the Cairo Geniza. The find in Masada opened a new chapter in the research of that book.

There are many codices and uncials that we could list and that could be the basis of a book on its own. That is not the purpose of this publication. Rather, our purpose is to show the depth of evidence we have in proof that the word of God has remained true as if written only yesterday. I will mention some of these works in this chapter and provide a short historical narrative as we go along. The continuation of manuscript copies was undertaken over several centuries, in order for God's word to be passed down to the present day.

As we have acknowledged, thousands of manuscripts have been documented.

The uncials manuscripts alone number over 300. These contain both Old and New Testament writings. Of this number, four are known as the four great uncials and these comprise of the:

Codex Alexandrinus
Codex Ephraemi
Codex Sinaiticus
Codex Vaticanus

Of these four three have prominence with Ephraemi being neglected as a member of the great uncials which we will see why later.

Before we go on to discuss the great uncials, it is worth noting that two other important documents are worthy of mention.

The Nash Papyrus was a collection of four papyrus fragments acquired in Egypt in 1898 by Dr. Walter Llewellyn Nash, the secretary of the Society of Biblical Archaeology. He presented them to the Cambridge University Library in 1903. They comprise a single sheet and are not part of a scroll. The papyrus is of unknown provenance. The text was first described by Stanley Arthur Cook (1873-1949) in 1903. Though dated by Cook to the 2nd century AD, subsequent reappraisals have pushed the date of the fragments back to about 150-100 BC. The papyrus was by far the oldest Hebrew manuscript fragment known at that time, before the discovery of the Dead Sea Scrolls in 1947.

Twenty four lines long, with a few letters missing at each edge, the Nash Papyrus contains the Ten Commandments in Hebrew, followed by the start of the Shema Yisrael prayer [the Shema prayer consist of the first two words of a section of the Torah, and is the title of a prayer that serves as a centerpiece of the morning and evening Jewish prayer services]. According to the Talmud it was once customary to read the Ten Commandments before saying the Shema.

The text of the Ten Commandments combines parts of the version from Exodus 20:2-17 with parts from Deuteronomy 5:6-21. Some (but not all) of the papyrus' substitutions from Deuteronomy are also found in the version of Exodus in the ancient Greek Septuagint translation of the Hebrew Bible, which we will discuss later in this chapter.

The second document worthy of mention is the Aleppo Codex.

The Aleppo Codex is a medieval bound manuscript of the Hebrew Bible. The codex has been dated to the 10th century AD as to the time of its writing and as such it is considered to be the most authoritative document in the Masorah (Masoretic Text). Up until the middle of the 20th century the codex remained in good condition. It was the oldest known copy of the complete Hebrew Bible and as such was considered to be the most important Hebrew manuscript in existence.

Jews from afar, across all of the Middle East consulted the Aleppo Codex and many still regard it today to be the most accurate representation of Masoretic principles in any extant manuscripts.

The Karaite Jewish community of Jerusalem purchased the Aleppo Codex about a hundred years after it was created. During the First Crusade (1099), the synagogue was plundered and the codex was transferred to Egypt. The Jews paid a high price for its ransom. It was preserved at the Rabbanite synagogue in Cairo, where it was trusted by all Jewish scholars. It is rumored that in 1375 it was brought to Aleppo, Syria, leading to its present name.

The Codex remained in Syria for five hundred years. Then, in 1947, rioters enraged by the UN decision to establish a Jewish state in Palestine burned down the synagogue where it was kept. This led to the disappearance of the codex but it re-emerged in 1958, when it was smuggled into Israel. On arrival, it was found that parts of the codex had been lost. The Aleppo Codex was entrusted to the Ben-Zvi Institute and the Hebrew University in Jerusalem. This finally gave scholars the chance to examine the document.

In modern times, several complete or partial editions of the Tanakh based on the Aleppo Codex have been published over the past three decades in Israel, some of them under the academic auspices of Israeli universities.

The largest organized collection in the world of Old Testament manuscripts is actually housed in the Russian National Library in Saint Petersburg, Russia.

The oldest manuscript in complete form of the Old Testament is the Codex Leningradensis which is in the Hebrew language.

The Leningradensis Codex is dated to around 1008 AD and is the only text that was reproduced in Biblia Hebraica in 1937 and then the later work, the Biblia Hebraica Stuttgartensia of 1977. Scholars also consult the Leningradensis Codex for the missing parts of the Aleppo Codex.

One interesting fact of the Leningradensis Codex which still remains in very good condition (considering it is over a 1000 years old) is that there is a page that lists the scribes who worked on the manuscript.

As we learned in our first chapter of this book, the Masoretes scribes were renowned for their accuracy. The Leningradensis Codex is also a Masoretic text. The Ben Asher family of scribes who are said to have been the Codex' copyists were no less unaware or careless than their ancestors. They too knew the importance of accurate copying. One of the ways they adopted their accuracy in ensuring the copy followed the sacred text was to use notes in the margins. They would write little letters as symbols by the side of the Biblical text. These symbols in turn told the scribe who was copying the text, of unusual formation of words that were not to be changed. An example of this was they might put a circle over a word that did not appear anywhere else in the Bible. Then in the margin they would put the letter "I" which informed the scribe that the word or wording was unique and it was not an error and the scribe was to copy the text as it was. Additional notes could be and were included at the top and bottom margins of a page to explain in more detail the symbols that were written in the side margins.

One point of note is that the very fact the Codex was a Codex meant it was a copy. The Hebrew 'Bible' used in the synagogues were scrolls. These would generally be made up of twenty or so leaves of papyrus or parchment and glued together to form a scroll some thirty feet long. Therefore the synagogues never had a complete Bible in one scroll but rather would have had several scrolls that comprised the Bible in separate works. These never left the synagogues. The Codex would not have been used in the synagogue. Rather it was used for personal study by students and scholars. It was not allowed [under strict punishment] to mark or write in, or on, the scrolls in any way as they were viewed as sacred.

In many [if not all] of the Old Testament manuscripts the order of books are somewhat different to the 39 books of the Old Testament we have today and the Leningradensis Codex is no different in this regard. History of the Codex is somewhat vague. According to its colophon [imprint on title page] the codex was copied in Cairo from manuscripts written by the Jewish scribe Aaron ben Moses ben Asher. No evidence exists if Asher ever saw it. Now housed in the Russian National Library, its previous owner by the name of Abraham Firkovich (1786-1874) did not disclose where he had acquired it. He took it to Odessa in 1838 and it was transferred to the Imperial Library in St.Petersburg, Russia sometime after this date.

There is also now an online digital version of the Leningradensis Codex called the Westminster Leningrad Codex which is maintained by the J. Alan Groves Center for Advanced Biblical Research at the Westminster Theological Seminary, Philadelphia, USA.

There are, or were, known to be some seventeen Masorah manuscripts, but many of these have been lost.

Now, let's get back to the New Testament Uncials and those that comprise the four Great Uncials. As we mentioned before there are over 300 manuscripts or pieces, fragments and the like scattered around the globe in various establishments ranging from specific buildings of Antiquity, Libraries, Seminaries as well as personal ownership. As a result, upon looking at the references of these, I counted some 364. But this figure is not correct as, many of the dating of these items of ancient antiquity share more than one century as the date they were written, hence there is a degree of repetition. Suffice to say, we can be safe in declaring there are at least 300 or so in existence in one form or another.

In terms of the activity [based on the dating of the documents] there is a variety of periods in which scribes were active. Let me explain by way of the following:

2nd Century - 1 Manuscript
3rd Century - 6 Manuscripts
4th Century - 27 Manuscripts
5th Century - 66 Manuscripts
6th Century - 95 Manuscripts
7th Century - 45 Manuscripts
8th Century - 39 Manuscripts
9th Century - 60 Manuscripts
10th Century - 23 Manuscripts
11th Century - 2 Manuscripts

Again, for clarification when I use the word manuscript this may only relate to one sheet or document or even only a fragment.

What it should and does tell us is that scribes faithfully executed the copying of God's word so that it would not be lost but past down to this day. This should give us confidence of God's promise when he wrote in Isaiah 55:11b concerning his word, ***"but it shall accomplish that which I purpose, and shall succeed in the thing for which I sent it" (ESV).*** Jesus also told us in Matthew 24:35 that, ***"Heaven and earth will pass away, but my words will not pass away" (ESV).*** I especially like how the Message Bible words this Scripture saying, ***"Sky and earth will wear out; my words won't wear out" (MSG).*** This gives the Christian the assurance that God's word cannot fail and will fulfill everything that it says.

The four Great Uncials were discovered at different times and places, they share many similarities. They share a uncial style of lettering that only adopts capital letters and each word is a continuous script without any breaks to separate the words.

No expense was spared in creating the documents both in material and labor. The material was vellum and the scribes employed to write the text created work based on the most accurate texts of their time.

The first of the greater manuscripts to be made accessible to scholars was Alexandrinus Codex.

The Alexandrinus Codex is a 5th century manuscript of the Greek Bible. It contains the majority of the Septuagint [LXX] and the New Testament and is dated between 400-440 AD. One story of the origin of the Alexandrinus Codex was that it was written by a notable lady of Egypt by the name of Thecla who was born around 30 AD and became a follower and disciple of the Apostle Paul. It is believed she was later martyred. However, we run into a problem with this theory in that it is believed Thecla died in the 1st century and the Alexandrinus Codex is not older than the late 4th to early 5th century.

Along with the Sinaiticus Codex and the Vaticanus Codex the Alexandrinus Codex is one of the earliest and most complete manuscripts of the Bible.

By its name it is easy to derive that the manuscript resided in Alexandria which appears to have been for a number of years. Cyril Lucaris (1572-1638) who was born Constantine Lukaris was a Greek theologian who later became Cyril III, the Greek Patriarch of Alexandria.

The Alexandrinus Codex was brought from Constantinople to Alexandria between 1308-1316 and it remained in Alexandria until the year 1621. It was Cyril Lucaris who arranged for the Alexandrinus Codex to return to Constantinople after this date. Lucaris had trouble with both the Turkish government and the Catholic Church, not to mention his own subordinates. This may well have been the reason why he was murdered on a ship and his body tossed into the sea. Prior to these troubles he had the support of the British government and by way of thanks he decided to present the Alexandrinus Codex to King James I of England. Unfortunately, James died before he could receive it and his son Charles I accepted it in 1627.

It is now one of the prized possessions of the British Museum and is on display in the manuscript department. Since 1973 the British Museum and the British Library have had separate buildings and the Alexandrinus Codex can be found in the latter. The contents of the Alexandrinus Codex consist of 773 vellum folios (630 are of the Old Testament with the remaining 143 being that of the New Testament). All 773 folios are bound in four volumes. The Alexandrinus Codex was written a generation after codices Sinaiticus and Vaticanus, but it may still belong to the 4th century AD. It certainly is not later than the 5th century. The current date was determined by the Institute for New Testament Textual Research (INTF).

According to the English scholar, critic and theologian Richard Bentley (1662-1742) he considered the Alexandrinus Codex to be the oldest and best in the world. Bentley attempted on more than one occasion to prove by several different readings that he could triangulate back to the single recension. In other words, he was attempting to perform a critical revision of a text incorporating the most plausible elements found in varying sources. Bentley presumed this format existed at the first Council of Nicaea but he was never able to confirm his theories and eventually any further attempts were abandoned.

Codex Ephraemi Rescriptus is a palimpsest [a manuscript that has had its original text scraped off so the manuscript material can be used again], and was deciphered by Constantin von Tischendorf (1815-1874) in 1840-1841 and published by him in 1843-1845.

Ephraemi Rescriptus was written around 450AD and is a Greek manuscript of the Bible.

Of the 209 leaves that survive, 145 belong to the New Testament and 64 to the Old Testament. The origin of the manuscript is possibly Egyptian (or Palestinian) and prior to the middle of the 5th century. After its journey to Constantinople the manuscript is believed to have become the property of Niccolo Ridolfi (1501-1550) who was the Cardinal of Florence. After Ridolpho's death it was possibly bought by Piero Strozzi (1510-1558) an Italian military leader to present to the French Queen Consort, Catherine de' Medici (1519-1589). Catherine is believed to have brought it to France as part of her dowry and the manuscript is now housed in the Bibliotheque nationale de France in Paris, France.

Unfortunately, in 1834-1835 potassium ferricyanide was used to attempt to bring out faded or eradicated ink. The result was the vellum [the manuscript material] defaced from green and blue to black and brown. This is likely to be one of the reasons the Ephraemi Rescriptus is not regarded worthy of being utilized like that of its three relatives [the four Great Uncials].

Tischendorf worked by eye only and his deciphering is less than perfect due to the poor quality caused by overlaid text on the palimpsest. This may be another reason why this manuscript became a neglected member of the family of great Uncials.

The Sinaiticus Codex is a celebrated historical treasure. It is thought to have been written soon after or around the same time as the Vaticanus Codex in 330-360AD.

Upon its discovery by Tischendorf it became known as one of the best Greek texts of the New Testament.

Scholars had to wait until the 19th century for the Sinaiticus Codex discovery at the Greek Orthodox Monastery of Mount Sinai, hence its name.

So valued is this document that no fewer than four libraries across the world hold part of its contents, the majority of which is housed in the British Library in London, England.

The vellum was harvested mainly from calf skins and secondarily from sheep skins. It is estimated that 360 animals were slaughtered for the making of this codex assuming all the animals yielded a good enough skin. When you add the cost of the material, the time it took for the scribes to write and bind the documents, it equates to a lifetime's wage for one person at the time.

The portion held by the British Library constitutes about half of the original work and covers 694 pages. These are represented as folios with approximately 199 belonging to the Old Testament and approximately 147 belonging to the New Testament.

In general, both the Sinaiticus Codex and the Vaticanus Codex agree. A large number of differences are due to iotacisms [pronunciation of certain letters] and variants in transcribing Hebrew names. They were not written in the same scriptorium [place of writing]. The Sinaiticus Codex, believe it or not, contains 4,000,000 uncial letters, which can only be seen as credit to the scribes who painstakingly copied the work.

Fenton Hort (1828-1892) commented that he believed both the Sinaiticus Codex and Vaticanus Codex were derived from a common original and much older source, but he felt they could not be later than the early part of the 2nd century or even slightly earlier.

That said, dating of the Sinaiticus Codex mentioned earlier is tantalizingly accurate in that it could not have been written prior to 325 AD because it contains the Eusebian Canons. Nor could it have been written after 360 AD because its margins contain references to certain Church fathers.

Together with the Vaticanus Codex, the Sinaiticus Codex has proven to be one of the most valuable manuscripts for establishing the original text of the Greek New Testament along with the Septuagint. It is the only uncial manuscript with a complete text of the New Testament. Despite a potential 300 years between the writings of the two Codices, the Sinaiticus Codex is considered to be highly accurate.

The complete publication of the Sinaiticus Codex was undertaken by Kirsopp Lake (1872-1946). He completed the New Testament in 1911 and later in 1922 the Old Testament.

In 1862 Constantine Simonides (1820-1867) attempted to discredit Tischendorf's discovery by saying he had written the Sinaiticus Codex. This was hotly disputed by the celebrated British Librarian, Henry Bradshaw (1831-1886). Bradshaw was very influential within scholarly circles and his support of Tischendorf's claims gave much weight to the Sinaiticus Codex authenticity. After Simonides died the story lay dormant for a number of years. Eventually, Bradshaw was able to show that the Sinaiticus Codex was indeed authentic and that the claims made by Simonides were a complete fabrication.

The complete document can now be viewed online at the Codex Sinaiticus website (www.codexsinaiticus.org).

The Vaticanus Codex is one of the oldest manuscripts of the Greek Bible containing both the Old and New Testament. Its name is, as you might have guessed, is from its place of conservation which is the Vatican Library. It has been held in the Vatican Library since the 15th century. Containing 759 leaves of vellum it has been dated to the 4th century (325-350 AD).

It became known to scholars as a result of communications from Desiderius Erasmus (1466-1536) and prefects of the Vatican Library. It is currently considered to be one of the best examples of Greek text of the New Testament and is only challenged in this value to that of one of the other Great Codices, the Sinaiticus.

The Codex Vaticanus originally contained virtually a complete copy of the Greek Septuagint (LXX). Of the 759 leaves, 617 are of the Old Testament and 142 of the New Testament.

Its original place of writing is uncertain, with likely proposals being Rome, Alexandria and Caesarea. Because the Vaticanus Codex does not contain any Eusebian Canon tables and the Sinaiticus Codex does it is believed that the Vaticanus Codex is the older of the two manuscripts.

It is believed that originally both the Vaticanus Codex and the Sinaiticus Codex were housed in Caesarea, probably in the 6th century. At some point, after the Council of Florence (1438-1445) the Vaticanus Codex arrived in Constantinople.

The Vatican Library was founded by Pope Nicholas V (1397-1455) in 1448 and it is understood that, since this time, the Vaticanus Codex has remained in the library. In fact, the earliest it appeared in the library catalog was in 1475 with just a simple shelf number to index its place. In 1481 the catalog gave a full description describing it as a "Biblia in tribus coumnis ex memb" or Three-Column Vellum Bible, referring to its page content of three columns of text.

Despite evidence of Erasmus consulting with the Papal Librarian Paulus Bombasius in the 16th century as to the manuscripts content, no scholars prior to the 19th century were allowed to study or edit its contents. As a result, many scholars did not ascribe any value to it. But in 1809 Napoleon Bonaparte (1769-1821) brought the manuscript to Paris as part of his trophies of victory. Six years later, in 1815 it was returned to the Vatican Library. Whether because of its theft by Napoleon or other reasons, the Vatican Library purposely obstructed scholars who showed an interest in studying the Vaticanus Codex for the better part of the 19th century.

In 1861, The Reverend Frederick Henry Ambrose Scrivener, LL.D. [1813-1891] said, "Codex Vaticanus 1209 is probably the oldest large vellum manuscript in existence, and is the glory of the great Vatican Library in Rome. To these legitimate sources of deep interest must be added the almost romantic curiosity which has been excited by the jealous watchfulness of its official guardians, with whom an honest zeal for its safe preservation seems to have now degenerated into a species of capricious wilfulness, and who have shewn a strange incapacity for making themselves the proper use of a treasure they scarcely permit others more than to gaze upon".[1]

It ...is so jealously guarded by the Papal authorities that ordinary visitors see nothing of it but the red morocco binding".[2]

The following year in 1862, Thomas Law Montefiore said, "The history of the Codex Vaticanus B, No. 1209, is the history in miniature of Romish jealousy and exclusiveness". [3]

Prior to this date, Cardinal Angelo Mai (1782-1854) had prepared the first facsimile edition between 1828 and 1838 but it did not appear until after his death in 1857 and it was considered unsatisfactory by whoever suggested it to be so.

Other facsimile typographical editions followed and eventually in 1889-1890 a photographical facsimile published by Giuseppe Cozza-Luzi (1837-1905) appeared of the whole manuscript, followed by a New Testament facsimile published in Milan in 1904-1907. As a result of these works the Codex Vaticanus then subsequently became widely available.

Finally, with scholars at last having access to the manuscript and its contents it is now considered to be one of the most important manuscripts for the text of the Septuagint and the Greek New Testament. It was used by Westcott and Hort in the edition, The New Testament in the Original Greek (1881), as the basis for their text. It is considered by critics to be the most important manuscript of the gospels with its stature being considered equal to that of the Sinaiticus Codex.

The Septuagint is sometimes referred to as the Greek Old Testament. It was written sometime between 300-200 BC and was widely used by Hellenistic Jews. More accurately described, Hellenistic Judaism was a type of Judaism in ancient times that combined the religious tradition of the Jews with that of Greek culture, which by default caused additional language integration. This culture and new colonization's created a process of cultural change called Hellenization. This, in turn, was the start of the Hellenistic age which attempted to create a universal or common culture. The Septuagint became the major literary product that in essence connected Second Temple Judaism to Hellenistic culture. It was produced primarily as a result of many Jews losing their Hebrew language due to the spread of the Jewish race throughout the Roman Empire. It also gave non-Jews a glimpse into Judaism by the translation being written in Greek.

Story has it that Ptolemy II Philadelphus (309-246 BCE) sponsored the translation and that between 70 and 72 Jewish scholars were commissioned to carry out the translation of Hebrew into Greek to form the body of work. The Babylonian Talmud is said to contain a story of this event.

Philo (20 BC - 50 AD) was believed to have relied heavily on the Septuagint and it is said he was quoted as saying that the number of 72 scholars chosen for the work represented six scholars from each of the twelve tribes of Israel.

The term "Septuagint" is, in fact, Latin for "seventy" as are the Roman numerals associated with the Septuagint [LXX].

Many early Christians used the Septuagint as their source during the 1ˢᵗ and 2ⁿᵈ centuries. The New Testament writers would have possibly relied heavily on the Septuagint, as a large amount of Old Testament quotes cited in the New Testament are directly quoted from the Septuagint. As time went by, the Septuagint became synonymous with the Greek Old Testament or Christian canon of writings of all the books of the Hebrew Old Testament. As Christians adopted the Septuagint, the Jews viewed it with some suspicion. They preferred to consult the original Hebrew/ Aramaic Targum manuscripts which were later copied by the Masoretes.

For Christians, it was natural for them to use and consult the Septuagint. They used Greek in everyday language. The Apostles are believed to have used the Septuagint, although Jerome (347-420) pointed out certain Scriptures that the Apostles referred to were missing from the Septuagint. This would indicate the Apostles would have had access to the Hebrew text also. This would not be unusual, given the fact that most of them were Jews and would no doubt have gone to and spoken in the synagogues where the Hebrew text in scroll form was preserved for service.

Interestingly, Jerome used the Septuagint in defense of him being declared a heretic. This was because he had checked the old Latin translations of the Septuagint against the Hebrew text. He was severely criticized for doing this no doubt because he uncovered text that the Catholic Church had corrupted. The Eastern Orthodox Church to this day still prefer the Septuagint translation as the basis for the Old Testament and for translation purposes.

The Septuagint contains all 39 books of the Old Testament as well as certain Apocryphal books. These latter books were retained in the Septuagint for historical and religious purposes but are not recognized by certain denominational bodies as being canonical [inspired by God].

All of these extant manuscripts combined give the Christian certainty of their faith in the words God has spoken to His chosen people. We have seen that despite differences in individual manuscripts the meaning has remained the same. God cannot and does not err. Neither does His Holy written word.

"The incongruity of the BIBLE with the age of its birth; its freedom from earthly mixtures; its original, unborrowed, solitary greatness; the suddenness with which it broke forth amidst the general gloom; these, to me, are strong indications of its Divine descent. I cannot reconcile them with a human origin"

William Ellery Channing (1780-1842)

CHAPTER 4

Biblical writings of the early Church

Until the Jews were dispersed over the entire Roman Empire the Hebrew language remained intact. Up to that point there was no reason to enter into translation of the Old Testament and eventually the New Testament, at least while only one language for the Jews remained. But translation was certainly required if the Christian faith was to expand, and it was only a matter of time.

As many Jews forgot their original Hebrew tongue and began speaking Greek, there was a need for a Greek translation which appeared as the Septuagint that we mentioned in the previous chapter.

We know from historical records that the Old Testament was translated into Greek sometime between 300-200 BCE and continued through to the 3rd century AD. In our last chapter we discussed the Septuagint being sponsored by King Ptolemy II of the Ptolemaic kingdom of Egypt sometime after the death of Alexander the Great in 323 BCE. If it was so ordered by Ptolemy II [and there is good evidence it was] then it had to have been after 309 BCE and before 246 BC, which was the timeline of Ptolemy II life. His reign began in 285 BCE and lasted until his death in 246 BCE. So we have a degree of certainty that the sponsorship of the Septuagint was ordered in this 40 year time span.

By the 3rd century AD the early Christians (Jews and Gentiles) read, wrote and spoke Greek, in relation to the New Testament. They wanted to read, write, speak and translate into the Greek language, the Old Testament as well. This was so as to have a full and accurate understanding of the original writings in the Hebrew language.

This requirement led to the beginnings of why the Bible manuscripts that we learned of in the previous chapter came into being as translations of the original text.

Although we are specifically looking at how the Bible was eventually translated into a person's native tongue, it would be a dereliction of duty if I did not mention the historical reference of followers of Christ, who in their own way supported true teachings of Jesus, but took little or no part in translation. Some writings only refer to their agreement of key doctrines, while others have their verbal testimony recorded as to their faith in our Lord and Savior.

That being said, we should also remind ourselves of the letters to the Corinthians that Paul wrote warning of church members following wrong teachings. He deals exclusively with this and other problems facing the early Church in 1 Corinthians.

We see Paul addressing the point of divisions among the church and admonishing that the one who should be followed is Christ, and Him alone. In view of the subject matter of this book I would be neglectful if I did not record Paul's words at 1 Corinthians 1:10-17 where he wrote, "*I appeal to you, brothers, by the name of our*

Lord Jesus Christ, that all of you agree, and that there be no divisions among you, but that you be united in the same mind and the same judgment. For it has been reported to me by Chloe's people that there is quarreling among you, my brothers. What I mean is that each one of you says, "I follow Paul," or "I follow Apollos," or "I follow Cephas," or "I follow Christ." Is Christ divided? Was Paul crucified for you? Or were you baptized in the name of Paul? I thank God that I baptized none of you except Crispus and Gaius, so that no one may say that you were baptized in my name. (I did baptize also the household of Stephanas. Beyond that, I do not know whether I baptized anyone else.) For Christ did not send me to baptize but to preach the gospel, and not with words of eloquent wisdom, lest the cross of Christ be emptied of its power" (ESV).

In view of the above, anyone mentioned in this chapter is not an endorsement by me of their activity or works [apostles not included], but merely a reference to what part they themselves played, if any, in the formation of translation of the scriptures or their specific teachings. Paul rightly points out that to speak or write contrary to the scriptures in effect weakens the position of Christ. This is a serious matter and we need to be vigilant in our belief in Jesus as our Savior and of the instructions written in God's holy word for our direction, trusting His word explicitly and without question.

Polycarp (69-155 AD) was believed to have been a disciple of the Apostle John as was his companion Papias (c.70-155 AD).[1] Whether this belief is fact or fiction, we are left to decide for ourselves. Suffice to say, we do know

75

historically that Polycarp was an early Christian Church leader and at one point lived approximately 30 miles from where the Apostle John was residing.

If someone told me the Apostle John was 30 miles away, I would make it a priority to travel and meet him. So I think I personally would err on the side that the two probably met at the very least, or even spoke at length. Certainly, we can assume with the Apostle John nearing the end of his earthly life, if he was aware of a Christian leader [John died when Polycarp was approx. 31 years of age] following Christ he would have wanted to have met and spoke to him, if only to ensure the teachings of Jesus were in good hands.

Eusebius references Polycarp in the writings of Irenaeus quoting, "But Polycarp also was not only instructed by apostles, and conversed with many who had seen Christ, but was also, by apostles in Asia, appointed bishop of the Church in Smyrna, whom I also saw in my early youth, for he tarried [on earth] a very long time, and, when a very old man, gloriously and most nobly suffering martyrdom, departed this life, having always taught the things which he had learned from the apostles, and which the Church has handed down, and which alone are true". [2]

Polycarp was martyred for his refusal to renounce Jesus as Lord, saying it would be blasphemy on his part.

Justin Martyr (100-165 AD) who converted to Christianity after meeting an old man, wrote of his new found faith and beliefs. The discussion he had with the mysterious character evidently left such an impression upon him that he became a stoic defender of Christians. In his writings [one known as The First Apology] he wrote to the Roman Emperor Antoninius Pius (86-161 AD) arguing against the persecution of Christians. He defended his arguments with the sound philosophy of Christianity, its practices and rituals. He was a firm believer in prophecy and is known to have cited scriptural prophecy of Jesus being the Messiah from writings in Matthew and Luke in reference to Isaiah 7:14. His writings are likened to a storehouse of early interpretation of prophetic scripture.

Irenaeus was born in the early part of the 2nd century (probably 130 AD). We have already mentioned he knew Polycarp as a boy and his family was thought to be Christian. Much of the history of Irenaeus is lost, especially after he became Bishop of Lyon, but one thing of lasting tribute is that he is thought to have been the loudest voice in his era in supporting the four gospel accounts. It appears in the early Christian church some Christians would only recognize or use one of the Gospel accounts which they favored. Irenaeus called for all four Gospels to be read and appreciated equally.

Irenaeus is believed to have died a martyr around 202 AD in Lyons, France.

Tertullian (160-225 AD) born Quintus Septimius Florens Tertullianus was a prolific early Christian author from Carthage. He is the first Christian author to have produced a large volume of Latin Christian literature. As a result, some call him the "father of Latin Christianity" and the "founder of Western theology". Despite being conservative, Tertullian advanced new theology to the early Christian church and is also famous for using the term "Trinity". His doctrine of the trinity was at first rejected and consider heresy but 100 hundred years after his death his doctrine was adopted at the council of Nicea.

Thirty One works of Tertullian are extant, covering the whole field of theological thought of his time. Despite not officially leaving his original faith of Catholicism he did not escape controversy as is evident by the rejection by the Catholic church of the typical canonization given their most avid teachers. Tertullian certainly did not fully agree with all of their teachings, hence his omission from sainthood.

Symmachus (lifetime unknown) translated the Old Testament into Greek around the end of the 2nd century. Jerome is believed to have used Symmachus' translation as a base for his Latin Vulgate translation. Origen was also thought to have used it.

Symmachus' intention and desire was to preserve the meaning of the Hebrew source text as a more literal translation than that of the Septuagint. Scholars have since remarked of the purity and elegance of his Greek translation which is said to have followed a theory and method.

Origen (182-254 AD), or Origen Adamantius was the son of Leonides. He was an early Christian theologian who spent the first half of his career in his birth city of Alexandria. His vast experience and prolific writings consisted of multiple philosophies on theology, textual criticism, Biblical exegesis and hermeneutics as well as preaching and spirituality. He was well versed in Hellenistic education, but was also similarly versed in the scriptures due in part to the insistence of his Christian parents.

It appears that his father Leonides was somewhat affluent but in 202 AD he was martyred and his fortune confiscated. This led to Origen having to support himself, his mother and six younger brothers. He certainly did support his family by becoming a teacher and selling his manuscripts, as well as being aided by a rich woman who admired his work.

Our chief historian to Origen's life, Eusebius, says that in 203 AD Origen revived the catechetical school [school of Christian theology] in Alexandria.

So successful was his teaching of the Christian doctrine that eventually Bishop Demetrius of Alexandria restricted Origen to instruction in Christian teachings only. Demetrius, at first a supporter of Origen, eventually opposed him, which led to Origen relocating to Caesarea.

Origen excelled in theological scholarship and eventually produced a work called the Hexapla [meaning an edition of the Bible in six versions]. This work included Hebrew, Hebrew in Greek characters, the Septuagint and the Greek writings of Aquila, Symmachus and Theodotion. We could liken the Hexapla to an early example of what we know today as a parallel Bible. One can imagine if six versions were in one Bible today it would be extremely large in book form!

Depending on one's actual religious belief a person may not entirely agree with many of the doctrines that Origen suggested or promoted. But in any event, Origen appeared to rigidly adhere to the Bible and is said to have not uttered any statement without support of the scriptures as its base. To him, and rightly so, there was no doubt, the Bible was divinely inspired and proven to be so, by fulfillment of prophecy.

Unfortunately, Origen interpreted scripture allegorically. Allegory is a form of literal interpretation that departs or becomes the imagination of a person.

There are numerous examples we could cite where scriptures have been allegorized and have sadly become the main doctrine of some faiths. We should not be surprised, as allegorizing the scriptures became the main method for over a thousand years of interpreting scripture. We can rest assured that God will not allow his word to be corrupted and always leads a person to the truth.

Allegorical interpretation does have some positives, in that it does teach the Bible is spiritual and not just historical.

But the negative side to allegorical interpretation is that it divorces itself from the Biblical text and its history. This type of interpretation opens the way for false teaching based on the person's religious faith and purports their own imagination as to the Bible's interpretation.

Many of Origen's views were eventually considered heretical and he is therefore remembered more as an ecclesiastical writer than a Church father.

About the same time period as Jerome [who will be our next character] there appeared another Bible translator who was a Goth by the name of Ulfilas (310-383). What is fascinating about Ulfilas, is that he translated the Bible from Greek into the Gothic language despite there being no such gothic alphabet to establish a translation. Ulfilas decided to create a gothic alphabet (c. 360 AD) in order to translate the Bible from Greek. He had to write down a language that, until then, was only oral. Then he devised a completely new alphabet to capture the sounds spoken in Gothic. He used a total of twenty-seven letters that he adapted from the Greek and Roman alphabet. You'll be excused if you have to read that last paragraph several times. I still find the concept mind boggling. But it speaks to the testimony of the brilliant mind of Ulfilas that God gave him, in order for him to teach his people God's word in their own language.

We have already established that Greek had become the language of the early Christians but living in the Roman Empire covered a vast area and there became a growing need for a Latin version of Bible texts. Those texts that became available became more and more corrupted and by the 4th century the leading Biblical scholar of his time, Jerome, said that there were 'almost as many texts as books' in his letter to Pope Damasus I. [3]

Pope Damasus I (305-384) [who became head of the Catholic Church in 366 until his death] commissioned Jerome to provide a definitive Latin version. It is Jerome's Latin Vulgate of the Bible that he is most famous for.

Eusebius Sophronius Hieronymus or simply, Jerome, was a priest and historian. He was baptized in Rome sometime between 360-366 AD and became a Doctor of the Church. He studied Latin under Aelius Donatus. Eventually arriving in Constantinople, he pursued a study of scripture under Gregory Nazianzen (330-390 AD). Two years later he was back in Rome working for Pope Damasus I. It was during this period in 382 AD that his commission began. The completion of his Vulgate took longer than expected, being completed around 405 AD. One of the many reasons for the delay was the death of Damasus in 384 AD before Jerome completed his work. Whether it was wise or not, during the beginning of his work, Jerome was tendered by several women which, after Damasus' death, turned into accusations of an improper relationship with one of the women. These accusations led to Jerome fleeing from Rome to Antioch.

Oddly enough, the same woman who was accused followed him. It is she who provided amply for his livelihood and book collection in later years.

Jerome is second in importance to Catholic philosophy to Augustine of Hippo (354-430 AD), who himself furthered the doctrinal teachings of Catholicism. Jerome's intent was for the Hebrew text to be recognized as the inspired text of the Old Testament and not the Septuagint. It was this view that he is believed to have employed to translate the Vulgate. This was slowly accepted by the Catholic faith. But later, more extant copies of the Hebrew text, which became available to scholars, have provided a larger window of knowledge for Christianity. The Vulgate naturally associates Jerome with that of the Catholic doctrines. This is also evident by the fact that Martin Luther and eventually the Protestant community are not generally inclined to accept his writings as authoritive or correct.

Whether Jerome had any part to play in the Catholic Church's attempt to 'seal' the scriptures from the common people and lead a false path of teaching can only be conjecture but unlikely. Augustine could be seen far guiltier on this premise.

One thing we can say about Jerome is that it was never his intention for ordinary Christians not to have access to God's word. He is quoted as saying, "Ignorance of the scripture is ignorance of Christ". [4]

Sadly, this perception is changed partly due to two reasons - one innocent, and the other unforgivable.

After the collapse of the Roman Empire people were scattered over far wider geographical areas than before, resulting in the people of Christian Europe speaking many different varieties of languages. The Vulgate, on the other hand was only understood by the minority, the learned, most of whom were priests.

They chose to keep the truths of God's word for themselves with the privilege of interpreting it for the people. Now, any suggestion of a translation being provided in the vulgar tongue of the people is discouraged.

Several hundred years passed without hindrance of this 'law'. There does appear a few exceptions. King Charlemagne (742-814 AD), who became the Holy Roman Emperor in 800, had parts of the Bible translated for missionaries to convert Germans.

Similarly, Cyril (827-869 AD) and Methodius (815-885 AD), two Christian missionaries who were brothers, were sent from Constantinople at the request of Prince Rastislav of Great Moravia to translate portions of the Bible into Slavonic in 863 AD in order for his people to learn the Bible in their own language. The brothers devised an alphabet known as the Glagolitic alphabet that enabled the Slavic language to be matched to Slavonic manuscripts.

Still, neither of these examples are out of the grasp of the Catholic faith and any suggestions now made for vernacular translation was against church hierarchy!

Around 200+ years later, a sect known as the Cathars were termed heretical by the Pope. They emerged largely as a homegrown group and a Western/Latin European movement. Their beliefs would be unrecognizable to a Christian today. Nevertheless, all that the Cathars were guilty of was simply wanting to serve God freely without the order and demands of the Catholic church. They eventually formed an anti-sacerdotal [against priests or priesthood] opposition to the Church of Rome. They accused the Roman church of being immoral and spiritually and politically corrupt.

Translation is not the subject in relation to the Cathars, but rather what they endured at the hands of the order of Pope Innocent III (1161-1216 AD). Due to one of the Pope's Cistercian monks being murdered on a visit to meet a ruler in the area of the Cathars, the full weight and power of the Roman church advanced on the

Cathars. The Cathars were protected by Southern French Nobles. In turn, their enemies were the Northern French Nobles, effectively creating a semi civil war of sorts. The King of France did not intervene and eventually the Cathars were massacred along with common people of the Catholic faith who chose to stay in defiance of Rome and defend and fight along with their neighbors.

Atrocities continued with 7000 men, women and children being dragged out of one church alone to their deaths. The Cistercian commander Arnaud-Amaury is said to have written to Pope Innocent III, "Today your holiness, twenty thousand heretics were put to the sword, regardless of rank, age or sex". [5]

By 1234 The Inquisition was established to rid Rome of the remaining Cathars.

On March 16 1244 another atrocity took place. Two hundred Cathar Perfects [Leaders] were burnt together in one giant pyre. Hunted down like animals the papal authorities continued to burn Cathars at the stake who would not recant. Those that did were subjected to sewing a yellow cross onto their outdoor clothing, forcing them to be segregated from other Catholics. When I was researching this portion, I could not help but recall the Jews having to sew a yellow star onto their clothing during their own persecution by the Nazi's in World War II.

The voice of the common people having a Bible in their own vernacular language would not be silenced. But any thought that the persecution of those who fought for such freedom was about to end would be mistaken, for it would continue on for three more centuries.

If you're a lover of history then you would agree that English Bible history [which is one of the primary reasons for this book] is a fascinating one. How we got it, when we got it, what it took to get it, and so on and so forth.

This work and the various chapters are by no means an exhaustive account of the Bible's history in terms of its translation, from manuscripts and different translations, to versions and editions that we have today. I'm sure someone reading this book may identify others who were just as involved in the Bible becoming available, especially in one's native language.

One example to this is Anton Koberger who was born between 1440/1445 and died in 1513. Koberger isn't identified as a theologian. His chosen career for many years was a goldsmith. But eventually he became a printer and publisher and, at one point, employed 100 workers, ran twenty four presses and owned two paper mills.

This story serves my point that I have not exhaustively included every single publisher or printer. Rather I have purposely stuck, for the main part, to those who were involved in translation, irrespective of whether they printed or published their work themselves.

Koberger did go on to print and publish his Koberger Bible in 1483, thought to be a ninth edition, originally from the German Bible that was printed by Gunther Zainer, who printed his about 1475. The Koberger Bible was a beautiful work, consisting of colorful woodcuts depicting various Bible scenes. Sadly, to research every printer or publisher would take too long and it would not serve the point of this book, which, as noted already, is to identify those involved in transcribing and translating the works that eventually became a Bible available in our native tongues.

Neither could we possibly identify original documents of the writers who were inspired by God to write His

Holy word. It is already established no one has seen those documents since being lost to time and decay. That should not surprise us at all in that the entire contents of what we know as the sixty-six books that form the Bible today, spans a period of time from around c.1450 BCE to c.95 AD. From around 400 – 1400 AD, which included the Dark and Middle Ages, God's word was locked away and only available in Latin.

Before we delve deeper into the English portion of Bibles that were translated, we do have several examples of Old English Bibles being translated long before more recognized works that we are perhaps more familiar with. To be fair, none of these were complete Bible contents.

Aldhelm (639-709 AD) was Bishop of Sherbourne, England and it is considered that he may have written an Old English translation of the Psalms.

Bede or Venerable Bede (673-735 AD) was an English monk in what is now modern day Jarrow, Northern England. He was a skilled linguist and translator and contributed significantly to English Christianity. He wrote several commentaries on both the Old and the New Testaments and at the time of his death he was working on a translation of the Gospel of John into English.

A manuscript known as the Vespasian Psalter was produced in the mid to late 8th century. Its contents are an interlinear gloss of the book of Psalms.

Eleven other 9th century Psalms are also known to have existed.

Aldred the Scribe, also known as Aldred the Glossator [a Glossator was a scholar who added text to explain the written word as in a document or manuscript]. He was believed to be a 10th century priest and a provost [academic administrator] for the monastic community of St. Cuthbert, Chester-le-Street, England in 970 AD. Aldred is best known for his 'gloss' of what we now know as the Lindisfarne Gospels. He translated Latin texts into word-for-word Old English language in order to provide more access for the common people to read and understand the scriptures. This was significant for the community at that time as Latin text could not be understood or described. Aldred made it clearer to understand by translating the text. In a time when very few even had the idea to do it, Aldred added descriptions or notes of explanation [known as a colophon] to assist in teaching the people. But his colophon was not just about descriptions or notes but recognition also. He identified the original writer of the Lindisfarne Gospels to be Eadfrith who was a bishop of Lindisfarne in 698. Binding of the manuscript was supplied by Ethelwald, who later succeeded Eadfrith a few centuries later. The fact that the Lindisfarne Gospels were still being read and bound over 200 years after Eadfrith translated them show the importance of them to the Lindisfarne community.

About the same time as the Lindisfarne Gospels it is said that a priest named Farman also wrote a 'gloss' of the Gospel of Matthew. This is in fact preserved as a manuscript called the Rushworth Gospels.

King Alfred the Great (849-899 AD) was King of Wessex but became the dominant leader of all England. He is thought to have commissioned a number of Bible passages including the Ten Commandments and the Pentateuch.

In 1066 the Norman conquest of England saw the Old English language disappear and replaced with what became known as Middle English. Just like partial writings of the Bible in Old English were made, so too were partial writings made into the Middle English. The period of time these events cover was generally around the years 1066-1500 AD. Yet again, English speaking, and more importantly, English translation, was abruptly halted. Along with the Norman's came not only alien rule, but also French as the preferred language. In fact French was generally reserved to those of a higher status while Latin was used as the preferred status for those who lived primarily as the scholars and theologians of the time.

The document known as the Ormulum, which consisted of partial translations of the Gospels and the book of Acts, was translated by the Augustinian monk Orm, who lived in the county of Lincolnshire, England.

The Cursor Mundi [which is Latin for "Runner of the World"] was written approximately in 1300 AD, anonymously in the Middle English language. This work is a religious poem of close to 30000 words and describes the world's history as seen through the Bible.

The religious writer Richard Rolle (c.1295-1349) was a partial Bible translator and a hermit. Known as Richard Rolle of Hampole (an area in Yorkshire, England), he actually studied at the University of Oxford and was sponsored by Thomas de Neville, who was the Archdeacon of Durham. Rolle was only interested in theology and biblical studies and before he received his Masters degree he dropped out of college at the age of about 19 to become a hermit!

His life and whereabouts from 1321 to his death in 1349 are somewhat sketchy and incomplete, but he may have even been ordained in Sorbonne, Paris for there is a record of a Ricardus de Hampole registered in their records for 1320 and 1326. Whether or not he was in Paris is part conjecture but, nevertheless, he did write several works of religious text and translated some glosses of the Latin Bible text, which included the Psalms, into a

Northern English dialect, which could have perhaps been similar to what we term Middle English.

We could go on recalling several more miniature works but, suffice to say, the thirst and desire for vernacular manuscripts and biblical text translated into even a muddled form of English were a continual, sought after, source of documents for further learning of the scriptures.

Affectionately known as the "Morning Star of the Reformation" John Wycliffe (1328-1384 AD) handwrote manuscripts of the Bible into the English language beginning in the 1380s. As mentioned already, the English language at that time was primarily a language used by the common man. In Wycliffe's time the Middle English language had several dialect accentuations due to geographical locations and was both varied and wide. To the modern observer, it would be very difficult to even identify it as the English language as we know it today. Given the fact that the majority of the populous was illiterate in the later 14th century and beyond education would also eventually become a factor in the common people being able to read and write in their native tongue. As noted, theologians and other various scholars predominantly spoke Latin and were well versed both in verbal and written works.

It should be considered testimony to John Wycliffe that, despite the masses not being able to read and write, at the very least they could begin to understand words spoken in English, for they certainly had no understanding of Latin. At least a Bible written in English could be read aloud by church leaders for their congregation to understand God's word and it is evident from history there was plenty of thirsty souls.

The tireless work and consistency that drove Wycliffe is also evident from the fact that one of his associates, John Purvey (1361-1421 AD) [who later produced the 2nd edition of Wycliffe's work] said that he (Purvey) would sit at the opposite end of the table to Wycliffe, both sharing an inkwell set in the middle of the table with each working on their manuscripts. What is significant about this comment lost to most is Purvey mentions Wycliffe writing his own portions of manuscript despite his palsied arm.

If we were not already impressed with this man's devotion to provide the word of God in English then this is yet another example of his determination and faith. Any form of palsy can be very debilitating and I'm referring to our day and age. Wycliffe was dealing with his abnormality over 630+ years ago!!

It isn't hard, when one reads the history of the Bible being written in English, to know what it was that motivated such men as Wycliffe. Long before the Reformation began, Wycliffe held weekly meetings of Bible study somewhat like to an underground movement. This movement was later known as Lollardy and was seen as the political and religious movement formed by followers of John Wycliffe. These members or associates in turn, became known as Lollards. The name Lollard was by no means out of respect or a socially respected identifying mark. It was however purposely meant and used to identify, or mark, followers of Wycliffe. The term was actually a derogatory nickname given to those who had, in general terms, no academic background. Lollards were considered to have a below standard education in English. More importantly, it earmarked those who believed in an English translation of the Bible. By the 1450s the nickname became associated with one being a heretic. What is also interesting is that despite the inference that a Lollard was a follower of John Wycliffe, this was not necessarily true or, at the very least, had some form of inaccuracy. Lollards had no central belief system and they certainly had no central doctrine. Individually they had many ideas and beliefs. But they did believe the Catholic Church to be corrupt and they looked to scripture for answers. Up until this point, the authority of religion or rather the church was the only recognized body. The Lollard movement challenged this authority in essence by becoming lay-preachers outside of any church authority. Hence, one of their main desires was to secure a Bible translated into English so that those who were literate could read the Bible in their own language without the need for the authority of a church or priest.

In 1395 the Lollards petitioned the English Parliament with a text known as the Twelve Conclusions of the Lollards. They presented the text to Parliament and also nailed them to the doors of Westminster Abbey and St Paul's Cathedral as a placard [which was a usual method of advertising in medieval times]. The Lollards had actually prepared a manifesto that contained a total of thirty seven conclusions [or thirty seven articles of corruption in the church]. This expanded number was for those who required more in-depth information. For the most part, the Lollards requested those that are called the Twelve Conclusions to be recognized and adopted by Parliament. The church was able to acquire land, most notably the Papal States surrounding Rome, convert pagan temples and claim relics for itself. Over 300 years, it became one of Europe's largest landowners.

For the next thousand years, tithes and tributes flowed in from all over Europe. Non-Christians and even fellow Christians were killed and their property confiscated. For example, the Fourth Crusade and the sack of Constantinople in the early 13th century brought it gold, money and jewels.

The first conclusion by the Lollards put them on an immediate collision course with the Catholics. Their petition was for parliament to reject the wealth that the church was accumulating by its leaders.

One can understand the argument of the Lollards with regard to the vast wealth the Catholic Church had accumulated. Since the early part of the 4th century Catholicism had become the official religion of the Roman Empire. For the next 300 years the church acquired land which became the Papal center and state around the city of Rome. The enormous accumulation of relics taken from what originally were pagan temples automatically made the Catholic Church the largest landowners. Priceless art, gold, precious stones and investments all added to the wealth. Like an ever flowing tap, tithes and tribute flowed into the coffers of the Catholic Church for over a millennia. This not only increased their wealth, but it also gave them religious and political power.

The Lollards conclusions only lit the powder keg of accusations of heresy and demands for burning at the stake. They directly attacked many of the main doctrines of the Catholic Church and argued that its claims to be the true church was wrong and incorrect due to their corruption.

Although the inevitable accusation of heresy followed, both John Wycliffe and the Lollard's were protected by John of Gaunt (1340-1399) who was a member of the House of Plantagenet and the third son of King Edward III of England (1312-1377). This protection could have continued had it not been for the Peasants' Revolt of

1381. Wycliffe and the Lollards, in general, opposed the revolt but, when it was found that one of the revolts main leaders was John Ball (1338-1381), himself a Lollard preacher, this changed everything. Ball, for his part was subsequently hung, drawn and quartered at St. Albans, England in the presence of the then king, King Richard II, on 15 July 1381. Both church and state believed that Lollardy was a threat to society and state and any protection quickly evaporated and disappeared. In 1401, King Henry IV, who despite being John of Gaunt's son passed, the De heretic comburendo which, although not banning Lollards, may just as well have.

This law that was passed by Parliament punished heretics with burning at the stake. It was one of the strictest religious censorship statutes ever enacted in England.

The statute read, "...diverse false and perverse people of a certain new sect...they make and write books, they do wickedly instruct and inform people...and commit subversion of the said Catholic faith...that this wicked sect, preachings, doctrines, and opinions, should from henceforth cease and be utterly destroyed...that all and singular having such books or any writings of such wicked doctrine and opinions, shall really with effect deliver or cause to be delivered all such books and writings to the diocesan of the same place within forty days from the time of the proclamation of this ordinance and statute. And if any person...such books in the form aforesaid do not deliver, then the diocesan of the same place in his diocese such person or persons in this behalf defamed or evidently suspected and every of them may by the authority of the said ordinance and statute cause to be arrested. If they failed to abjure their "heretical" beliefs, or relapsed after an initial abjuration, they would...be burnt, that such punishment may strike fear into the minds of others...". [6]

The sect this ugly law alluded to was none other than the Lollards, followers of John Wycliffe.

From then on King Henry IV's declaration banned any translating of the Bible or even owning one. The penalty of disobedience to this rule was, as stated, burning of such people as heretics at the stake. By the beginning of the 15th century the Lollards were now only able to continue their activities underground. So many of those who were burned at the stake for being a Lollard have been lost in time. The only remembrance of them is of a small infamous plaque which now stands at the Bridge House Pub in Norwich, England where it states, "Lollards Pit. The site of a place of execution for heretics and other offenders in the sixteenth century".

In Wycliffe's case, his crime was he dared suggest that people should learn about God themselves and not leave it to what the Catholic Bishops were telling them. In effect, he was telling people to ignore the law of the Pope and follow the law of God, but he knew the only way the people could do that was if they were taught, and eventually shown, how to read the Bible in their own language.

You may think Wycliffe was promoting Protestant teachings but he was not. His initial endeavors were simply to provide the Bible in a language that people could understand and learn the will of God for themselves. Wycliffe and his team of fellow scholars and followers were translating from the Latin Vulgate which had already become corrupted. One could ask why the religious authorities in Rome were so angry and vicious in their assault on Wycliffe. The answer is a simple one. Rome knew that the Latin Vulgate was corrupted because it was they themselves that had begun the corruption. If people began to challenge the Latin Vulgate by understanding the writings in their own language then Rome could lose all of its positions of authority and finance. Sound familiar?

It should.

This was almost, if not exactly, how the Chief Priests and the Sanhedrin had acted during the time that they had Jesus crucified. They knew if they did not put an end to this person who they accused of being a heretic, they too would lose all power and authority and worse, face financial ruin. In other words, they cared more for their own positions and finances than the Jewish nation they were supposed to lead by following God's commands.

The Catholic establishment (and let us not forget later the Church of England establishment) committed the same offenses against God.

Another practical reason Wycliffe had to rely on the Latin Vulgate was because at that time in history people knew Latin but they were not familiar with Greek. In any event it appears the Greek manuscripts during the time of Wycliffe were not available to him in England.

Wycliffe's initial intent was to formulate an English translation to be used for public gatherings. I would suggest to you (as it is not my intention to make the Roman Catholic faith the enemy here) that had the religious authorities been acting as true servants of God in the first place then why would they have had a problem in proclaiming God's kingdom as commanded by Jesus in Matthew 24:14 where he said, ***"And this gospel of the kingdom will be preached in all the world as a witness to all the nations, and then the end will come" (NKJV).*** This was the command of followers of Christ in the first place, no matter what the language was.

Because many of the words in Wycliffe's translation had no English meaning they substituted Latin. This meant the translation was Latinate, meaning that it was taken from the Latin. This would have still created difficulty in some of the understanding, hence the reason why, after Wycliffe died, his faithful student John Purvey did a revision of Wycliffe's work to make it more understandable.

As there was no printing presses during the time of John Wycliffe his translation was a series of handwritten manuscripts.

Despite papal condemnation, John Wycliffe never had to endure the terror of being burned at the stake during his lifetime. He was no doubt declared a heretic while alive by those who in fact had the mirror of condemnation facing directly at themselves. We do know that Wycliffe's corpse was dug up and 'ceremoniously' defrocked and then burned to somehow elicit in some way justification of the established church being right all along. But he had already spent 44 years in the presence of the Lord when this ridiculous action took place.

One person who did not escape being burned at the stake was the Czech Jan Hus (1369-1415) who actively supported many of Wycliffe's ideas. Like Wycliffe, Hus was not denouncing his Catholic faith but rather, the false teaching that was not in the Bible. Born in Bohemia he traveled to Prague where he sang and served in several churches to support himself. His commitment to study was said to be remarkable and by 1393 at the age of 24 he received his Bachelor of Arts at the University of

Prague. Three years later he earned his Master's degree and in 1400 was ordained a priest. He later served as rector of the University for one year before becoming a preacher to the people. Hus was influenced by John Wycliffe' writings and he attempted to reform several aspects of the teachings of the church. He attacked the moral failings of clergy, bishops as well as the Pope, from his pulpit. For a time, the Archbishop of Prague (Zbyněk Zajíc) made no attempt to stifle Hus's teachings. Pope Innocent VII (1339-1406) later intervened and condemned the teachings of Wycliffe (that Hus readily accepted and read in his sermons). From then on it was only a matter of time before Hus would be silenced. The period of time that Hus lived was both politically and religiously charged. The Western Schism existed where both Gregory XII of Rome (c.1326-1417) and Benedict XIII of Avignon (1328-1423) were making claim to the papacy. Added to this, Sigismund of Hungary (1368-1437) who was King of the Romans wanted to end the religious dissention. Sigismund was also heir to the Bohemian crown held by Wenceslaus (1361-1419) who was Sigismund's brother. It was Sigismund who suggested a council to be convened and this was held on 1 November 1414 in Konstanz (Constance). Hus, in fact, was happy to go to Constance to help eradicate the dissentions and was promised safe passage and protection under Sigismund. At first Hus moved freely, but when he began preaching to the people he was quickly imprisoned. Sigismund was livid with Hus' imprisonment but when the prelates of the council convinced him that a King's promise could not be extended to a heretic, any support quickly evaporated.

When Hus argued for proof of his heresy he demanded that he be shown proof of his fault by scripture. His demand was ignored, because his accusers could not point to any.

Again Hus, like Wycliffe, was condemned simply for promoting the idea that people should be allowed to read the Bible in their own language. It is said that Hus was burned at the stake in 1415 with Wycliffe manuscript Bibles used as the kindling for the fire. The story goes that the pyre was stacked up to his chin and as the pyre was set ablaze people could hear Hus singing "Jesus, Son of the living God, have mercy on me" three times before he was consumed by the flames. If the papal authorities thought the murder of Hus would stifle the people [so that they could continue their idolatrous acts] they were sadly mistaken. Responding with horror, and indeed anger, at Hus being burned at the stake, the people of Bohemia moved rapidly against and away from papal teachings. This led to what became known as the Hussite Wars.

One interesting piece of trivia is in Czech, the word Hus means Goose. One of the last words attributed to Hus were, "Today you will roast a lean goose, but a hundred years from now you will hear a swan sing, whom you will leave unroasted and no trap or net will catch him for you" [7]

That 'swan' was Martin Luther. In fact another strange connection to Luther was the fact that his coat of arms bore a swan.

Luther became the first person to translate and publish a Bible in the German people's common language which was more appealing than any previous German Bibles prior to his publication.

If we thought for one moment, however, that the fight to provide God's word in the common people's language was over we would be wrong. In fact the same year that

Luther nailed his 95 Theses to the doors of the Castle Church in Wittenberg in 1517, the Roman Catholic Church burned seven people at the stake.

They were burned, not for possession of a Bible, but merely for teaching their children to recite the Lord's Prayer in English.

"The BIBLE is the truest utterance that ever came by alphabetic letters from the soul of man, through which, as through a window divinely opened, all men can look into the stillness of eternity, and discern in glimpses their far-distant, long-forgotten home"

Thomas Carlyle (1795-1881)

CHAPTER 5

The Bible arrives in Print

If we thought the handwriting of the Bible was to continue for much longer we would be wrong. The year 1450 saw Johann Gutenberg (c.1400-1468) inventing the printing press. His invention of a movable mechanical press revolutionized printing. Using oil-based ink and a wooden press, similar to a wine press, allowed for the first time, printing of books on a mass scale. Gutenburg's experience with metals [he was previously a German blacksmith and goldsmith] evidently gave him the skills, knowledge and ability for making metal alloy type for text. The first book ever printed was a Latin language Bible, printed in Mainz, Germany.

The Bibles Gutenberg produced not only were printed but each leaf was colorfully hand-illuminated. Sadly, Gutenberg's contribution to history was somewhat blunted by the fact that one of his business associates (Johann Faust who helped finance his venture), accused him of not paying the loan back, with the result that the court fined Gutenberg and ordered the business to be handed over to Faust. Gutenberg was perhaps master of his own downfall. He was certainly a successful inventor and printer but not a clever businessman. Even though Gutenberg never realized the fortune his invention should have provided him, his fame is not clouded by the fact of acknowledging his contribution to the growing Renaissance. His movable printing press was a major catalyst that would sprout a later scientific period of printing. History will not allow anyone to take anything away from Gutenberg's contribution to printing. His invention of moveable type printing presses revolutionized the thoughts and dreams of those wanting to mass produce the Bible. This in itself would mean success for the Reformation.

Thomas Linacre (1460-1524) was an Oxford Professor and later the personal doctor to Henry VIII. He was born at Brampton near Chesterfield, Derbyshire, England to an ancient family recorded in the Doomsday Book. His early education was under the direction of William Celling [or William Tilly of Selling] at the Canterbury Cathedral School. Canterbury Cathedral is still one of the most inspiring and majestic architectural buildings of English Gothic architecture and several well-known historical figures are buried there such as Thomas Becket, Edward the Black Prince, Henry IV of England and many more. Under his care, Celling charged himself with Linacre's education.

Linacre later traveled to Italy remaining under the training of Celling who had been sent to the papal court as an envoy to King Henry VII. Linacre only went as far as Bologna. Here Linacre became the pupil of Angelo Ambrogini (1454-1494) who was more commonly known by his nickname Poliziano and shared instruction along with two brothers who were the sons of Lorenzo de Medici (1449-1492). The younger brother, Giovanni di Lorenzo' de Medici (1475-1521) later became Pope Leo X who would later remember Linacre.

Linacre eventually learned Greek and after reading the Gospels in the original Greek and comparing them to the Latin Vulgate he recognized that the latter was so corrupt that it no longer bore any truth or relation to the Holy Scriptures. The backdrop to this was the church threatening to kill anyone who read the scriptures by any other means than Latin. Interestingly, this again shows the sins of mere men who ordered the reading of scripture only in Latin [which was not even the original language of the manuscripts of the scriptures] and then allowing it to be read only by scholars or priests.

One of Thomas Linacre's friends was another Oxford professor, John Colet (1467-1519). The Colet family motto is "Semper Erectus" which is Latin for "Always Upstanding". This can be certainly applied to John Colet who eventually became Dean of St. Paul's Cathedral in London, England. Colet's desire was for people to see the scriptures and apply them in their lives. He preached a message of restoration and rejuvenation for Christianity and he actively pursued reforms in the church. His famous convocation sermon in 1512 was direct and to the point. He reminded the listeners that the church needed reform and openly criticized the living style of priests. He likened them to figures of darkness rather than being beacons of light and urged them to set examples. His admonition was for them to stop being puffed up with pride, looking for honor and dignity, but instead to humbly serve the church. Colet's attack was far from over, citing many of the works of the flesh being conducted by priests and eventually telling them to stop serving men but rather to serve God. He ended his convocation sermon telling all to return to God. No doubt he may have quoted or referenced Romans 12:1-2 which reads, ***"I appeal to you therefore, brothers, by the mercies of God, to present your bodies as a living sacrifice, holy and acceptable to God, which is your spiritual worship. Do not be conformed to this world, but be transformed by the renewal of your mind, that by testing you may discern what is the will of God, what is good and acceptable and perfect" (ESV).***

It is believed Colet translated the New Testament into English for his Oxford students in 1496 and then later for the public at St. Paul's Cathedral. This was not the majestic building we see in London today. The current building was built and completed by Sir Christopher Wren in1770. Wren had been commissioned to rebuild 52 churches in the City of London after the Great Fire of London in 1666 which included St. Paul's Cathedral. In Colet's time, this building, also known as St. Paul's Cathedral was no less magnificent. Stories suggest that people were so hungry for God's word in their native tongue that six months after his writings 20,000 people packed into St. Paul's Cathedral just to hear his sermons, with a similar number outside trying to get in!!

That would be, what we call, having to put on extra services to preach to the many, which some churches are doing now. One of which is the church my wife and I attend, which you can view at www.mbcocala.com.

Isn't it ironic that today in the majestic architecture of St. Paul's Cathedral [that still remains in our modern day and continues to display its dominance on the London landscape] that church services only attract a few hundred people for a Sunday morning service and most of those are tourists?

For Colet, given the nature of his call for reform and his direct attack of priests, one would think he would have become another victim of the burning stake. Fortunately, he had powerful friends which evidently enabled him to avoid execution and he died of a sickness in 1519.

Desiderius Erasmus Roterodamus (1466-1536) known as Erasmus of Rotterdam or simply Erasmus said of John Colet that he was "a man for the ages and a true Christian". I think Erasmus was correct in his belief and statement for a true man of God. Erasmus was so moved by the examples of John Colet and Thomas Linacre who both stood up and proclaimed the Latin Vulgate to be so corrupted, that it led Erasmus himself in 1516 to publish a Greek-Latin Parallel New Testament with the Latin portion free of the corruption of the Vulgate.

Erasmus whose birth name some claim was Geert Geerts (or Gerhard Gerhards), but no proof exists of this, was the illegitimate son of Gerard, a Catholic priest and curate in Gouda. His mother, Margaretha Rogers, was the daughter of a physician and may have in fact been Gerard's housekeeper. Although being born out of wedlock it appears both he and his older brother Peter were loved very much. Their mother in fact moved to where they were both studying [Deventer in the Netherlands] to provide a home for them while at school and while there she contracted the plague and died in 1483.

By 1492 Erasmus was in poverty and decided to become a Catholic priest and was ordained at the age of 25. Much later he received special dispensation from the Pope to relieve him of his vows so he could take up the work of secretary to the Bishop of Cambrai due to his immense skill of Latin. One can track Erasmus' movements throughout Europe for several years. After this he took up a variety of positions of teaching and theology in Paris, Basel, Cambridge etc. What is refreshing and a pleasant relief to the killings of religious opponents is that Erasmus, although being a Catholic priest, became good friends with several reformers of his day such as John Colet and Thomas Linacre.

His dedication to learning the Greek text was one of a man on a mission. Undeterred, Erasmus did not stop the lack of money from keeping him from his studies. He practically begged his friends for money and books and studied day and night for three years.

Erasmus used at least a half dozen or so old Greek New Testament manuscripts. This became the first non-Latin Vulgate text of the scriptures in over a thousand years, as well as the first to be printed on a press. Erasmus' 1516 work focused attention on just how corrupted the Vulgate was and its inaccuracies. He showed the importance of going back and using the original Hebrew for the Old Testament and the original Greek for the New Testament to ensure accuracy so that, when translated, they would faithfully detail God's written word.

Although Erasmus, translated the New Testament only from Greek into Latin, in the preface of his 1516 edition he expressed the desire that "Would that they were translated into each and every language so that they might be read and understood not only by Scots and Irishmen, but also by Turks and Saracens. Would that the farmer might sing snatches of scripture at his plough, that the weaver might hum phrases of scripture to the tune of his shuttle, that the traveller might lighten with stories from scripture the weariness of his journey". [1]

This was perhaps Erasmus' attempt to suggest the reading of the scriptures be available to all classes and cultures. The quote is merely a fleeting comment of Erasmus which may be concluded that he meant all men should be able to read in their own tongue. The population of the Scots and the Irish was far less than that of the English, and still is to this day. In his singling out these national people, I would suggest he was saying even nations with a minority voice, in terms of population, deserved to have the Bible translated in their own tongue. Likewise, his comment to Turks and Saracens may have been his desire to see people of other faiths and cultures learn of God's word.

Because of his independent stance on matters concerning doctrine he was somewhat ostracized by both the Catholic and Protestant faiths but did remain a Catholic priest all his life. He preferred a life of an independent scholar, shunning any effort to cause him to choose sides that could perhaps infringe on his freedom to express his intellect and teachings. Only after he had fully mastered Latin did he embark on his greatest work of translating the New Testament into Greek in 1514. However this work had to await his publication of the Old Testament that was awaiting the approval of the Pope in 1522. Erasmus was dedicated to ensuring that the Greek and Latin of the New Testament was unified or, simply put, his Greek translation was not just the basis of his Latin translation but the other way around also. Later versions of his Greek text became known as the Textus Receptus and it was this document that was used extensively for the King James Version in 1611. He had great respect for Luther and Luther expressed similar comments, but the two never really enjoyed a lasting or mutual friendship. Perhaps this was in part due to his resistance to embrace the Christianity the reformers were preaching. This we do not know, but when the city of Basel was officially reformed, Erasmus gave up living there and relocated. Neither did he oppose the punishment of heretics but called for moderation, saying, "It is better to cure a sick man than to kill him". [2]

As ill health began to impede him he was invited to move from Freiburg to Branant by Mary, Queen consort of Hungary and Bohemia (1505-1558). Sadly, prior to taking up her offer, on a visit to Basel, Erasmus died unexpectedly as a result of dysentery. He was buried in Basel Minster with great ceremony.

Although this book predominantly follows how we arrived at obtaining the Bible in English, it would be remiss, if not neglectful of me, if I did not mention Martin Luther who became one of the central figures of the Protestant Reformation.

Martin Luther (1483-1546) arrived into history just prior to William Tyndale.

Luther's father, Hans Luder [it changed to Luther later on] wanted his eldest son to become a lawyer. He sent Martin to Latin schools in Mansfeld, Germany and later to Magdeburg in 1497 and the following year to Eisenach. All three schools focused on grammar, rhetoric and logic and Luther describes his education as purgatory and hell. At age 19 he entered the University of Erfurt and in 1505 received his master's degree. As per his father's wishes, he enrolled in law school at the same University but almost immediately dropped out due to his belief that this type of occupation was insecure.

Despite Luther's interest in Aristotle and the subject of philosophy this proved to be unsatisfying for him and he began looking at scripture. He later related a primary reason for his decision to embark on a life to God to an event that happened on 2 July 1505. While riding on horseback, as he was returning to University, a lightning bolt from a thunderstorm struck close by to him. He recalls telling his father he was terrified of dying and divine judgment and decided there and then he would become a monk. Hans was furious and believed his son was wasting his education. Despite this outburst from his father, Luther left law school, sold all his books and entered a closed Augustinian friary and became a monk. Luther dedicated himself to his new life and fasted, spent hours in prayer, went on pilgrimages and frequent confession.

But Luther felt almost as if he was a prisoner, chained to religious rites and did not feel this was the way to serve Christ. One of his superiors, Johann von Staupitz, taught him that true repentance did not involve self-affliction nor penances but rather a change of one's heart.

In 1508 Staupitz became the first dean of the new University of Wittenberg. Luther had been ordained a priest the year before and Staupitz wasted no time in appointing Luther to teach theology. Four years later in 1512 Luther was awarded his Doctor of Theology.

Life went on for Luther until an event that would change his life in 1516. A Dominican friar and a commissioner to the Pope by the name of Johann Tetzel was sent to Germany to sell indulgences. If one still thinks indulgences were something that helped one's salvation, we only have to look at the reason for these indulgences being sold. The money raised was to rebuild St. Peter's Basilica in Rome! Completely contradictory to scripture, Rome sold indulgences on the basis that faith alone could not justify man, but rather such faith depended upon charity and good works. Good works were interpreted by the Catholic Church to be the donating of money in the form of indulgences.

On 31 October 1517 Luther wrote to his bishop Albert of Mainz to protest. These writings became known as the Ninety-Five Theses. The boldness of Luther in these writings can be seen by Thesis 86 which he asked, "Why does not the Pope, whose wealth is to-day greater than the riches of the richest, build just this one church of St. Peter with his own money, rather than with the money of poor believers?". [3]

There is some controversy with regard to Tetzel suggesting, or even saying, that "as soon as a coin hit a bowl it would ring, and a soul from purgatory would spring". Let us examine this for a brief moment in answer to those who defend Tetzel. After a somewhat shady career as a priest [he was condemned for immorality but surprisingly pardoned] he was appointed 'Inquisitor' of Poland in 1509 and later appointed by Pope Leo X as commissioner of indulgences for all of Germany in 1517. Inquisitors were agents of the Roman Catholic Church whose purpose was to eliminate heresy. Heresy against what? None other than those who spoke against the Catholic Church and exposed their corrupt teaching of such things as indulgences. The fact that Tetzel then became the commissioner of indulgences for all of Germany shows his commitment to promote the teaching of indulgences, a teaching that is NO WHERE found in scripture. Irrespective of whether Tetzel said the words mentioned is mute and irrelevant. As a priest he was supposed to follow God, not a mere mortal. He was certainly supposed to preach the word of God accurately and live a life as a true follower of Christ. History shows this not to be the case. For one, he promoted the practice of indulgences according to his faith. Second, he actively had people tortured or put to death by the fact that he was an Inquisitor appointed by the Pope. His faith was man's faith, not God's. On this subject alone, it was too much for Luther which I can fully appreciate. Luther had not suddenly, out of the blue, erupted into revolt or indignation. One can imagine his own theology had built itself to the point that he was already asking himself, if not others, about the things he felt were contrary to the word of God. This is what led to the famous nailing of Luther's 95 Theses to the church door at Wittenberg. In January of 1518 friends of Luther translated his 95 Theses from Latin to German and they became widely printed and spread like wild fire across Germany in less than two weeks and throughout Europe within two months. The result was students packed the pews to hear Luther's sermons. During the next decade Luther wrote extensively and preached his beliefs to people only too willing to listen. He was convinced the church was corrupt and had deviated from the word of God on several important doctrines, the main one being justification through faith. He preached to the roof-tops of the Grace of God being given and not earned and that only through Jesus Christ was salvation possible.

Meanwhile, Archbishop Albrecht of Mainz and Madgeburg did not reply to the 95 theses Luther had sent him. Instead he had the documents checked for heresy and sent them to Rome. Albrecht also secretly needed money from indulgences to pay off papal dispensation for the employment of another bishopric. This didn't escape Luther's notice who said both Abrecht and the Pope had their fingers in the pie so to speak.

Pope Leo X had already been accustomed to heretics and decided to deal with Luther slowly, or so he thought. Over the next three years he sent several papal theologians [if indeed you could call them theologians which I would suggest was an insult to those who were true theologians] and envoys to speak against Luther. Luther was ordered to Rome, which he ignored, and the Elector Frederick persuaded the Pope to have Luther examined at Augsburg where the Imperial Diet [assembly] was held. Luther did indeed attend and the result was that it ended in a shouting match. Luther by now was cast as an enemy of the Pope. The original instructions by the papal authorities was that if Luther did not recant he was to be arrested. Luther managed to escape and did, in fact, agree to remain silent if his opponents did. Johann Eck, a staunch supporter of the Pope, however, was determined to expose Luther in a public debate. But Luther defended himself explaining that the Pope had no exclusive right to interpret scripture. Eck's outburst branded Luther as a new Jan Hus.

In the middle of 1520 the Pope warned Luther one last time with the papal bull [letter sealed by the Pope] that he would be excommunicated if he did not recant no fewer than 41 sentences from his 95 theses within 60 days. Luther replied to the Pope with a copy of "On the Freedom of a Christian" and publically burned the papal bull and decretals [orders] in Wittenberg.

Luther was excommunicated by the Pope on 3 January 1521. I can attest to how Luther must have felt from my own experience. Being brought up as a Jehovah's Witness from the age of five until my mid-twenties I too spoke out against the false doctrines this sect believed and preached. Despite a letter informing them of my desire and decision not to be recognized as a member of their church, they foolishly still met as a body of elders to formally excommunicate me from their church. I am in no way saying my situation was the same as Luther.

For one, I did not face the possibility of death. But I share this point merely to suggest that by now Luther [like myself] probably could care less what decision had been made, for it bore no importance as to what he believed to be true.

In April 1521 Luther appeared at the Diet of Worms. This assembly ran from the end of January to the end of May and Emperor Charles V presided over proceedings. Prior to Luther attending, Frederick III [Elector of Saxony] had obtained safe passage for Luther. Despite the fact that by this time he had already been excommunicated, Luther was ordered to recant, which he refused, and over the next five days his fate was to be determined. Finally, Charles declared Luther an outlaw, banning his literature and requiring his arrest. Anyone supporting Luther was also guilty of a crime and permission was granted to anyone to kill Luther with the assurance they would not face any charges for doing so. Presumably, the promise of safe passage obtained by Frederick III prior to Charles' declaration was sufficient to allow Luther to return to Wittenberg. However, Luther's return trip to Wittenberg was intercepted, but there is a good ending to this part of the story. Frederick had arranged for masked horseman to act as highwaymen and to 'kidnap' Luther, who escorted him to Wartburg Castle where he remained in relative security. He later likened this period to his "Patmos" in reference to the Apostle John's time of captivity while writing the book of Revelation.

During his time at Wartburg Luther translated the New Testament from Greek into German. He also wrote several doctrinal and polemical [critical] writings with the result that one particular writing renewed the attack on Archbishop Albrecht and actually shamed him into halting the sale of indulgences.

Almost a year later, Luther returned to Wittenberg. This was in part due to a particularly nasty group of visionary zealots [called the Zwickau prophets] who arrived in Wittenberg and preached revolutionary doctrines. Augustinian monks had also revolted, smashing statues and effigies of the church. Luther felt duty bound when the council invited him back.

Despite returning secretly to Wittenberg he immediately preached eight sermons during the period of Lent and the effect of his intervention was immediate. He set about reversing and modifying church practices and was successful in having the Zwickau prophets banished, but he was unable to stifle such radicalism further afield. It transpired that two Zwickau preachers, Nicholas Storch and Thomas Munster, were responsible for helping instigate the German Peasant's war in 1524-5 during which many atrocities were committed in the name of Luther. Although Luther sympathized with some of the grievances of the peasants, he insisted that the people should obey the local authorities. He was angered at the burning of convents, monasteries and libraries, and condemned the work as being that of the devil. He also charged the rebels with blasphemy for calling themselves Christian.

By 1526 Luther was increasingly occupied with organizing the new church, but avoided too much change so as not to anger the people. He did, in fact, base his services on a similar fashion to that of the Catholic service, which over time caused some reformers to accuse him of being too papistic. Modern scholars also make the comment that he was too conservative on his approach and reforms.

Luther used Erasmus' translation, which we read of earlier, to translate the Bible into German which as previously noted Luther successfully published in 1522. In 1518 Luther had been joined by a young professor, Philip Melanchthon who had helped Luther with learning Greek. Melanchthon went on to become a strong ally and supporter of Luther and provided Luther with advice and direction to his translation in 1522. Luther went on to publish a German Pentateuch the following year and a new edition of the German New Testament in 1523.

All of these works were the forerunners to the complete Bible published in German in 1534 and Luther continued to work on refining this work for the remainder of his life.

The years of fighting against the Roman papal authorities, the antagonistic situations with his fellow reformers etc., all took its toll on Luther's health and he suffered from an array of health problems as a result. He preached his last sermon three days before he died at Eisleben, his birthplace, on 15 February 1546. After successfully concluding business in Mansfeld to protect his family and their future livelihood, he returned to his home in Eisleben and died in the early hours on February 18 1546 at the age of 62.

It was against this backdrop which the work Luther and Melanchthon had created that quickly spread to England and caught the attention of one William Tyndale.

William Tyndale (1494-1536) wanted to use the same text that Erasmus had used to translate and print for the first time in history, the New Testament in English. If you are not already aware of it, we of the English language use the words of Tyndale daily in our everyday lives and certainly in our reading of the scriptures. Tyndale was referred to as the "Architect of the English Language" and is referenced far more widely than even William

Shakespeare. Many of Tyndale's phrases are still used by us all today which should come as no surprise as we shall learn.

The man himself was not only a magnificent scholar but a genius. He was so fluent in the eight languages he had learned that anyone of them could be considered his native tongue.

Not refusing advice, help and likely companionship, Tyndale eventually showed up on Martin Luther's doorstep sometime around 1524-1525 and within a year he translated and produced the New Testament from Greek into English. 3000 copies were printed at Worms, Germany in 1526 and were sent on their way to England. Upon arrival, the bishop of London had every copy that his agents could lay their hands on confiscated and subsequently burned. Despite the fact that only two of the original 3000 copies are said to exist, Tyndale was undeterred.

Tyndale had been forced to flee England for the very reason of his publication. He had attempted to seek both support and financial backing from certain people in England, but they had refused him. This led Tyndale to becoming a marked man and for the next 11 years he played a cat and mouse game of hiding from those who wanted him dead. Henry VIII had even invited him back to England under the rouse that he would give Tyndale royal protection, but Tyndale did not trust neither the crown nor the church. This is not surprising. Tyndale had previously written "Practyse of Prelates" which opposed Henry VIII's divorce on the grounds of scripture. To suddenly give Tyndale protection would not have appeared to have been legitimate in Tyndale's eyes. He would have immediately been suspicious.

In some ways Tyndale's life mirrored Luther's. Both men were wanted dead. In Luther's case he had strong backing, but nonetheless Luther was considered an outlaw, even to the point of people being threatened if they helped him. There does not appear in history anything to suggest that the German authorities decree [that anyone who killed Luther would not face charges] ever being rescinded.

Tyndale was practically facing the same fate. Bounty hunters and inquisitors were now on the lookout daily for any mention or sight of Tyndale.

With his New Testament complete, Tyndale set to work on translating the Old Testament from Hebrew to English. It had been his original plan to have translated this work in England. A fact that escapes the notice of many of us is in the 16th century, any attempt to translate the original languages of Hebrew and Greek was, to say the least, extraordinary and almost impossible. This wasn't due to a shortage of scholars in the ancient languages but because English (believe it or not) was not considered to be a serious language. This may seem unheard of in our day for English is now a widely accepted international language. But in the 1500's those who were able to read and write considered English barbaric and lacking the correctness of all grammatical pronunciation whatsoever.

In 1401 Richard Ullerston (died 1423) who was a Vice-Chancellor, then Chancellor of Oxford University, participated in a debate in Oxford defending the use of English as a language and as a base for translation. The debate finished with the decision that English was not to be used for translation and in 1407 the Archbishop of Canterbury, Thomas Arundel, ordered that any translation of the scriptures into English either by means of a book, pamphlet or tract, was not to be read in public or private. Arundel date stamped it to include any such literature from 1407 back to the writings of John Wycliffe.

As far as Tyndale was concerned, it appears at the time of his living in England he had not learned Hebrew. Those that knew Hebrew whom he could have called upon to teach him the language, namely the Jews, had been expelled from England long before Tyndale was born.

King Edward I in 1290 issued the Edict of Expulsion of all Jews from England. The Jews first arrived in England in 1066 when large communities of Jews came with William the Conqueror. Jews enjoyed being direct subjects of the King rather than feudal Lords, but with each passing King a royal charter had to be reviewed and passed. This led to a precarious situation for the Jews depending if they found favor with the current presiding King or not. Neither did Jews have any protection under the Magna Carta. Jews became very wealthy by providing loans to Jews and non-Jews which was strictly forbidden by the church. This created resentment of the Jews by church leaders, but for a time, because the King could levy taxes directly from the interest made on the loans, this gave the Jews some protection. However, Jews became more and more resented by both the church and the general public and this resentment was fueled by some extortionate Jewish moneylenders. Jews became hated by the English and were portrayed as a diabolical race who hated Christ. Many false beliefs started to appear, accusing Jews of even hunting children before the Passover to kill them for their blood. In 1275 the Statute of Jewry outlawed any lending of money by Jews and gave them 15 years to readjust to an alternative lifestyle and work. Heavy taxes were imposed and in 1287 Edward I ordered all local Jews expelled which was enforced by the year 1290. For over 365 years Jews were absent from the soil of England.

As a result, William Tyndale learned Hebrew in Germany and eventually started work on his translation. Sadly, Tyndale would never see his complete work of the Bible published but it would be completed by his faithful friends and scholars. While in Antwerp in 1535 he was betrayed by a fellow Englishman, Henry Phillips, and was arrested and sent to the cells at the castle Vilvoorde, not far from Brussels. Thomas Poyntz, who gave Tyndale safe lodging in Antwerp, had also been fooled by Phillips, although he had told Tyndale of his concerns or misgivings as to this 'new' friend. Despite all the academia we admire of Tyndale, this one solitary lapse of judgment spiraled into the events of his downfall and demise.

Wallowing in the dark damp cells of Castle Vilvoorde, Tyndale continued to write if only a few hours per day. His imprisonment would last for the next 18 months. Eventually brought before the authorities, with a long list of charges brought against him, Tyndale knew his fate. The mock proceedings of course found him guilty of heresy and like those ordained before him who met the same fate, he was led out to the town square and de-frocked of his church robes. The church, believing they had done their duty of excommunication, handed him over to the secular authorities for execution.

Again, we can see parallels of the way the chief priests and elders denounced Christ but handed him over to the Romans for execution.

Strangely, instead of being executed there and then, Tyndale was led back to prison where he would spend a further two months.

Differing accounts relate that Tyndale was strangled prior to being burnt, while others say he was strangled but revived. Either way, his death was the same debauched level of inhumanity heaped upon innocent men and women who followed the words of Christ in Matthew 24:9 which reads, ***"Then you will be handed over to be persecuted and put to death, and you will be hated by all nations because of me" (NIV).***

No doubt Tyndale also had the words of our Lord Jesus from Luke 9:24 on his mind, ***"For whoever desires to save his life will lose it, but whoever loses his life for My sake will save it" (NKJV).***

William Tyndale died a martyr with the resolve and bravery of a soldier of Christ. His last words were, "Lord! Open the King of England's eyes". [4]

Little did Tyndale know how prophetic that cry would be. Just three years later, King Henry VIII eyes would indeed be opened to accept an English Bible translation.

Thomas Poyntz, despite his stoic and brave defense for his friend was unable to save William Tyndale despite records showing his exhaustive efforts in writings to his brother John Poyntz. Thomas was himself held under house arrest being questioned by authorities regarding Tyndale but he delayed their endeavors for several weeks to assist in attempts to release Tyndale but to no avail. Knowing he was likely to face the same fate he managed to escape his captors and fled to England. He would live with the guilt of Tyndale's capture for the rest of his life and this, along with heavy debts incurred in Antwerp all took its toll. He died in England in 1562.

The traitor, Henry Phillips, fared even worse, himself becoming hunted by authorities of Henry VIII. Evidence suggests Phillips wasn't even acting on the orders of Henry VIII. Records indicate that Phillips hated the king as much as he hated Lutheranism. It appears he was no more than a sad figure whose only thought was money and he didn't care who he betrayed as a result of it. Clearly this was proven earlier with the theft from his own father. No more is heard of him after 1542 where he is a prisoner in Italy, disowned by his family, his King, and his country. A parallel to Judas if ever we needed one.

If Henry or his henchmen, or the church leadership thought they had heard the last of Tyndale, they were very much mistaken.

Despite his Bibles being burned, the money proved a regular source to print more, with one even ending up in King Henry VIII bedroom!

For all of the vilification of Tyndale and his English Bible, the more the authorities resisted its distribution, the more people wanted it. Church leaders even suggested the translation had thousands of errors. This would arguably be a case of calling the kettle black coming from such, considering their adherence to the Vulgate version they had insisted on for so long. They burned the translation of Tyndale because they knew they could find no errors and hence, would expose their lying and deceit.

People could themselves face being burnt at the stake for just owning a Tyndale Bible.

Here, laid bare in plain sight is the real reasoning behind these false teachers. Heresy would be too mild a term for them and I would doubt they would be free of punishment or retribution if they faced a court of their peers now. They knew of their wrongdoing [just like the Pharisees] and they knew if the common people could read the true word of God themselves their falsehood would be exposed. No longer would they be able to control the scriptures, as if they ever thought they could. They should have known they were fighting Almighty God himself!

If people read the Bible themselves the church's income and power would crumble. Indulgences would be seen for the false doctrine they were. Purgatory would be shown it did not belong in scripture, and the contradictions of the priests would be fully exposed for all to see. Everything the church had built their vast wealth on to the detriment of the people in the name of Christ would come back to haunt them. No. These things were indeed the biggest threats to their existence and they would not give up without a fight. But neither would those on the right side of God give up either.

Tyndale's New Testament flowed into England like a never ending torrent, hidden in bales of cotton and sacks of flour. No matter what orders Henry gave his men, the thirst for God's word would not be muted. It had been tethered and for far too long did not have a voice of its own. Tyndale's legacy was that forever the people of England would learn of God's word as it was intended. By their own might they themselves would discern the scriptures and feed on the truth and light of Jesus Christ.

Tyndale's last words were indeed answered, when in 1539 King Henry VIII allowed, and even funded, the printing of an English Bible which became known as the "Great Bible". If Henry or his band of crooked lieutenants thought they had silenced Tyndale they were wrong. The Great Bible for the most part was all Tyndale.

Two key figures emerged who had helped Tyndale with his translation and they both went on to fulfill the will of Tyndale in producing a complete Bible. We know that in the last years of William Tyndale's life his two faithful lieutenants and fellow disciples where Myles Coverdale and John Rogers.

Like a soldier seeing the standard bearer killed in battle, Myles Coverdale (1488-1569) immediately picked up the 'flag' to finish translating the Old Testament that Tyndale had begun. Known as the Coverdale Bible, it was completed in 1535 and printed in October of that year.

Born to Yorkshire parents [possibly Cover Dale near Richmond in the County of Yorkshire] Coverdale studied philosophy and theology at Cambridge. In 1514 he was ordained a priest at Norwich, England and it was here that he came under the influence of Robert Barnes. He also counted as either his friends or, at the very least acquaintances, Sir Thomas More and Thomas Cromwell. Cromwell was indeed a friend of Coverdale and had protected him, but when Cromwell was executed in 1539 Coverdale was compelled to flee England once again.

We can picture Coverdale as being a trusted and faithful friend, not only by the information from Cromwell, but also from the account that when Robert Barnes was charged with heresy, Coverdale went to London to aid Barnes with his defense. Soon after this he left the convent he first joined and began a life predominantly preaching against confession and the worship of images.

Around the time of the death of Cromwell, who had employed Coverdale to produce the "Great Bible",

Coverdale continued this work in Paris until the French government banned it. Returning to England he completed it in the same year.

Due to Coverdale defying The Act of the Six Articles of 1539 by marrying Elizabeth Macheson, his Bible was prohibited by proclamation in 1542 and he once again found himself in Europe. In 1545 he was pastor and schoolmaster at Bergzabern, Germany and then lived for a time in Frankfort three years later. By 1548 Coverdale was staying at Windsor Castle where Thomas Cranmer and others were preparing the First Book of Common Prayer.

Coverdale became almoner [chaplain] to Queen Catherine Parr and preached at her funeral in September 1548. He was also understood to have been the chaplain to young King Edward VI and evidently assisted [presumably] Cranmer with reforming measures.

During Mary's reign he was again in Europe, this time in Denmark. It is said he fled England with two servants, one of them being most likely his wife in disguise.

Finally he returned to England in 1559, no doubt believing it safe to do so after Elizabeth I succeeded Mary in 1558. He remained in England for the rest of his life.

Coverdale had used Luther's German text and the Latin as his source. Coverdale hoped his Bible would be approved by Henry. Instead, Henry decided that a new English translation was to be kept and read in every church in the land. One thing Coverdale did succeed in was to be nominated the author for what would become known as the "Great Bible".

One endearing and perhaps forgotten fact of Myles Coverdale was that despite lacking the charisma and style of Tyndale, he still showed great determination in dealing with authorities and was able to escape execution.

As a translator, he was faithful despite his puritan values which he extolled later in life. Myles Coverdale perhaps had more involvement over translations of several Bibles than anyone of his contemporaries of his day.

In 1537 Tyndale's other faithful supporter John Rogers printed a second complete Bible in English. However, Rogers' translation was from the original Hebrew and Greek. If you thought it would be called the Rogers Bible you would be mistaken. Possibly using a pseudonym that Tyndale may have employed himself, John Rogers (1500-1555) called his Bible the Matthew's Bible claiming the author was one Thomas Matthew who did not in fact exist [not at least in any real sense of any known Biblical scholar or translator as far as history is concerned].

The Matthew's Bible was, if you will, a mix-match of Tyndale's Pentateuch and New Testament, Coverdale's Bible and some translation of Rogers himself. To all intense and purposes it was a Tyndale Bible under a different name.

John Rogers was born near to the metropolitan City of Birmingham in Central England. After attending the local school there he went to Pembroke Hall, Cambridge University where he graduated with a B.A. in 1526. Later he became the rector of Holy Trinity the Less, in the City of London. In 1534 he left for Antwerp where he became chaplain to English merchants, and it was during this time that he met William Tyndale whose influence caused him to leave the Roman Catholic faith. He met and married an Antwerp native in 1537.

Despite Rogers being described as a translator it is believed he did very little, if any, translating himself but collated several known translations to form what would become the Matthew's Bible.

Rogers would later attend the University of Wittenberg and there he became good friends with Philip Melanchthon. By 1548 he was back in England and three years later was reader at St. Paul's Cathedral. Here, Rogers was no different from John Colet in his outspokenness, but his was denouncing the greed shown by certain courtiers who had suppressed the property of monasteries. Rogers also refused to wear the church vestments in favor of a simple round cap.

Imprisoned in January 1554 by the Bishop of London, Edmund Bonner [a particularly nasty inquisitor and murderer] who was known better as Bloody Bonner, Rogers was again defending himself for the charges brought against him a year earlier. Refusing to recant, his one request was to see his wife before his execution. Bonner would not even grant this request of the condemned man. Rogers was not even allowed to say goodbye to his wife nor comfort any of his 10 children. John Rogers was burned at the stake on 4 February 1555 at Smithfield, London.

Bonner never stopped nor repented of his crimes against Protestants. Referring to Bonner in one of his letters to Peter Martyr, Bishop Jewel wrote, "Being confined to the tower of London upon accession of Queen Elizabeth, the highest punishment inflicted, he went to visit some of the criminals kept in that prison, and wishing to encourage them, called them his friends and neighbors." [5]

Upon this, one of them is believed to have answered, "Go beast, into hell, and find your friends there, for we are none of them. I killed but one man upon a provocation, and do truly repent of it; but you have killed many persons of all sorts, without any provocation from them, and are hardened in your impenitence." [5]

John Rogers is believed to have been the first English Protestant martyred under Mary I of England.

Richard Taverner (1505-1575) is known, vaguely, for his Bible translation called the Taverner's Bible. This Bible is mentioned briefly as one which the King James Version translators could review as part of their work. It was purported to be 'The Most Sacred Bible' but was really only a small revision of John Rogers Matthew's Bible.

Still, young Taverner got into trouble early in his life for reading William Tyndale's New Testament work which was being circulated by Thomas Garret. Taverner later came under the direction of Thomas Cromwell and actively became engaged in producing works to promote the reformation in England. He was once arrested and placed in the tower of London but was restored to favor. Still, martyrdom was not on the mind of Richard Taverner and he disappeared from public life during the reign of Mary I. Eventually serving as justice of the peace for Oxfordshire and later as High Sherriff, Richard Taverner died in July 1575 without event.

George Joye (1495-1553) could be perhaps a name lost to history. Only by accident, while doing further research for this book, did I 'meet' the man who actually translated and produced the first printed translation of several books of the Old Testament into English.

Born in Salpho Bury, Renhold, Bedford, Bedfordshire, England he studied at Christ's College in Cambridge and graduated as B.A. in 1513-14. In 1515 he was ordained a priest and two years later received his Master of Arts. Five years later he graduated as Bachelor of Divinity and during all these years he undoubtedly came into contact with several of the men who later became the voices of the Reformation. It was during this period of association and influence that Joye embraced the thoughts and beliefs of Luther. Evading several near misses of being caught by the papal authorities with religious propaganda, he was finally ordered to appear before Cardinal Wolsey at Westminster along with Thomas Bilney and Thomas Arthur. Whether Joye was purposely kept in his Wolsey's antechamber [a smaller room serving as an entryway into a larger room] for several days the record is unclear. But during this time he witnessed or certainly heard the interrogation of Bilney and Arthur which persuaded him to flee to the Continent. Where he first arrived is conjecture. It may have been Strasbourg. Wherever it was, he likely met up with other like-minded individuals also in hiding such as Tyndale, Hitton, Barnes, Roye and Coverdale. He may have also been employed, as was Coverdale, as a proofreader or translator in the printing business. He worked tirelessly on translating several books of the Bible into English and these were among the very first to be printed in the English tongue. He also corrected an edition of Tyndale's New Testament that had been printed three times, without any English speaking corrector, by a Flemish printing firm. He corrected typographical errors and made some other changes which resulted in Tyndale bringing out his own revised version in 1534. Tyndale inserted a second foreword attacking Joye and his editorial work, which to some could be considered unfair, although Tyndale's attack was due to accusing Joye of denying the bodily resurrection of Christ and causing divisions among Protestants. Joye later published an apology but refuted Tyndale's accusations.

Henry Phillips, who we read earlier betrayed William Tyndale, may also have attempted to apprehend Joye and Robert Barnes. But Joye managed to escape. Interestingly, at the time of Tyndale's betrayal by Phillips, some English merchants were accusing Joye of assisting Phillips. Phillips however did not know Joye and had never met him. After other periods of exile in mainland Europe, Joye finally returned to England for good in 1547 and was given several appointments. He died in 1553.

As we stated earlier, Tyndale's last words were prophetic. Three years after Tyndale had been murdered, the Archbishop of Canterbury, Thomas Cranmer (1489-1556) hired Myles Coverdale in 1539 at the request of Henry VIII to publish a Bible that would be chained to every pulpit in the land. Sometimes referred to Cranmer's Bible, Coverdale completed this work in 1539. It was better known as we have previously mentioned the "Great Bible" due to its size, measuring over 14 inches tall.

To be clear, Henry VIII did not suddenly have a change of heart to have the Bible printed in English. His motives were far more personal and selfish. No longer giving spiritual allegiance to the Pope, Henry was still, at heart, a Catholic. But declaring himself head of state and the church meant he no longer had the support of Rome. As a result, Henry's world gave birth to a church that at the time was a mixture of both Roman Catholic and Protestant doctrines. This poor mixture, like a spoiled cake mix, became known as the Anglican Church or Church of England. Henry, already being aware of the contention of having an English Bible and how the Pope felt about it, knew exactly how he could defy Rome and therefore did not have to think twice about approving and funding an English speaking Bible. This action was pure spite, but God fulfills his promise in many more ways astounding to us than this example.

If Henry was the master of ceremony for an English Bible for his new Anglican Church, his daughter Mary I was the wicked ruler portrayed in many fairy tales. Except this ruler was all too real and upon her ascension to the throne she immediately ordered confiscation of English Bibles again. Her reign brought about the "Marian Exile" that we have mentioned, where refugees fled England for the Continent to escape religious persecution and death, once more, all in the name of religion. Almost 300 Christian martyrs were sent to their deaths [mostly by burning at the stake] by her direct orders. Thomas Cranmer is just one example of her murderous rule. Cranmer had previously recanted to save himself several times, only for Mary to ignore his recant and insist an example should be made of him. Before being sent to the stake Cranmer denounced his recantation and called the Pope the enemy of Christ, and was pulled from the pulpit and dragged to the site of his death. As a symbol of his earlier error in recanting [presumably by writing] he placed his hand in the fire first, as though he was placing his hand there as the offending item of recantation.

Mary's obsession with turning England back into a kingdom of Roman Catholics bordered on insanity and she rightly earned the title "Bloody Mary". This, we have already established by the burning at the stake of John Rogers and Thomas Cranmer in 1555 and 1556. These men were just two of the many hundreds of reformers attributed to being executed on the orders of Mary.

It was during this period that we eventually move into our discussion of our next chapter, The Geneva Bible.

John Foxe (1516-1587) is famous for his recordings written in his book Foxe's Book of Martyr's and was one of several men who sought and found safe haven in Geneva. The others were Myles Coverdale, Thomas Sampson and William Whittingham, who all enjoyed the protection of the theologian John Calvin.

Calvin and Foxe determined that they would produce a Bible while in exile that would offer the education of the scriptures their families desired.

The Geneva Bible was the Englishman's choice for over 100 years and enjoyed at least 144 editions between 1560 and 1644.

It should not be considered unusual to associate Foxe with the Geneva Bible. It would no doubt be a Bible he would refer to constantly as he grew more and more into the Puritan ideal.

Born in Boston in Lincolnshire, England, Foxe was a child who was industrious in his studies and entered Brasenose College, Oxford at age 16. A year later he transferred to Magdalen College School and successfully attained several degrees thereafter.

By the age of twenty five Foxe had read both Latin and Greek writings and had acquired the skills of reading the Hebrew language. His life was clearly one of being an academic but in 1545 he resigned his college post after becoming a Protestant. His resignation was perhaps hastened by papal authorities, who still had much influence with the college authorities.

His career prospered under Edward VI rule and he was later ordained deacon by Nicholas Ridley in 1550. But this life of security did not last upon the accession to the throne of Mary I after Edward succumbed to tuberculosis. Believing his life was in danger, Foxe sailed, along with his pregnant wife from Ipswich, England to

Nieuwpoort, Belgium. This was a closer call than one imagined. Officers had already been dispatched to effect his arrest and his escape was a timely one. In Basel, along with John Bale and Lawrence Humphrey, Foxe worked as a proofreader. During this time Foxe was getting reports of persecutions in England and wrote a pamphlet asking English nobles to intervene, but without success.

Foxe was perhaps more astute than some of his contemporaries, who upon learning of the death of Mary rushed back to England. Foxe on the other hand waited to see if religious changes would be both recognized and instituted by Mary's successor Elizabeth I, and remained in Europe.

Although he was later ordained a priest by the new Bishop of London and friend Edmund Grindal, Foxe, like many reformers, refused to wear clerical vestments which had been ordered by the Queen. Here, his Puritan ideals again surfaced and he remained in defiance of the order.

His famous Book of Martyrs began in 1552 but it was not until 1563 that he published his first edition which was called Actes and Monuments which the public named Book of Martyrs. The publication made Foxe instantly famous in name only. There were no such things as royalties then and he remained as poor as before, at least from a financial standpoint. It immediately came under attack by the Catholics. But new material flooded in so that Foxe was never short of adding additional stories or verifying ones he already had written. This constant stream of new material allowed him the opportunity to produce several editions.

Foxe's Book of Martyrs has garnered criticism ever since it was published. First by the papal authorities and later by critics who claim some of the stories lack a certain element of fact. Stories can indeed become inflated over time and Foxe was not immune or ignorant of this. He took great strides to prove many of the accounts listed in his book. One fact that cannot be denied is that many of the accounts occurred during his lifetime and Foxe had eyewitness testimony from people of the atrocities. He consulted episcopal registers and reports of trials and used many of these sources for his content.

The fact that we have Foxe's publication stands as a witness to those who falsely accused good men, women and children whose only crime was to serve the true God and apply His written word in their faith and their lives. These butchers of the devil proved by their idolatry whose side they were on and happily carried out the devils work, just so they could attempt to keep a strangle hold on the people with their false doctrines.

But the last word of this chapter is to those who kept the faith, who fought the fine fight in boldly going to their deaths rather than renounce their Savior Jesus Christ. They won far more, both then and now.

They paid for their faithfulness to God with their earthly lives, but exchanged it for a crown of glory in heaven.

"Centuries of experience have tested the BIBLE. It has passed through critical fires no other volume has suffered, and its spiritual truth has endured the flames and come out without so much as the smell of burning"

William Edwin Sangster (1900-1960)

CHAPTER 6

The Geneva Bible of 1560

The Geneva Bible preceded the authorized version of the King James Bible by some 51 years. The historical significance of the Geneva Bible cannot be minimized by time nor circumstance. For the very first time, the Geneva Bible was a Bible that was mass produced by the invention of mechanical printing, which made the Geneva Bible available directly to the general public.

If you have a copy of the 1560 edition you will note the entire Bible is a facsimile version of the original text. I hope, like me, when you open and look at it, you will get just a little excited that you are actually directly staring at over 450 years of history in the making. Hopefully too, you will appreciate its pages, no matter how difficult it is to read or decipher, knowing brave men and women literally gave up their lives for the translation in your hands. If you do not own one, then you can do an internet search and view some of the facsimile online.

It was certainly one of the Bible's taken to America on the Mayflower by the pilgrims, which consisted of puritans who fled religious persecution from several governments and entities. More on this later.

139

Many famous names read and used the Geneva Bible which became the primary source and Bible of choice amongst 16th century Protestants. Some of those names were William Shakespeare (baptized 1564-1616), who interestingly was virtually ordered to become part of King James I court.

Oliver Cromwell (1599-1658), known as the Lord Protector of Protestant England used the Geneva Bible and Cromwell's soldiers still respected this version at the time of the English civil war, its contents being included in the Soldier' Pocket Bible.

John Knox (c.1513-1572) who is considered to have founded Presbyterianism in Scotland, was believed to have had a copy of the Geneva Bible. This would not be unusual given the fact he spent several years in Geneva along with John Calvin.

John Bunyan who wrote Pilgrim's Progress also read and used the Geneva Bible.

Because of the mechanical process employed in printing the Geneva Bible the publisher was able to include a variety of study guides and aids. This included verse citations that allowed the reader to cross reference scriptures for their enlightenment of the word of God. Introductions of each book of the Bible allowed the reader to read a summary of each particular book which contributed to the readers understanding of the Bible text.

The language of the Geneva Bible was preferred over that of the Great Bible due to its force and vigor.

At the time of Queen Mary I of England' reign (1553-1558) many Protestant scholars had little choice but to flee from England for fear of persecution and death. Many of these learned scholars ended up in Geneva

Switzerland which at the time was a Republic. Prominent spiritual leaders such as John Calvin resided there and later Theodore Beza.

John Calvin, born Jehan Cauvin (1509-1564) was actually a Frenchman from the town of Noyon in the region of Picardy, France. Perhaps because of having the influential family, the Montmors, as his patrons, Calvin was able to attend the College de la Marche in Paris, France. It was here that he learned Latin from the famous teacher Marthurin Cordier (c.1479-1564). Upon completion of this course he began studies in philosophy at the College de Montaigu, also in Paris. In 1525 or 1526 Gerard Cauvin [Calvin's father] withdrew young Calvin from Montaigu and enrolled him in law school in the University of Orleans. Calvin's father evidently felt his son would earn more money as a lawyer than a priest. This period of time played a significant role in Calvin's life later. When he finally returned to theology he applied his teaching of law whenever he applied himself to scripture. Not unlike Luther, Calvin experienced a religious conversion around the year 1533. Two accounts are suggested for his conversion. In one he speaks of God bringing upon him a sudden change of mind, while the second he mentions a period of inner turmoil which was followed by spiritual and psychological anguish. Whichever version it was, it marked the end of John Calvin's association with the Roman Catholic Church. The year before this occurrence Calvin had received his license to practice law and he returned to Paris. Only a month after arriving in Paris, Calvin's close friend Nicolas Cop (c.1501-1540), who at the time was rector of the College de France, Paris, was embroiled in a heated debate as a result of his inaugural address where he called for the need of reform by the

Catholic Church. Cop was denounced as a heretic and forced to flee to Basel. For whatever reason, lost to time, Calvin was also implicated and for the next year was forced to hide from the authorities. By 1534 the Affair of the Placards had taken root. Reformers had posted placards attacking Catholic mass which had provoked a violent reaction against Protestants. Calvin took little time in deciding to finally join Cop in Basel. It was here that he published his first edition of The Institutes of the Christian Religion in 1536. That same year saw Calvin leave Basel for Geneva after being recruited by William Farel (1489-1565) to assist in reforming the Geneva church. However, the council of Geneva rejected both men's ideas and they were both expelled. Calvin then traveled to Strasbourg on the invitation of Martin Bucer (1491-1551) to become a minister there for French refugees. Calvin preached to 400-500 members of the church and he preached or lectured every day, as well as performing two services on Sunday. By now his friends were playing matchmaker and several ladies were presented to him. Reluctantly he agreed to marry on the condition his new wife would learn French. However less than 5 months later he refused to marry the lady in question and married instead Idelette de Bure who was a widow with two children.

While in Strasbourg he continued to support the efforts of reformers in Geneva and this led to him being invited to return to Geneva which he did. Strasbourg in fact 'loaned' Calvin for six months prior to him taking up a position in Geneva permanently in 1540. During his time in Geneva, Calvin preached over 2000 sermons. His sermons would last an hour, without the use of notes. In 1545 Idelette died and Calvin, heartbroken never married again.

If we imagined Calvin's tenure in Geneva was without opposition we would be wrong. He faced opposition many times, perhaps due in part to his personality which he unashamedly assumed was of a higher level and intellect than that of his opponents or peers. One can easily see that many of the oppositions that Calvin faced were due in the large part to political or religious rivalry as to worship or position. One particular unpleasant incident was the appearance of an unsigned threatening letter found at the pulpit where Calvin preached. The Geneva Council, believing there was a plot against church and state, appointed a commission to investigate and report back with its findings. Jacques Gruet who was a libertine and atheist, belonged to a group opposed to Calvin and confessed under torture to writing the letter as well as other crimes. The civil authorities condemned him to death and with Calvin's consent he was beheaded on 26 July 1547.

I mention this sad tale for two reasons. One was the folly of writing falsehood which scripture warns one of not doing which Gruet suffered the ultimate penalty for. It could be argued that Gruet deserved what he got. He was known to mock the scriptures and ridicule Christ and said immortality of the soul was a fairy tale. With the religious hotbed of the day, Gruet's condemnation was assured. The second reason I mention is when I read this story in my research I could not help but sigh that Calvin [in my personal opinion] showed no better mercy than that of the Catholic persecutors before him. Indeed, this would not be the last time that Calvin was to approve of the execution of others who opposed him. By 1552 opposition to Calvin was so intense that he believed he was defeated and offered his resignation to the council the following year, but they refused to accept it. Those who opposed him [some of which in previous years had actually supported him] now knew their battle was in vain. They had succeeded in curbing Calvin to a degree but they had failed to have him banished.

Calvin's fortunes and support appear to have been invigorated by the events of his contact with the Spaniard Michael Servetus (1511-1553). Servetus who was a theologian, physician and cartographer appears to have been someone who was not afraid to speak his mind or to challenge theories or doctrines of other likeminded theologians or faiths. In 1553 that could have been and was interpreted as heresy. Calvin's friend, Guillaume de Trie had denounced Servetus as such. He was already a fugitive from ecclesiastical authorities and had previously and brazenly criticized the teachings of the Trinity as well as infant baptism. He had quarreled with Johannes Oecolampadius (1482-1531) and had been expelled from the city of Basel only to then travel to Strasbourg where he published a pamphlet against the Trinity. Martin Bucer objected to this work and quickly asked him to leave also. One could say that Servetus didn't know when to hide or when to keep quiet. It is honorable for a person to believe in his or her convictions but when both main religious factions agreed to disagree with Servetus' beliefs his days were numbered. Upon returning to Basel from Strasbourg he published his Two Books of Dialogues on the Trinity which caused an immediate sensation. Perhaps Servetus was simply a man who was too proud or puffed up with his own importance. In any event, his next target was Calvin. At first the two corresponded by letter [Calvin used a pseudonym while Servetus did not sign his letters]. Calvin eventually grew tired of the writings and refused to reply. Servetus had sent him over 30 letters but when Servetus sent a copy of Calvin's own work of the Institutes of the Christian Religion heavily annotated with comments declaring errors, Calvin was incensed. Servetus wrote Calvin that he would come to Geneva if Calvin was agreeable. Calvin, by now feeling greatly offended by Servetus, wrote to his friend William Farel stating that, "Servetus has just sent me a long volume of his ravings. If I consent he will come here, but I will not give my word; for if he comes here, if my authority is worth anything, I will never permit him to depart alive". [1]

It is clear from Calvin's letter to Farel that he was more than offended. His own tone was such that it suggested he would seek Servetus' execution. The fact that Calvin made the point in his letter that if his own authority was sufficient he would not allow Servetus to leave Geneva alive, places Calvin in a position contrary to scripture. Calvin knew that it was God who was, and is, a man's judge and not a fellow man. To disagree with another person or to hold a strong opinion was one thing. But to suggest having someone killed for their beliefs because they disagreed or argued with another person's belief [in this case Calvin] made them no better than those who had committed the same atrocities themselves in the name of religion.

Strangely [or perhaps not] the French inquisitor-general learned of Servetus' whereabouts and had him arrested. His letters to Calvin were used as evidence against him for heresy, but he denied writing them. There is no suggestion made by me here that Calvin conspired with the Catholic authorities. However, it appears Servetus was convicted by the Roman Catholics under one of his other known names Michel de Villeneuve on the basis of 17 letters sent by Calvin. One may draw their own conclusions. Likely, one could also ask why Calvin was cooperating with Catholics, unless one assumes it may have been the ideal in Calvin's mind to have Servetus murdered by the Catholics and thereby thwarting any accusations made against Protestants being involved with the whole sordid affair. Whatever the cause of Servetus' arrest and subsequent conviction he managed to escape and was sentenced to death in absentia by the Catholics by burning. This episode has some irony to it, in that the Catholic authorities sentenced Servetus to death on the evidence of the writings sent to them by Calvin, who was no longer of the Catholic faith.

Regardless of his narrow escapes Servetus did not employ a jot of commonsense. On his way to Italy he decided to stop off in Geneva for reasons unknown and actually attended one of Calvin's sermons. He was, not surprisingly, recognized and arrested. This time, Calvin's secretary drafted a list of accusations that was brought before the court in Geneva. After receiving further information from Zurich, Basel, Bern and Schaffhausen, Servetus was condemned to death. Calvin along with other ministers asked that he be beheaded as a traitor rather than be burned as a heretic, but their request was denied and Servetus was burned on top of a pyre of his books at the Plateau of Champel. Again, we could argue that this act was no better than what Catholics had done. Tyndale was himself burnt with copies of his books piled on the pyre.

Following Servetus' execution one of Calvin's close associates, Sebastian Castellio (1515-1563) finally ended any vestiges of friendship with Calvin stating that he did not agree with Calvin's treatment of heretics. This led to Castellio writing his Treatise on Heretics in 1554 where he argued for more restraint and focus on the moral teachings of Christ in place of what he called theological vanity. He later developed a theory of tolerance based on principles of the Bible.

Sebastian Castellio is possibly one of those gallant voices of history that has been lost to us over time. Many in his day considered him Calvin's equal. I would suggest that is somewhat of an insult to his memory in terms of his sheer knowledge of Hebrew, Greek, Latin and later German, which certainly exceeded Calvin's experience. Calvin knew of Castellio's brilliance first hand.

After meeting by chance in Strasbourg the two men struck up a solid friendship with the result that Calvin invited Castellio to Geneva to become rector to the College de Geneve. Castellio also became commissioned to preach in the Geneva suburb of Vandoeuvres. In 1543, Castellio was the only minister to visit those afflicted with the plague and to console the dying. Calvin and the rest of the Consistory refused to visit with excuses of being indispensable, saying that it would not help the church but weaken it if Calvin and others were lost to the plague themselves. It irreversibly smacks of double standards on Calvin's part. Nevertheless, the council recognized Castellio for his kind works and deeds and the people of Geneva rewarded him with the permanent position of preacher at Vandoeuvres. Only a year later his treacherous friend Calvin launched a campaign against Castellio. It appears Castellio had decided to translate the Bible into French and in 1544 asked Calvin for his endorsement. Calvin not only rejected his request but publically and privately rebuked Castellio. Their disagreements widened when at a public meeting Castellio stood up and said that clergy should not persecute those who disagree with them on Bible interpretation and should be held to the same standards that all believers where held to.

As a result, the political machine of Calvin again came into play and Castellio was forced to resign. Before doing so he asked the council for a letter stating that he had resigned of his own accord and that anything spoken or written contrary to the letter was false. Castellio's fall was heavy and quick. Though one of the leading lights of theology in his time, he was left to beg from door to door for food for himself and his eight dependents. Surviving by digging ditches, begging and the occasional proof reading, he eventually was restored to a position he should never have lost. In 1553 [9 years after asking Calvin for his endorsement of the French Bible] Castellio was made Master of Arts of the University of Basel with all the prestige the position carried. It was while in this position that Castellio exchanged the war of words with Calvin regarding Servetus' execution which ended any possible reconciliation of the two men. He even went as far as to accuse Calvin of murder. Calvin defended his actions in a treatise [exposition or argument in writing] explaining the need to defend the orthodox faith, in which he said Servetus' execution was justified by Servetus' diverging from the orthodox Christian doctrine. Three months went by and Castellio wrote that Servetus had 'fought' with reasons and writing and should have been repulsed by the same manner. He even reminded Calvin [indirectly] that Calvin had written several years before to the Catholic church regarding his own persecution saying that it was unchristian to use arms against those expelled from the church and to deny a person such common rights.

Castellio argued that Calvin was interpreting scripture to fan the fire to justify his own actions and suggested that a heretic was obviously one would argue against Calvin. Given the evidence we have already read of

Calvin's actions toward Servetus one could be forgiven at arriving at the same conclusions as Castellio. He strongly argued for separation of church and state and declared that no one was entitled to attempt to control another man's thoughts. He called for tolerance and peace and an allowance for different sides to disagree, while still showing love for one another.

Ten years later, in 1563 Castellio died and was buried in the tomb of a noble family in Basel. That should have been the rightful end for this man of faith, but his enemies in one final insult unearthed his body [just like Wycliffe before him] and burned it and scattered his ashes.

Calvin [no different than the Catholics] insisted that the Consistory [the ecclesiastical council] should rule over matters of excommunication which was agreed. In January 1555 the council announced that the Swiss churches retained their authority of power over such matters as that which related to the church.

Calvin's staunch defense against Servetus and his subsequent arguments that the Consistory should retain their authority led to him being acclaimed a defender of Christianity. Others [primarily the Libertine's] continued to attempt to stage Calvin's downfall. On another occasion the Libertine's planned to burn down a house full of Frenchmen. The plotters who stayed in the city were rounded up and executed. This marked the beginning of the end of opposition to Calvin. His authority was virtually unchallenged during his final years in office. He even enjoyed an international reputation as a reformer. This, one could ponder, was the bad side of Calvin. Or was it? Was he merely trying to protect those who argued for reform? Or did he engineer those who opposed him to be killed?

Arguably, we will never know the full answer to this and many questions regarding not just Calvin, but a plethora of people who had, or ordered others to be killed who opposed them or their faith. The true answer lies with Almighty God. Man ultimately is not answerable to man, but we are all answerable to God and He will be everyone's judge.

Fortunately, Calvin is remembered more for his positive actions with regard to the reformation. After all, it was Calvin who gladly provided safe haven to the Marian exiles [those who had fled England from Queen Mary I persecution]. And it was Calvin who arranged for them to be able to form their own reformed church under the leadership of John Knox and William Whittingham. English church services are conducted each week in Geneva right up to the present day. Calvin, in fact, was more interested in reforming France and he supported the building of churches and sending literature and arranging for its printing all from funds from Geneva. He was especially interested in the building of a college for children in order for them to be educated. His wish was for his old tutor in Latin, Mathurin Cordier, to be one of the primary teachers. The other was Emmanuel Tremellius who was a professor of Hebrew. Neither were available and his next choice fell to Theodore Beza, who became rector. Beza is one of the main characters we can thank for the little information Calvin left us to understand the man. Despite all of the preceding information [good or bad] Calvin's theology hardly wavered from his youth to old age. He wrote in Institutes, "the sum of human wisdom consists of two parts: the knowledge of God and of ourselves". [2]

He also said that for anyone to believe that God is their creator, one only had to read scripture. He fully believed the church to be the body of Christ with the Lord as Head of that body, and denied the primacy of the papal system. As to sacraments, he accepted two, namely baptism and communion, while the Catholics believed in seven. He completely rejected transubstantiation, but argued also his belief in predestination. During his lifetime Calvin wrote commentaries on every book written by the Apostle Paul and eventually wrote commentaries on every book in the New Testament with the exception of 2nd and 3rd John and Revelation. He had also increased the twenty-one chapters of his book Institutes, to eighty and his drive in this also contributed to his ill health. After recovering sufficiently to conduct a sermon he strained his voice which resulted in a severe coughing fit, which burst a blood vessel in one of his lungs. His health steadily worsened and within six months he died in 1564. So great was the number of people who came to see his body laying in state that his associates were concerned of fostering a form of hero worship. As a result they arranged to have Calvin buried in an unknown grave keeping its location secret. Other thoughts, which may be more accurate, is that Calvin was a deeply private person outside of his circle of close associates. Little, if anything, is known as to his personal life. It has been suggested by some that it was his wish that he be buried in the manner it was. It could also be considered that he was probably aware of what the authorities in England had done to the body of Wycliffe 40 years after his death. Remember also that a year prior to his death the body of his opponent Castellio had suffered the same or similar fate. It may be that he did not desire the same fate or at least the historical narrative of Wycliffe or Castellio's final resting place.

It is true, under men such as Calvin spiritual leadership and theology thrived. William Whittingham (1524-1579) who actually married John Calvin' sister, would later be the one who supervised the translation that became the Geneva Bible.

Born in Chester, England, Whittingham entered Brasenose College, Oxford, at the age of 16. The college entry states he was listed as a "commoner". He graduated with his B.A. and five years later was elected fellow of All Saint's College. Two further years saw him become the senior student at Christ Church College, Oxford, where he subsequently began his M.A. In the summer of 1550 he was granted leave of his studies for three years in order to travel. Whittingham went to the University of Orleans in France as well as Lyon and Paris. In 1552 he visited Germany and Geneva. Whether his travels were the result of him adopting extreme Protestant views is uncertain. This could have been the reason for these trips where he would have undoubtedly come into the company of those proclaiming the reformation. After all, mainland Europe was indeed the hotbed for the establishment of the Reformation.

Whittingham did in fact return to England in 1553, honoring his three year absence. However, his theology had now changed and in 1554 he was living in Frankfort, Germany, after previously leaving England, with some difficulty perhaps due to his stance on doctrine. Whittingham succeeded in interceding on behalf of Peter Martyr Vermigli (1499-1562) who himself was forced to flee from England upon the ascension of Queen Mary I. This action and support of Vermigli by Whittingham may have made him a marked man and Whittingham was indeed one of the first Marian exiles to arrive in Frankfort. He wasted no time in sending invitations out to likeminded exiles to join him. He would have probably remained in Frankfort permanently had it not been for a disagreement of which prayer book to use in their church services. Whittingham, along with John Knox, insisted on revising the current prayer book to that of John Calvin's teachings. But when Richard Cox (1500-1581) arrived in Frankfort dissention became unavoidable. Cox originally had been consulted on the compilation of the Communion office in 1548 which later included the first and second books of Common Prayer. He was also a member of the commission who sat to reform canon law. No doubt Cox felt he was the more knowledgeable personage than that of Knox. Cox favored the continuation of the Common Prayer Book of 1552. The result was Knox was suspended and expelled from the city. Although Whittingham attempted to accept Cox's influence, he soon realized he could not, and departed to Geneva to join up again with Knox.

For the next four years Whittingham enjoyed several positions of leadership within the church at Geneva. He became an elder, a deacon and finally succeeded Knox as minister in 1559. Despite receiving no previous ordination to minister he was encouraged by Calvin to accept the post which he did. When Queen Mary I died the majority of the Marian exiles returned to England, but Whittingham remained in Geneva, primarily to complete the translation of what was to become the Geneva Bible.

In this endeavor he was assisted by William Cole, Myles Coverdale, Anthony Gilby, Christopher Goodman, Thomas Sampson along with several others.

The result was the first edition of the Geneva Bible of 1560, but it would be another 15 years before it was printed in England in its entirety. No less than 144 editions were produced, the last around the year 1644.

The first Bible to ever be printed in Scotland was in fact the Geneva Bible and likely John Knox (1514-1572) may have had some influence in this. In 1579 Scotland actually passed a law that required every household who was able to buy a copy of the Geneva Bible to own one.

Although Knox is not mentioned as being part of the translation team of the Geneva Bible he does in fact still warrant mention. Due to his influence and, indeed, his leadership as the minister of the Geneva church, it would be somewhat of a stretch to suggest he had no involvement in the production as such, if only perhaps proof reading some of the work. The same could be true, I would suggest, regarding Calvin. Rather, Knox appeared to busy himself with reforming theology and his daily experience and knowledge gained [some perhaps from Calvin] would go on to formulate his theology based upon Presbyterian polity [the church government or constitution]. There is no historical record as to why Knox first adopted Protestant teachings. It may have been as a result of George Wishart (1513-1546) who had previously fled Scotland due to his reformation beliefs and upon returning, Knox became his bodyguard. Later however, Wishart would be added to the martyrs list when he was burned at the stake in 1546 accused of heresy. Knox himself somehow escaped execution by Wishart's accuser Cardinal David Beaton (1494-1546). It is interesting to note that Beaton himself was murdered less than three months after the death of Wishart by a gang of several people in revenge for Wishart's execution. Eventually, after suffering imprisonment by the French for two years, Knox took refuge in England and in April 1549 he was licensed to work in the Church of England. He served in several positions in England until leaving for the continent in the beginning of 1554 on the advice of friends due to the ascension of Mary to the throne of England. Disembarking in Dieppe, France, he apparently made his way to John Calvin. He, as previously mentioned, then took up a position in Frankfort before he left Frankfort returning to Geneva in 1555. Despite being a leading reformer himself, what many do not realize is upon leaving Frankfort, Knox ceased his association with the Church of England. This may be the reason how the Presbyterian faith came into being. Despite various faiths being born to the Reformation, one can sense the closeness these men of faith had by their personal interactions with one another. For example, Knox's two sons who were born in Geneva had as their godfathers none other than William Whittingham and Myles Coverdale.

Knox eventually returned to Scotland and he is perhaps best remembered for his contribution in establishing the Presbyterian doctrine through Scotland. He is also noted in history of speaking out both publically and to the face of Mary Queen of Scots rebuking her actions and dogma. When he died on 24 November 1572 the 4th Earl of Morton, James Douglas is said to have pronounced at his grave "Here lies one who never feared any flesh". [3]

In his will Knox insisted that "None have I corrupted, none have I defrauded; merchandise have I not made". [4]

To corroborate his words, his wife and children would have been left in abject poverty had it not been for the General Assembly agreeing to continue to pay Knox's stipend to his widow for the following 12 months.

In the end, Knox was not so much remembered for his overthrow of the Catholic Church in Scotland, but the predominance of Presbyterianism over Anglicanism. In Europe, Knox is remembered in the 'Reformation Wall' in Geneva depicting the stone carvings of William

Farel, John Calvin, Theodore Beza and Scotland's own John Knox.

The annotations recorded in the Geneva Bible is perhaps what led to State and Religious authorities requesting its removal. The Geneva Bible was considered to be both Calvinist and Puritan in its character. Both the Anglican Church along with King James I of England disliked it intensely.

The prior ruler of England, Elizabeth I, disliked it too, for much the same reasons and this was what motivated in part the production of the Bishops' Bible. Likewise, during Mary's reign demand was sought for the Rheims-Douai edition that was favored by Catholics.

The Geneva Bible, however, continued to be the choice of the Puritans and continued to be used widely until after the English Civil war.

As you delve into the history of the Geneva Bible and, for that matter, the King James version, you will be faced with the amazing facts that despite all of the persecution, the burnings at the stake, the untold tortures people were subjected to in order to have them recant their new found faith, the truth of God's word moved forward like a steam train at full throttle. It burned a trail so wide and so fast that within just a few lifetimes the strangle hold of the Catholic Church and sadly the Anglican Church, who at times were just as guilty, were no longer able to continue to teach false doctrines and stifle the true word of God.

The refreshing breeze of truth was felt in the Geneva Bible with translations made from scholarly editions of the Greek New Testament and Hebrew Scriptures.

The English rendering alone comprised of more than 80% of the original translation of Tyndale.

The Geneva Bible was also the first Bible to use verse numbers based upon the work of Frenchman Robert Estienne (1503-1559) who was originally a Catholic and later became a Protestant. Estienne had previously printed the French Bible with verse numbers and the writers of the Geneva Bible adopted this style as well as including notes and annotations in the margins.

In addition to all of this was the selection of size for the Geneva Bible. For example, the 1560 edition was in quarto size but there were also pocket size versions printed as well. All of this added to the benefit of the common people. By now the Geneva Bible was becoming more affordable and could easily be purchased for less than a person's weekly wage even for those who received the lowest of wages.

I'm sure the common people would have been grateful to receive a Bible that had just the text in their language, but the Geneva Bible went way beyond that. It included an index of names as well as topics and maps together with explanatory notes. It had tables and wonderful intricate woodcut illustrations as well as study aids. We can only imagine the delight in a person seeing all of this and in their language! If you own a facsimile version of the 1560 edition of the Geneva Bible you will be instantly amazed how simple it is to read once you master the style of lettering used in that era. If that is not to your taste then I can also recommend the 1599 Geneva Bible Patriot's Edition which is somewhat like the King James Version in its language style and is more readily understandable. One thing that fascinates my wife and I every time we gaze into the 1560 edition is we are directly looking at a copy of a Bible that was finally in the hands of people who could read and understand it, over 450 years ago. A person cannot help looking through its pages and not remember the good men and women arrested and, in some cases, put to death just for possessing or owning a Geneva Bible.

No less was this seen during the reign of Mary Tudor who subsequently was known unofficially as Bloody Mary and perhaps deservedly so.

So determined was she to reinstate Catholicism, the persecution of Protestants inevitably followed. Having strong ties to the Spanish Catholics she eventually married Phillip II of Spain and forced Parliament to once again recognize papal Rome. Despite the fear of persecution and death, these actions met a great deal of resistance from the Protestant Reformers in England, but Mary showed no signs of compromise. This resulted in what was known as the Marian Exile which we have touched on, where one historian believes that upward of 800 or more Protestants fled England for continental Europe. Given the fact that many of those fleeing were Clergymen and theological students' one can only imagine the vacuum it created in spreading the truth of God's word amongst the people of England. Likewise, many gentry also fled and the number of skilled workers and the trades they had were all lost to the mainland.

Of course many of those who took shelter in Europe would go on to become some of the loudest voices proclaiming the truth of God's word.

So it was that the Church of Geneva that now had the benefit of these men of God, set about to produce an English Bible without the required permission of either the English throne or papal Rome. The birth of the Geneva Bible was inevitable.

The theological scholars we have mentioned previously began the work of translation in 1557. Essentially, they were revising and correcting the New Testament version done by Tyndale in his 1534 edition. No sooner had the Geneva New Testament come off the press that work began on creating an entire Bible containing both Testaments. This took a further two years in which they checked their work with that of Theodore Beza's work of the Greek text.

Finally, in 1560 a complete and revised Bible was published and translated according to the Hebrew and Greek and was dedicated to Queen Elizabeth I.

Elizabeth was crowned Queen in 1558 which saw the return of Protestants to their native land.

The Geneva Bible was finally printed in England in 1575 only after the death of Archbishop Matthew Parker, editor of the Bishop's Bible. This Bible had been published ironically because Elizabeth had also taken offense to some of the marginal notes written in the Geneva Bible.

Despite this, for all of the aforementioned features and benefits, the Geneva Bible became an instant success among the British public.

Let us briefly mention here that when the Pilgrims arrived at Plymouth, Massachusetts in 1620 they held in their hands Bibles [most likely the Geneva Bible] and a conviction derived from those Bibles of the establishment of a new nation. When James I ascended to the English throne in 1603 there were two Bibles in use. One was the very popular Geneva Bible and the other the Bishops' Bible which primarily was kept chained in churches as a pulpit Bible.

King James I as we have previously said, disliked the Geneva Bible because he felt it was seditious in nature to his rule and position. He frowned upon its marginal notes that suggested that anyone should disobey a king or his orders. As a result he considered, quite erroneously, that the marginal notes were a political threat to his kingdom. What he failed to recognize and accept was the fact that his kingship was only given to him by the Lord and Sovereign Almighty God.

The conference King James I called at Hampton Court in 1604 originally did not have any mention nor desire of a discussion for a new translation of the Scriptures. Ironically, a suggestion was made by the Puritan scholar John Reynolds [Rainolds] (1549-1607) that a new translation was needed. Due to the king's dislike of the Geneva Bible this suggestion grew in intensity through the king's desire to replace the Geneva Bible altogether.

Actually, the Puritans were considered radical Protestants and extremists. They had made petition to the king on a variety of items but many in regard to religious services, teaching and theology. Their petition stood little to no chance of success of even being heard, let alone listened to. They had originally petitioned the king in April 1603 and finally the conference was called nine months later in January 1604.

One only has to consider King James I mind in the matter of who would win his ear at the conference. First and foremost, it had to be what he as king wanted and decreed. Second, if you read the history of James I, especially that of his childhood and upbringing, it is not difficult to see why he hated the puritan movement. James had been subjected to some of the worse treatment a child could receive during his formative years. His teacher was strict Presbyterian George Buchanan (1506-1582) who was a member of the Scottish Kirk (Scottish Church). Buchanan constantly snarled at his royal charge and engaged in the cold denouncement of the young James at every opportunity, which surprisingly included striking the young royal. Given the fact that neither parent was there to protect him, it is not surprising that Buchanan did not fear any retribution. Buchanan represented the strict disciplinarian that James came to hate [albeit which he himself adopted throughout his life] and the puritans, as far as James was concerned, were no different than his childhood teacher.

James saw the puritans very similar in nature to his teacher. In contrast, the Anglican Church had bishops who were much friendlier. James much preferred the friendly disposition he saw with the bishops.

Due in part to its marginal notes, the Geneva Bible may have been seen as a threat to the king of England and to the church. One example of this can be seen in the 1560 edition of the Geneva Bible citing Revelation 11:7. In the marginal notes for this scripture the Pope is named as the beast that comes out of the bottomless pit.

The marginal notes for this scripture was referencing the Pope, so why would King James I be unhappy with the marginal notes in the Geneva Bible?

Despite what you hear from supporters of the King James Bible, James was known not to like the Geneva Bible, declaring it to be the worst Bible as far as he was concerned.

Five marginal notes of scriptures contained in the Geneva Bible could certainly have irritated the King.

In Daniel 6:22 we read the story of Daniel disobeying the King and receiving God's approval for doing so. The marginal note states, "For he disobeyed the king's wicked commandment in order to obey God, and so he did no injury to the king, who ought to command nothing by which God would be dishonored" [anglicized]

In Daniel 11:36 in referencing the King shall do according to his will the marginal note refers to the king as a tyrant. It states, "So long the tyrants will prevail as

God has appointed to punish his people: but he shows that it is but for a time" [anglicized].

Exodus 1:15-19 records for us the story of Pharaoh wickedly commanding the murder of Hebrew newborns. The marginal note for verse nineteen in the Geneva Bible refers to the Hebrew midwifes disobeying Pharaoh as lawful. It says, "Their disobedience herein was lawful but their dissembling evil" [anglicized].

The story of King Asa in 2 Chronicles 15:15-17 was perhaps another text King James objected to. Asa's mother, Maachah, had committed idolatry. Despite Asa removing his mother from being Queen it appears he did not remove some items from the high places. Questioning the king's zeal the marginal note for this scripture states, "He showed that he lacked zeal, for she ought to have died both by the covenant and by the law of God, but he gave place to foolish pity and would also seem after a sort to satisfy the law" [anglicized].

Finally Psalm 105:15 speaks of those anointed by God. The King James Version identified James as the anointed one whereas the Geneva Bible marginal note states, "Those whom I have sanctified to be my people" [anglicized].

Given the nature of James' personality and his dislike of the Puritans it is easy to conclude why he would want a translation that would not challenge his authority and royal position. The scriptures did not offend him, but the marginal notes certainly could have or did for him to be so interested in ordering a new translation.

We will discuss more of the King James version of the Bible in the chapter of the same name but suffice to say, despite the suggestion made by a Puritan for a new translation, it was hardly a translation that was overseen by a body of men who were in agreement. Politics or religious affiliation aside, the 52 men recorded as translators gave due diligence to their work. There was however, still an air of suspicion as to whether this new work would be free of corruption. After all, the Puritans, despite being labelled radical, were perhaps the ones who were living their lives closest to the scriptures and being vilified for it. Previously, the Catholic authorities were the ones arguing about ownership and translation of the scriptures. Sadly, they had been replaced by a body who were hardly any better than themselves who were also trying to control what went into the new translation. We will read more of this later.

I'm reminded of the lengths the established church went, with the full blessing of and indeed orders of the Pope to dig up the bones of John Wycliffe 44 years after his death and to 'ceremoniously' take the corpse and destroy it. As Wycliffe was an ordained minister some have suggested this insane ceremony even went as far as dressing Wycliffe's corpse so they could 'defrock' him of his position. After tying the corpse, which surely was only bones by then, they burnt it at the stake as best they could and finally crushed the bones and threw them into the river Swift.

I cannot help but see the analogy of stupidity in these actions that reminds me of those who tried, and woefully failed, to stamp out any memory or record of our Lord Jesus Christ. The book of Acts reports, as promised by Jesus, that the Holy Spirit would be sent to the Apostles and those gathered in an upper room numbering 120. From that moment, the disciples and the body of Christ grew exponentially into thousands of believers who were baptized and saved by accepting Jesus as their redeemer.

Not only did the Geneva Bible find favor as the preferred choice for worshippers in England and Scotland but we also have history that records for us that it was also favored by the Pilgrims who arrived in America.

The secretary to the Virginia Company, William Strachey (1572-1621) used the Geneva Bible in the writings of his history of Virginia in 1609.

As mentioned earlier, the Pilgrims brought the Geneva Bible with them on the Mayflower in 1620 and the writings of the Plymouth colony suggest the Geneva Bible was used exclusively, certainly at the beginning of their settlement.

The Puritans it can be said were born out of the religious persecutions of their day, namely the 16th and 17th centuries. Many Protestant figures emerged after the mid 1500's due in part to the freedom they had in both their theology and translation of the Bible, notably the Geneva Bible in 1560.

Many Puritans were also Calvinists named after John Calvin who, as we have acknowledged, took a prominent lead in the Geneva Church and Reformation.

However, if the Puritans thought they would escape religious inferiority either by the Catholics or Protestants of the Church of England or the Anglican Church they were very much mistaken.

Puritans were seen as troublemakers, extremists and do-gooders of the day. They vehemently attacked the theaters that were popular in their time, due in part to the prominence of William Shakespeare and his group of players, who all had the blessings of King James I of England.

For these and similar actions and activities they were considered to be more of an activist movement within the Church of England which is somewhat ironic. King James I narrowly escaped assassination by a Catholic activist group who planned to blow him and his entire family up along with the entire members of parliament. This became known as the Gunpowder Plot, which was an attempt to restore Catholicism to England. Puritans, no doubt, were perhaps viewed, or considered, to be just as likely to commit acts of atrocities similar to the Gunpowder Plot. No evidence in history can support such opinions. Puritans, although strict, lived by a set of values far removed from that of the commonplace and in doing so were shunned by many. I wonder, if our conduct as true followers of Christ sets us apart from the majority? If it does then we should be proud we are being singled out as true worshippers of God.

Puritans were blocked from changing anything with regard to the Church of England's established practice. It was inevitable that they would seek a land that would allow them their religious freedom and doctrine. Inevitably, this is exactly what happened. Many, unfamiliar with their history, assume the Pilgrim Fathers left England for America. In part that is true to the extent that they returned to England from the Netherlands to make arrangements for their passage. But their place of origin after leaving England in 1608 to worship as they saw fit was first and foremost the Netherlands where they enjoyed more freedom.

For those of us wondering why they wished to leave the Netherlands after 12 years of relative religious freedom, one has to look to history once more in the records recording why they decided the way they did.

Two factors emerged, though not necessarily holding the same weight, but both equal in the eyes of the Puritan ideal.

Many Puritan parents began to worry that their children, and subsequently their children's children, would lose their English heritage, which could seem to many people as odd in that their decision to move back to England was a temporary one to leave England again. This could also translate that they wanted to build a society that would be Godly, a 'new' England if you will.

The second reason was that Holland was becoming a larger power to be reckoned with within Europe. In fact you may recall that John Adams sought a loan from Holland in the American War of Independence and eventually was successful in securing such.

This power that saw its beginnings in the early to mid-17th century led to the fear of the Puritan values.

These two reasons alone was sufficient cause in the eyes of the Puritans to find 'their' ideal in terms of a country of residence. In order to form the legal requirements of emigrating to the New World they first had to obtain permission from the King [then Charles I] and form a merchant company which they called the Virginia Company.

It should be noted their resolve was not political but a religious agenda. Moral and theological principles were involved from their perspective and they would not accept any compromise. They took 2 Corinthians 6:17 to literally refer to themselves where it says, ***"Therefore go out from their midst, and be separate from them, says the Lord, and touch no unclean thing; then I will welcome you" (ESV).***

Knowledge of the Scriptures and Divinity was of the utmost importance to the Puritans. They believed fully that the Bible was the revealed word of God and of His direct communication to humans by means of it.

The Geneva Bible played a full and active part in the developing stages of a new nation, a beacon of religious light and a model of spiritual promise. Of no doubt, Puritan John Winthrop had the words of Jesus in mind in Matthew 5:14 where Jesus said, **"You are the light of the world. A city set on a hill cannot be hidden"** **(ESV).**

That "city on a hill" would produce many translations of American Bibles, some of which are still with us today in one form or another and we will discuss these later.

"The BIBLE is superior to all other religious books in content. It sets up the highest ethical standards, enjoins the most absolute obedience, denounces every form of sin, and yet informs the sinner how he can become right with God. How could uninspired men write a book like that?"

Henry Clarence Thiessen (1883-1947)

CHAPTER 7

The King James
Version 1611-1789

The first edition of the King James Version arrived in 1611, some 7 years after the start of its translation. Other than what we have either been told or seen, either by writings, books, and television perhaps, what do we know of it?

We do know it was produced primarily for the Church of England and work started on this particular translation in 1604 after an almost casual comment made by the Puritan John Reynolds [Rainolds], that existing Bible translations written in English had perceived problems. When one reads the accounts of the Hampton Court conference, which was instigated by complaints made by Puritans, the fact that King James I even listened to Reynolds is, to say the least, remarkable. Unless of course, we imagine that James immediately sensed that a body of work such as the King James Version could leave a legacy. A legacy it indeed left. Not to the trumpets sounds of how great a King James was [which in fact he was not]. James was neither a good nor effective King. He certainly displayed signs of paranoia. He did not consider he needed to use Parliament in any decision making process and looked upon them as unnecessary [unless it favored him otherwise]. Perhaps, worse of all, he wasted the money collected from the public and elsewhere on his own selfish extravagances. Not with standing any of these failings, the King James Bible did become perhaps his one and only legacy of a work of art that would stand the test of time for over 400 years. That is, if indeed we agree with those who today still insist that the King James Version is, and should be, the only Bible read in church or used for private study.

I personally do not share that view, and although that is not the subject of this book, it still demands an answer as to why we have those who insist on the King James Version exclusively to be used for scripture reference and those who do not. While this chapter may not answer all those points, it will answer some. It is not my intention [or desire] to sway a person to use a certain translation or not. Neither, would I hasten to add, should it be the intent for those who insist on the use of King James Version to hold such strong, and in my view at least, unchristian views in rebuking those who hold to using a different translation. I might add, those that do subscribe to a different translation of the Bible as their personal choice do not have the same voice of condemnation as those who support a King James Version only being used.

The Hampton Court conference was held over 3 days. The first day, Saturday 14 January 1604, those in attendance were led into what was called the Presence Chamber. The Puritans did not even gain access to the chamber. James welcomed both bishops and deans but gave the command that Puritans were not even invited to observe or partake in proceedings. One can only imagine the anger and indignation they felt by the King completely ignoring them when it was their complaints and request to seek an audience with the King that instigated the conference in the first place. The Presence Chamber was where the King would meet people. It was somewhat like a public room, away from any of the royal household area. The Puritans were simply refused entry, even to this public area to meet the King.

The following Monday (day two of the conference) the Puritans were allowed to be present. Only four of their number were allowed to represent their cause. If the Puritans thought they could choose even the four picked to attend the conference they were greatly mistaken. James wasn't interested in allowing a fair hearing of the complaints made by the Puritans. He, or someone he ordered, ensured any argument made by the Puritans would easily be out voted. Not that they needed a vote. James was too enamored with his own self to allow anyone but himself to make judgment. He alone would be the one to decide any outcome and decisions of the conference. Who made the choice of the four we can only guess. Who ordered only four of their number was decisively the King's choice. Had it not been, the records would have shown James questioning why only four Puritans were present. This in itself was completely biased and unfair. Four Puritans versus something like over twenty bishops, deans as well as privy councilors. In the hotbed of English Politics this was not unusual. James had no sympathies for the Puritans or their cause and as we discussed in the previous chapter probably hated them and/or their very presence.

No Puritan with radical or extreme tendencies were allowed but, nonetheless, the four eventually picked were all shining lights in their observance of the word of God in their particular division of faith within the confines of the Church of England. The four men chosen consisted of John Reynolds who was Master of Corpus Christi, Oxford, and former Dean of Lincoln, Laurence Chaderton, Master of Emmanuel College, Cambridge, the Suffolk Rector John Knewstubs and a clergyman from Buckinghamshire, Thomas Sparke.

We can probably concede into thinking the King allowed some consideration to the Puritans. Reynolds and Chaderton would both become translators among the 47 [although 54 had been the number that James had ordered to work on the new translation].

At the end of the second day, the Puritans had not achieved anything. There had been much insult and offense leveled at the Puritans that all they possessed by the end of the second day was contempt. Reynolds was particularly singled out. When, as main spokesman for the Puritans, he informed the King that they objected to the traditional wedding ceremony stating, "with this ring, I thee wed", the King immediately rebuked Reynolds for such a request, especially since he himself was a confirmed bachelor. One can imagine the scene. James enjoying the ridicule and perhaps public laughter at the expense of Reynolds which James himself had purposely created in some debauched way of 'fun'. Had a subject done the same to James they would have been dispatched to the gallows post haste. But it was far from 'fun'. James never cared for anyone but James. To ridicule someone, especially in front of one's peers, was to illicit attacks on the person and to somehow elevate James into a false sense of importance and those in attendance were happy to oblige.

Day three became a mirror of day one. The Puritans again were refused audience or attendance into the conference. Eventually, they were allowed in, but only to hear the summing up of the conference.

It was after this point that it is believed Reynolds made his statement regarding a new Bible translation. His comment could be regarded as a casual comment, even bordering on a tone of sarcasm, in that of all the complaints the Puritans brought before the court, King James I rejected every single one of them. The bishop of London, Richard Bancroft, immediately condemned such a suggestion but it was too late. The spark had ignited into the mind of James that he could indeed leave a legacy of a work, that whether he knew it or not, would be a work still revered today. In fact by the early part of the 1900s, the King James Version was unchallenged as the translation to be used in the English Anglican and Protestant Churches. The evidence of how far reaching this translation has become is the fact that even today, the most used edition of the King James Bible closely follows the standard text of 1769 that was edited by Benjamin Blayney (1728-1801) of Oxford.

One has to remember that prior to becoming King James I of England James was King James VI of Scotland. His Scottish crown was a mere title. Prior to ascending the English throne James hardly had any power at all, being financed and supported by Queen Elizabeth I of England. His desire to unite both countries under his kingship perhaps would be realized with a new Bible that could possibly heal the wide divide of the clergy at that time. After all, he had overseen the General Assembly of the Church of Scotland at St Columba's Church in Burntisland, Fife, two years before as King James VI of Scotland. Proposals had been put forward for a new translation into English in May 1601. Time and circumstance would have to wait and in the following two years James would ascend to the English throne as

175

King James I of England, thus combining the two nations finally into one kingdom.

When the time came for the creation of the new translation it was not, however, the first English translation published to be approved by the English Church authorities but, in fact, the third.

If we thought the new translation would show no bias we would be wrong. Instructions [presumably by James] were given to ensure the limitation of any Puritan influence on this new work.

James also gave the translators instructions with the intent that it should guarantee that the translation would conform to ecclesiology [study of the Church] and reflect the episcopal structure of the Church of England in regard to its belief in an ordained ministry. This went as far as instructing that certain Greek and Hebrew words were to be translated in a way that justified the churches teaching and usage in the church. An example of this was the word "church" which was not to be translated "congregation" irrespective of whether it rendered the original text being incorrectly translated. Translators were also ordered not to add any marginal notes.

The translators were handpicked and as previously noted should have numbered 54 but some say this number was only 47. This number discrepancy may be due to seven members dying during the years 1603-1611. If this is the case the figure is still incorrect as there were in fact 52 named within their various committees. In a moment we will meet them. In any event, whatever the number was, all who participated in the translation of the King James Bible were members of the Church of England and all were members of the clergy with the exception of Sir Henry Savile.

The translation was to be translated from the Greek for the New Testament and from the Hebrew for the Old Testament, which was the common denominator of the day. The Apocrypha was translated from Greek to Latin and then obviously into English.

Despite any "Authorized" title, the first edition in 1611 was simply known as "The Holy Bible". If the translation that would eventually bear his name was authorized by King James, history is unable to tell us. Such records would have been kept by the Privy Council but all registers of this council from 1600 to 1613 were destroyed by fire in January of 1618/19. One tantalizing clue that it may have been authorized is contained in the title page of the first edition which read 'Appointed to be read in Churches'. Tradition in general did not give a specific name to a Bible, but the use of the name "King James Bible" can be found in historical records in Massachusetts in 1815 and in England in 1818. The term "Authorized" has been found as early as 1814.

If the King James Bible was authorized, this was not the first time a Bible had been officially authorized. Henry VIII had authorized what became known as the Great Bible which we have briefly discussed in a previous chapter.

Then in 1568 the Bishops' Bible appeared which Elizabeth I authorized.

There were 15 rules made to be observed in the translation of the King James Version [obviously by the King himself]. Briefly, these rules were as follows:

1. The Bishop's Bible was to be used as the reference Bible for the King James Version.

2. The names of the writers inspired by God was to be retained, as was the names ascribed to the prophets and any other names used in the text.

3. Old Ecclesiastical terms were to remain. For example the word "church" could not be changed to "congregation".

4. If a word differed significantly than that which ancient writers had used, but based on faith they agreed to keep it, then they were allowed to do so.

5. The division of chapters was not to be altered unless absolutely necessary.

6. No marginal notes were to be allowed other than to explain a Greek or Hebrew word.

7. Any quotations of places could be placed in the margin to cross reference scripture.

8. Every man of each Company was to take the same chapter(s), translate or amend them himself, and then meet and confer with the rest of the Company and agree what was to be kept.

9. When one book was finished by a Company it was to be sent to the other Companies for them to read and consider.

10. If a Company who received a book from another Company for review had any doubts or disagreements with the content they were to send their reasons, if they consented or not, and it would be further discussed at the General Meeting which consisted of the chiefs of each Company.

11. If there were any obscure parts that the Company could not reconcile they could send letters of authority to Learned Men in the land [Country] for their comments or judgment.

12. Letters were to be sent to every Bishop who, in turn, was to inform his clergy of the work of

the translation was in hand. If any one member was skilled in languages they could send their observations to any of the Companies.

13. The Directors of each Company were to be the Deans of Westminster and Chester and the King's Professors skilled in Hebrew or Greek in either University.

14. Other translations [presumably from point 12 and/ or 13] were to be used if such translations agreed better with the translated text versus the Bishops Bible, Coverdale's, Geneva, Matthew's, Tyndale's, or Whitchurch.

15. Apart from the Directors previously mentioned, three or four theologians/scholars from either University and not already involved with the translation, were to be appointed by the Vice-Chancellor upon conferring with the heads of each Company to be Overseers of the Translations to include Hebrew and Greek in order that point four was correctly observed and applied.

When one reads the fifteen rules it is easy to criticize and point out some obvious scurrilous decisions to essentially enforce the will of King James I of England. Had they not observed all that he commanded then the translation would have been rejected. This in itself is another reason why [in my humble opinion] the King James Version should not be considered the most accurate translation. One example is point three. What James was ordering was that even if the original translation from the extant manuscripts read "congregation" the translators of the King James Version were to write "church". This may seem to be trivial. But isn't this the same argument that those who insist that the King James Bible should be the only one read accuse others of in their choice of Bible translation?

Point four is another startling example. Here we see that despite what the ancient writers had written, if it did not support the current beliefs of the committee members the committee could reject it! This fact alone should make a person question the biased one-sided nature of the committee members. Think about it. They could actually agree to alter extant words or meanings from God's holy written word so that the wording they substituted could comply with their man-made faith!

The text of the Bishops' Bible was ordered to be used as the main guide but where any disagreement or confusion occurred the translators were allowed to consult with other translations which included the Tyndale Bible, the Coverdale Bible, the Matthews Bible, the Great Bible and the Geneva Bible. There is some evidence that has surfaced to suggest that translators may have also turned to the Taverner's Bible as well as the Douay-Rheims Bible. We clearly see from points 11, 12 and 13 of the King's fifteen rules that they could refer to many other sources, especially if it agreed with what James wanted written.

Six committee's or companies were formed. Two based from the University of Oxford, two from the University of Cambridge and two from Westminster.

Orders were made to provide these committee's with 40 unbound copies of the 1602 edition of the Bishops' Bible. Any agreed changes could be made in the margins of these copies for discussion and agreement before the final translation draft. Each committee had specific assignments as to scripture translation. The committees were known as "First" and "Second" companies of their respective university.

Once each company had completed their assignments their work was sent to the other committee's for review, comparison and any revision so that by the end of the exercise each company's assignments were in harmony with each other.

The committee's consisted of the following:

First Westminster Company (Consisted of ten men)
Translated from Genesis to 2 Kings and consisted of:
Lancelot Andrewes, William Bedwell, Francis Burleigh, Richard Clarke, Geoffrey King, John Layfield, John Overall, Hadrian a Saravia, Richard Thomson and Robert Tighe.

First Cambridge Company (Consisted of eight men)
Translated from 1 Chronicles to the Song of Solomon and consisted of:
Roger Andrewes, Andrew Bing, Lawrence Chaderton, Francis Dillingham, Edward Lively, John Richardson, Robert Spaulding and Thomas Harrison.

First Oxford Company (Consisted of eight men)
Translated from Isaiah to Malachi and consisted of:
Richard Brett, Daniel Fairclough, John Harding, Thomas Holland, Richard Kilby, John Rainolds [Reynolds], Miles Smith and William Thorne.

Second Oxford Company (Consisted of ten men)
Translated the Gospels, Acts and Revelation and consisted of:

George Abbot, John Aglionby, Richard Eedes, John Harmar, Leonard Hotten, John Peryn, Ralph Ravens, Thomas Ravis, Sir Henry Savile and Giles Thomson.

Second Westminster Company (Consisted of seven men)
Translated the Epistles and consisted of:
William Barlow, William Dakins, Roger Fenton, Ralph Hutchinson, Michael Rabbet, Thomas Sanderson and John Spenser.

Second Cambridge Company (Consisted of nine men)
Translated the Apocrypha and consisted of:
Richard Bancroft, William Branthwaite, Thomas Bilson, John Bois, Andrew Downes, John Dupont, Jeremiah Radcliffe, Robert Ward and Samuel Ward.

In the middle of 1604 King James sent a letter to Archbishop Bancroft asking him to contact all the churchmen of England for donations towards the work of the translation. The donations were not requested to provide payment to the translators. In fact all of them received no recompense for their work but rather, bishops were encouraged to employ these men in well paid positions within the church. This no doubt was also somewhat biased against the two puritans, Reynolds and Chaderton. Given the fact of the disdain of puritans by the mainline clergy their chances of successfully obtaining a position in payment for services was, to say the least, almost non-existent.

By 1608, after four long years of translation, all six companies had completed their translation with the Second Cambridge Company being the first to finish. Following this in the beginning of 1609 a General Committee of Review reviewed all work.

If the fifteen rules made by King James was not bad enough in hoping that the translation would be completely pure and unbiased, we now had another unscrupulous attempt to dictate what was put into the Bible by non-other than Bishop Bancroft. Without any authorization from James, Archbishop Bancroft insisted on having the final say and is said to have made fourteen changes, one of which we know of was the term "bishopricke" found at Acts 1:20.

If indeed there were fourteen changes the greater majority are not identified by the lead accusers, namely Myles Smith and Thomas Bilson. What is worthy of mention however to those who insist this never occurred is the following. Several publications refer to Myles Smith complaining that Bancroft altered the translation of the King James Version in fourteen places. Edwin Bissell, in his book Historic Origin, also notes that Bancroft was officially charged for making the fourteen changes, one of which was 1 Peter 2:13 to the *king as supreme* being one of the fourteen references. The king here inferred James, not our Lord Jesus Christ. [1]

Robert Barker, whose father Christopher secured the titled of Royal printer in 1589, was the original publisher of the King James Version in 1611. Despite the Barker family being granted 'perpetual Royal privilege' to print Bibles in England, Barker was not without controversy. Investing large sums, his firm soon began to drown in debt. He avoided his firm's total demise by sub-contracting the printing of the new translation to two rival London printers. This only delayed things and caused more problems, with litigation among the three companies dragging on for several decades. Despite the Universities of Oxford and Cambridge securing special license to print the Bible, the original three rivals continued to argue.

Two editions thought to have been published in 1611 also appeared with incorrect text in Ruth 3:15 with one saying "he went into the city" and the other stating "she went into the city". These became known as the He and She Bibles.

Once errors were identified and corrected the King's printer was ordered to issue no further editions of the Bishops' Bible and by default the King James version became the only standard lectern Bible in the English parish churches.

If James thought by producing the King James Version it would instill unity amongst English and Scots he was disappointed. In Scotland the Geneva Bible was still the preferred choice of the clergy and it would be for another two decades, before the King James Version appeared in 1633 in conjunction with Scotland's coronation of King Charles I.

Even in England the Geneva Bible refused to give up its hold of the general public and would not give way to the King James Version. It took the general public longer to accept the King James Bible (albeit they had no choice in any eventuality). Their love of the Geneva Bible ended in 1637 when the Archbishop of Canterbury, William Laud (1573-1645), prohibited both the printing and/or importation of the Geneva Bible.

I again reflect on this action of a man claiming to be a man of God 'banning' a Bible! When one reads some of the history of William Laud it isn't difficult to conclude that he put more emphasis on pomp and ceremony than in accurate Bible and Christian theology. He was later beheaded due in part to his divisions among both church and state.

Nevertheless by the 17th century there was no translation that was able to offer a serious threat to the

King James Version. This was partly because printers involved in printing Bibles saw no commercial advantage in printing anything other than the King James Version. Notwithstanding, this was also the fact that the same printers were competing with one another to become the Royal printer, in the hope of giving them the exclusive right to be the only printer of the King James Version. This position would give the ultimate victor prestige as well as guaranteed payments that would secure their financial future. Evidently, we must conclude that Barker's 'perpetual Royal privilege' had long run its course or presumably had been cancelled.

As a result of all of this competition and prior to a royal decree declaring who would be the Royal printer, in their haste to become the chosen company, printers became less careful in the printing of the 1611 edition.

Over the years, 1500 misprints were identified with one becoming famously notorious. Due to a misprint, one particular print run of the King James Bible became known as the "Wicked Bible" due to an error in one of the Ten Commandments rendering "Thou shalt not commit adultery" to read instead, "Thou shalt commit adultery"!

After the English Reformation it was proposed that a more thorough revision was necessary, although the evidence suggests this was not acted upon as Parliament eventually decided against it. Still, the King James Bible was not without its critics. Considered one of the most highly regarded Hebraist' of his time, Hugh Broughton (1549-1612) totally condemned the new version as early as the year it was first published. However, one could be forgiven if they accused Broughton of being bitter with regard to this new Bible. He had been excluded from any involvement in being one of the chosen translators despite his scholastic abilities and may have felt vengeful at the very least to dismiss a production he felt should have contained his expertise (and perhaps it should have). Still others voiced their condemnation also at what they considered an inferior translation.

Despite all of this the King James Version established itself as the sole translation used in Protestant churches and was unchallenged during the 18th century. Historical errors of printing forgotten, many people believed any challenge to the King James Bible was a direct assault on the Holy Scriptures. The immense variations of modernized text and the accumulation of misprints led to a situation of almost scandalous proportions. Both Oxford and Cambridge Universities began to produce an updated text. The first to produce a new edition was Cambridge which saw the culmination of 20 years work by Francis Sawyer Parris (1707-1760) who sadly died in 1760, the year of the edition. Parris' work was eventually superseded by the 1769 Oxford edition by Benjamin Blayney. It is Blayney' text which has virtually remained unchanged from 1769 to the present day.

One thing both Parris and Blayney sought was to standardize the wide variation in punctuation and spelling, resulting in thousands of minor changes to the text. Their work was not dissimilar to that of Thomas Bilson and Dr. Myles Smith who you will recall were appointed as the two men to finalize the 1611 original version. Despite Bilson not being part of the original translators he was highly regarded for his accuracy of languages and readings of the scriptures, and, the King liked him. He took on the task of correcting anything he saw as not correct in content. Smith was the one who could be called the copy editor inserting commas etc. where they were needed to give the page rhythm.

Blayney's 1769 text differs some 24,000 times in the text versus that of the 1611 edition of the King James Bible. Since that time a few additional changes have occurred that were introduced into the Oxford standard text. Editions printed by Cambridge contain further changes and these changes are considered more accurate.

For a period of time Cambridge continued to use the Parris text but when the market demanded a standardized edition they opted to use Blayney's work omitting some idiosyncratic Oxford spellings. As a result, by the mid-19th century virtually all printing of the King James version were taken from the Blayney text by Oxford in 1769.

The King James Version has enjoyed immense popularity for well over 250 years and became the dominant translation over that period of time.

Even to this day you will find either individuals or groups that go to the extent of forming movements that insist that no other Bible other than the King James Version should be consulted, read, or studied to understand the scriptures.

Of special note is the fact that despite the decisions, desires or reasons why the King James Version was created in the first place, at least 80% of the text is unaltered from that of Tyndale's translation. That in itself speaks volumes of the dedication and studious nature of William Tyndale and had he enjoyed greater freedom, who knows what further legacy he could have endowed upon his fellow man.

Although the 47 translators were given unbound copies of the Bishops' Bible as reference, when they did deviate they commonly favored the Geneva Bible which is somewhat ironic given the nature of reason for the King James Version replacing that of the Geneva Bible.

It can be hard to argue in some circles that the King James Version was any better than that of the Geneva Bible. Certainly, the King James Version is more Latinate [having the character of Latin] than the Geneva Bible and others. That in itself may have appealed to Latin scholars who would already be familiar with a Latinate text. But surely, as was evident by the time the King James Version was created, those entrusted with the translation knew the Latin Vulgate was corrupted. If not, why else did the Protestant Reformation occur in the first place?

One of the major reasons for the emergence of the Protestant Reformation was the disagreements the Protestants had with Catholic theology. By default the teachings that had been inserted into scripture via the Latin Vulgate is what the early reformers had challenged to begin with.

One could argue that the King James Version was born out of the whim of an English King who resented and rejected any idea that his royalty was not of a divine nature. Had James recognized the authority of God and that it was God Almighty who had placed James into the position as king, then perhaps James would be remembered more fondly. But King James I could not stand any criticism of his royal appointment and I would suggest a reading of the history and character of James will leave the reader describing him as somewhat of a sad figure, foul in mouth to the extreme and a temperament and mind bordering on obsessive compulsive disorder.

Strangely, in spite of the King James Version overwhelming success in its place in history, there was never any mandate for a person to use it. Given the banning of the Geneva Bible mentioned earlier by Laud we could challenge the fact that no mandate was required because the King James Version became the only source.

Reflection of its former dominance cannot be ignored and is to be admired.

In the United Kingdom it is still under license to the Crown to print, publish and distribute and the Crown licenses publishers to reproduce under letters of patent.

In England, Wales and Northern Ireland these letters are held by Queen Elizabeth II printers who are Cambridge University Press [at time of writing].

In Scotland it is published by Collins under license from the Scottish Bible Board [at time of writing].

These patents are the last ribbons of history where the Crown had a monopoly over all printing and publishing in the United Kingdom.

Still, from the early nineteenth century academic debate continued and the voices of concerns grew ever louder challenging the accuracy of the King James Version. Many argued that new and additional study of languages that have advanced since 1611 (or indeed 1769) supported calls for a revision of the Hebrew Bible. Scholars had identified Greek Text that had not been translated correctly from the original language. And last but perhaps more significantly, additional extant manuscripts had been discovered that called into question some of the renderings of the translation. For example the Textus Receptus used to translate the New Testament could no longer be relied upon as being the best example scholars now had for study. In fact the original translators of the King James Version appeared to have ignored first hand manuscript sources such as the Codex Bezae which would have been available in their day, relying instead on works of later copyists.

Over the centuries translators ignored the more up-to-date linguistic style that was already prevalent in their day. Examples of this are the words [still contained in the King James Version] 'verily', 'thou/thee' and the use of 'eth' as the third person speaking. All of these archaic words were already perishing in the days of King James I, to the new and commonly used words that are significant still in the English language today. The translator's habitually used and phrased words more in line with the Latin Vulgate which, as we have already seen, was corrupted.

We will discuss in a further chapter, some of the Bibles that have since been translated either as an alternative or a more up to date version than previous ones such as the King James Version. The likely one that comes to mind is The New King James Version by Thomas Nelson publishers.

Irrespective of what you personally think about the King James Version, one fact is undeniable. It was [and to some is still] a great Bible translation. We could get muddy in the waters of intellect and argue for and against versus other translations but the King James Version stood long, high and proud as the bastion of Bible translations into the English language for over two and one half centuries and continues to be read daily by millions to this day over four hundred years later from its conception.

Irrelevant to the readers' view of the King James Bible, God's word would translate exponentially through and into future generations.

"The empire of Caesar is gone; the legions of Rome are smoldering in the dust; the avalanches of Napoleon hurled upon Europe have melted away, the prince of the pharaohs is fallen; the pyramids they raised to be their tombs are sinking every day in the desert sands; Tyre is a rock for bleaching fisherman's nets; Sidon has scarcely left a wreck behind; but the Word of God still survives: All things that threatened to extinguish it have only aided it; and it proves every day how transient is the noblest monument that men can build, how enduring is the least Word that God has spoken"

Albert Baird Cummins (1850-1926)

CHAPTER 8

Biblical writings from 1611 to the Modern Day

In the last two chapters we saw the influence of the Geneva Bible and how it remained the favored translation among the English speaking people. Only by banning the Geneva Bible could the King James Version ever hope to overtake its main rival in the hearts and minds of the common people. One of the reasons, unknown to most who read the Geneva Bible, was its sparkle and shine to the testament of William Tyndale's genius of translation. The Geneva Bible, in fact, retained over 80% of his original translation.

The Geneva Bible holds the historical honor of being the first Bible taken to America by the Pilgrim Fathers and it became the Bible of the Protestant Reformation.

The influence of the Geneva Bible during the period between 1560 and 1611, followed by the introduction of the King James version in 1611, justified them both having their own chapters, due to their influence and affect each had on the people of the era.

Before we jump fully into the 1600s and beyond I'd like to mention some other translations that appeared between the Geneva Bible and the King James Version.

We read earlier of the appearance of the Coverdale Bible, Matthew's Bible and the Great Bible. One thing I did not mention regarding the Great Bible was it was also known by several other names. As Thomas Cromwell first directed its publication it was known also as the Cromwell Bible. Many called it the Whitchurch's Bible, named after the first English printer. As Henry VIII had ordered the Great Bible to be a large sized Bible and to be chained to the pulpit of every church in the land, it was also called the Chained Bible. A less accurate description for the Great Bible was also the Cranmer Bible. Cranmer had no involvement or responsibility for the Great Bible translation. Perhaps because his preface was in the second edition, this may have been the reason for the error of calling it by his name. The clergy of the 1560s were bleating their disgust and condemnation of the Geneva Bible when Elizabeth I ascended to the throne of England. The voices grew ever stronger and louder for yet another new translation.

This was not ignored by Elizabeth. Quite the contrary. She too disliked the Geneva Bible intensely due to its comments in the margin notes. Political games were also played out. The Geneva Bible had been compiled by William Whittingham who had succeeded John Knox as pastor of the English church in Geneva Switzerland. You may recall that Whittingham was also married to John Calvin's sister and the Geneva Bible was seen as too 'Calvinistic' by the Church of England. Knox had previously written a pamphlet condemning the Catholic Church and female royalty, in particular Queen Mary I and Mary of Guise. Although Elizabeth I was not included in the rhetoric and deformation of Knox' pamphlet, she never forgave Knox for his comments. Of note, Knox was by default associated with the Geneva Bible.

Against all of this scene of religious and political dallying it is of no surprise that Elizabeth gave her blessing and approval for a new Bible. She appointed her Archbishop of Canterbury, Matthew Parker (1504-1575), with the task to produce a new version, which wasn't really a new version at all. His instructions were for a new Bible free of any marginal notes that were considered contentious, and to be based upon the Great Bible.

The result was what became known as the Bishop's Bible and it appeared in 1568 and disappeared into history almost as quickly as it arrived.

By now, the Roman Catholic Church knew they had lost their battle in stopping an English Bible being readily available, but they were far from accepting defeat. It was a classic case of, "if you cannot beat them, join them". English scholars of Roman Catholicism who were connected with the University of Douai in France set about publishing a Roman Catholic New Testament and this was completed in 1582. Within a decade they had also created a new Roman Catholic Old Testament. The two works became known as the Douay-Rheims Bible.

I cannot resist the necessity to mention the double-standards of the writers of this work with regard to the notes they included in their version. In the notes a person can identify the strong anti-Protestant views. They further went to specifically mention in the preface explaining their stance saying the Protestants had been guilty of "casting the holy to dogs and pearls to hogs" [1]

Interestingly these Roman Catholic writers were evidently no different than their predecessors who had persecuted, tortured and executed those who spoke out against the Catholic faith with regard to twisting of scriptures to illicit somehow the justification of their doctrines. If ever there had been a time for such writers to put the record straight, as it were, now was such a time. Sadly, all they were interested in was to continue their false rhetoric and speak of their 'opponents' as 'holy dogs'. So much for Jesus' words as to the second commandment of "loving one another" for these men. Also of interest is the fact that certain portions of the Douay-Rheims version clearly included influences of both Coverdale and the Geneva Bible.

The fact that the Old Testament for the Douay-Rheims version was not completed until 1609-1610 together with the political and religious landscape changing to a distinct Protestant one, meant that this Catholic Bible did not have any significant effect upon the populace, but was distributed among the Catholic brethren. Still, the translation was updated in 1750 by Roman Catholic Bishop Richard Challoner (1691-1781) and remained the standard version for English speaking Catholics until 1941. This was [whether one agrees with it or not] a significant milestone, at least for Catholics, for this translation to last some 191 years as the Catholic standard.

You may recall the King James Version was not free of its faults in its infancy and went through a major modernization in 1769 but evidently faired far better than any other Bible in regard to its longevity and favor.

The sinful nature of man became just as evident as England transformed from a dominated Catholic nation to a Protestant one. In effect, the Protestant church authorities changed one cloak for another and were equally as guilty as their predecessors. Not so much in terms of execution [although that did also occur as we saw with the story of Calvin and Servetus] but for their arrests and imprisonment of those who did not conform to their new ideology of faith.

One historical account of note is that of John Bunyan (1628-1688). Many regard Bunyan as one of the first Baptists but Bunyan, above all else, was a non-conformist and of independent mind and belief. He could be likened today as one who led a nondenominational church but believed in the true faith of God and of Jesus Christ. In fact Bunyan shunned any title, preferring to be known simply as a Christian. He was also a prolific author, writing some 60 books or pamphlets in his lifetime and is famous for his book called Pilgrims Progress.

Deciding to follow his father as a traveling worker, then known as a tinker, he traveled the towns and villages of England repairing pots and pans. This occupation was far from respectable in the eyes of most. He was likened to a traveling gypsy, but at least the women of the households who could ill afford new pots welcomed the site of a tinker to repair the ones that they had.

Joining the Parliamentary army at sixteen Bunyan later records his despair of being wantonly sinful. For many years he struggled with the fear of his own salvation. He also claimed to hear voices saying "sell Christ" and said he experienced fearful visions. This experience led him to seek repentance believing fully that God had spoken to him. Sometime around 1650 Bunyan became what could be described as severely depressed and he began a four year spiritual journey with several poor women in Bedford, England, who belonged to a then, nonconformist sect. This eventually led him to being accepted into that church which was believed to be the Church of Christ under the leadership of Pastor John

Gifford. Soon after, in 1655 Gifford died and Bunyan was chosen as Gifford's successor and began the work of preacher to the congregation.

Bunyan was constantly targeted for slander and libel, even being called a witch. Just four years later, Charles II of England, who was restoring Anglicanism to his realm, ordered meeting houses closed and ordered all to attend Anglican Church services. It became punishable by law for a person to preach or conduct religious services outside that of the divine church, this being the Anglican or Church of England. Again England, who had fought so long against repression of their freedom of faith and will, was once again dictated to by a King and church authority that had no interest in allowing a person to serve God in the way and manner God desired.

John Bunyan was arrested on 12 November 1660 while preaching privately. His refusal to stop preaching led to a period of almost twelve years of incarceration. When asked to stop preaching his answer was that God's law obliged him to preach at any and every opportunity and therefore was duty bound to refuse any order not to preach.

What is ironic in this story is Bunyan was imprisoned for preaching to a small meeting or group of probably a half dozen people. In prison, he regularly preached to over sixty!

In 1672 Bunyan was finally released when King Charles II issued the Declaration of Religious Indulgence which basically meant people were free to worship how they saw fit. Bunyan finally received his license to preach as an independent preacher. Charles however reneged on the declaration and Bunyan was once again thrown into prison. With the help of the Quakers and others, Bunyan was set free for the last time and was never arrested again. He died in 1688 as a result of catching a cold which developed into a fever and is buried in Bunhill Fields cemetery in the London borough of Islington in England alongside other nonconformists such as George Fox, William Blake and Daniel Defoe.

I shared this story of Bunyan to highlight several points. An overwhelming one is that he truly recognized and experienced the free Grace of God and went on to be a staunch supporter and follower of Christ no matter what the consequences. For those of us who may think we are unworthy we only have to look at John Bunyan and see that God will never leave us, He will never forsake us. Bunyan is a great example of faith and conviction. Despite not being a scholar, he did know the Bible and he knew scripture thoroughly.

One brief point I mention now is regarding the Geneva Bible and the King James versions. I did not cover it in their respective chapters but I make mention of it now collectively.

We have already noted that the King James Bible could not overtake the Geneva Bible in popularity until the Geneva Bible was banned by authorities. One of the biggest ironies of these two translations is the fact that the Geneva Bible was produced by Protestants [for the Protestant Reformation]. Yet many Protestant Churches today embrace the King James Bible as the exclusive and legitimate English language translation. Here is the folly to that statement.

The King James Bible was not produced as a Protestant translation. It was printed to compete with a Protestant translation, the Geneva Bible. The King James Bible was ordered by the English King which, by default, was the

Church of England. The origin of the Church of England was not Protestant at all. It was King Henry VIII's way of creating a church state declaring himself as leader in defiance of Rome's Pope who would not agree to Henry's divorce from Catherine of Aragon. Henry had no intention, nor did he alter, any religious rites that the Catholics had previously taught. He ordered that everything taught was to be continued in the same tradition as that of the Catholic Church. He simply gave it a new name, the Church of England. Therefore, essentially, the Church of England, and by default the King James Bible, did not base its origin on the Protestant Reformation. I do not make this point to vilify the Church of England, but to point out that the only reason the Church of England came into being was for the personal interests of a King who wanted his own way. Henry wanted a divorce from Catherine of Aragon in order to marry Ann Boleyn and needed the Pope's permission, which we all know was refused. Irrespective of whether we agree with the Catholic faith or not, Henry's request for a divorce was not scriptural. Catherine had done nothing wrong. In fact, she remained faithful to her vows and declared her love for Henry until her death. The Pope [at least on this occasion] ordered God's holy ordinance of marriage remain intact.

One only has to look at history to see why the Puritans and Pilgrims fled to America. It was to flee religious persecution that was now being deployed by the Church of England. And what Bible did they take? The Geneva Bible.

Today, this little known fact is not known by many Protestants. They are unaware [even ignorant] of the Geneva Bible and do not even know that the content of the King James Bible is mostly that of the Geneva Bible.

On that basis one could argue that it is of Protestant origin but there is one more important point. The Geneva Bible is free of any influence of the Catholic Rheims Bible that King James I translators utilized and took into consideration when translating the King James Version.

While I have not chosen to discuss in depth all of the translations that appeared during the 19th century, I will mention here many of those that were published between 1808-1898. Some that are mentioned in this catalog of names have, or will, be discussed in this book. Also, let it be known that by mentioning the following list I am not endorsing any but stating the obvious, that there was a plethora of translations being created during this time.

1808 – Thomas Belsham et al, The New Testament, An Improved Version upon the basis of Archbishop Newcome's new translation with a corrected text and notes critical and explanatory. London: Richard Taylor & Co., 1808. Boston 1809. This work also saw a fourth edition in London in 1817.

1808 – Charles Thomson, The Holy Bible, containing the Old and New Covenant Commonly Called the Old and New Testament, Translated from the Greek.

1822 – Abner Kneeland, The New Testament, in Greek and English.

1826 – Alexander Campbell, ed., The Sacred Writings of the Apostles and evangelists of Jesus Christ, commonly styled the New Testament.

1828 – Alexander Greaves, The Gospel of God's Anointed, the Glory of Israel and the Light of Revelation for the Gentiles.

1828 – John Gorham Palfrey, The New Testament in the common Version, conformed to Griesbach's Standard Greek Text.

1833 – Noah Webster, The Holy Bible, Containing the Old and New Testaments, in the Common Version.

1833 – Rodolphus Dickinson, A New and Corrected Version of the New Testament.

1836 – Granville Penn, The Book of the New Covenant of our Lord and Savior Jesus Christ.

1840 – Samuel Sharpe, The New Testament, translated from the Text of J.J. Griesbach.

1841 – John T. Conquest, ed., The Holy Bible, containing the Authorized Version ... with twenty thousand emendations.

1850 - Spencer H. Cone and William H. Wyckoff, The Commonly Received Version of the New Testament of Our Lord and Savior Jesus Christ, with Several Hundred Emendations, edited by Spencer H. Cone and William H. Wyckoff.

1851 - James Murdock, The New Testament; or, the Book of the Holy Gospel of our Lord and our God, Jesus the Messiah. A literal translation from the Syriac Peshito version.

1853 - Isaac Leeser, The Twenty-four Books of the Holy Scriptures: Carefully Translated According to the Massoretic Text, On the Basis of the English Version, After the Best Jewish Authorities; and Supplied with Short Explanatory Notes.

1857 - George Moberly, Henry Alford, William G. Humphry, Charles J. Ellicott, and John Barrow, The Gospel According to St. John, after the Authorized Version. Newly Compared with the Original Greek and Revised by Five Clergymen. London: John W. Parker and Son, 1857. Followed by The Epistle of St. Paul to the Romans, after the Authorized Version Newly Compared with the Original Greek and Revised by Five Clergymen in 1858; The Epistles of St. Paul to the Corinthians, after the Authorized Version. Newly Compared with the Original Greek and Revised by Five Clergymen in 1858; and The Epistles of St. Paul to the Galatians, Ephesians, Philippians, and Colossians, after the Authorized Version. Newly Compared with the Original Greek and Revised by Four Clergymen in 1861.

1858 - Leicester Ambrose Sawyer, The New Testament, Translated from the Original Greek, with Chronological Arrangement of the Sacred Books, and Improved Divisions of Chapters and Verses.

1859 - Charles Wellbeloved, George Vance Smith, and John Scott Porter, The Holy Scriptures of the Old Covenant, in a Revised Translation, by the late Rev. Charles Wellbeloved, the Rev. George Vance Smith, B.A., the Rev. John Scott Porter.

1863 - Robert Young, The Holy Bible ... literally and idiomatically translated out of the original languages.

1863 - Herman Heinfetter [Pseudonym of Frederick Parker], A Literal Translation of the New Testament of our Lord and Saviour Jesus Christ, on definite rules of translation, from the text of the Vatican Manuscript.

1864 - Benjamin F. Wilson, The Emphatic Diaglott.

1864 - The New Testament of our Lord and Savior Jesus Christ. The Common English Version, Corrected by the Final Committee of the American Bible Union.

1865 - Samuel Sharpe, The Hebrew Scriptures, Translated by Samuel Sharpe, Being a Revision of the Authorized English Old Testament, in three volumes.

1866 - Henry T. Anderson, The New Testament Translated from the Original Greek.

1867 - John Nelson Darby, The Gospels, Acts, Epistles, and Book of Revelation: Commonly called the New Testament. A New Translation from a Revised Text of the Greek Original.

1867 - Joseph Smith, Jr., The Holy Scriptures, Translated and Corrected by the Spirit of Revelation.

1869 - George R. Noyes, The New Testament: Translated from the Greek text of Tischendorf.

1872 - Joseph Bryant Rotherham, Rotherham Version. The New Testament: newly translated from the Greek text of Tregelles and critically emphasized, according to the logical idiom of the original; with an introduction and occasional notes.

1875 - Samuel Davidson, The New Testament. Translated from the Critical Text of Von Tischendorf; with an Introduction on the Criticism, Translation, and Interpretation of the Book.

1876 - Julia E. Smith, The Holy Bible: Containing the Old and New Testaments; Translated Literally from the Original Tongues.

1881 - C.J. Ellicott, ed., The English Revised Version. The New Testament of our Lord and Savior Jesus Christ, Translated out of the Greek: Being the Version Set Forth A.D. 1611, Compared with the Most Ancient Authorities and Revised, A.D. 1881.

1886 - John Wesley Hanson, The New Covenant: Containing I. An accurate translation of the New Testament. II. A Harmony of the Four Gospels. III. A Chronological Arrangement of the Text. IV. A Brief and Handy Commentary.

1897 - Robert D. Weekes, The New Dispensation. The New Testament translated from the Greek.

1898 - Francis Aloysius Spencer, The Four Gospels: A New Translation from the Greek Text Direct, with Reference to the Vulgate and the Ancient Syriac Version.

1898 - George Barker Stevens, The Epistles of Paul in Modern English: A Paraphrase.

I mention these thirty four works or so to illustrate the point that translations will continually be published. Not, as some may suggest, to further a denominational thought but to attempt to translate the Bible as God intended them to translate it. Translations will inevitably be conceived and some will be found to be negligent and in direct opposition to God. Likewise, translations created by learned theological scholars and members of the church continue to diligently seek the full knowledge of scripture. God has provided man with the intellect and knowledge to search and discover things to their full potential. Therefore, it would be inconceivable to imagine that we will not continue to ensure translation of scripture and, more importantly, that interpretation of God's word is done as purely and as accurately as possible, in line with each nations language.

Until the 1880s most, if not all, Bibles contained 80 books, namely, the 66 books we know of the scriptures today and 12 books of the Apocrypha. King James threatened anyone removing the Apocrypha with jail time and heavy fines.

Only until recent times have the traditional Protestant churches removed and rejected these 12 books from the true word of God.

Looking at history, the English, who for so long fought with their blood and souls to ensure an English language Bible was their right, seem to have passed the baton to their American relatives. The preponderance of new translations and versions is never more noticeable than what has been produced across the Atlantic Ocean.

After the English Revised Version (ERV) was created by updating the King James Version in 1885, in America, scholars responded with an almost identical version called the American Standard Version (ASV) in 1901.

It is interesting that the English Revised Version was in fact derived by a 'movement' as early as 1870. This movement formed a large committee in order to revise the King James Version and immediately took on an international flavor of eminent Bible scholars both in England and the United States. The English committee formed itself into two groups. One group took on the task of the Old Testament and the other the New Testament with both groups regularly meeting in the Deanery of Westminster in London, England.

A year later in 1871 the American committee was organized by invitation from the English committee. The American committee also split into two groups and also regularly met together at the Bible House in New York, USA. Despite the separation of the Atlantic Ocean, both the English and the American committees equally held to the same principles and values of creating a unified revised work. This they accomplished by regular communication and correspondence with each other. What is also worthy of note is that over 100 scholars participated in this great work from across a wide selection of denominational faiths. The American contingent was in fact made up of many experts of Hebrew and Greek.

So what was the purpose of such a huge task of revision?

The answer is very simple but also protracted.

The simplicity of the requirement for such revision was the English language itself. When one reflects that the King James Version was written in 1611 we realize that it was in dire need of revision, if only for the change of the English language during the then 250 or more years since its inception. It is true that the King James Version had a major revision in 1789 but this was predominantly a work to 'fix' the mistakes and/or deviance from both the early works since 1611 [i.e. the "Wicked Bible", the "His, Hers Bible" references] as well as the competition of both the Oxford and Cambridge Universities vying for the right to have the correct translation/version.

Nevertheless, both committees were determined not to alter the message of God in a way that would not conform to the sacred scriptures. They insisted on making as few alterations as possible and to limit as much as possible any expressions of conflict. Like the original translators of the 1611 King James Version the English and American Revisers were to read their revised work at least twice. Once to verify what they had written and a final check to approve. This included revision to chapter headings, pages and paragraph markings, as well as italicize and punctuation settings. If they could not agree, they were to confer with their colleagues from either country.

This then, became the English Revised Version. It was the first, and remains the only, officially authorized and recognized revision of the King James Bible.

The 1901 version (ASV) grew in popularity for several decades by American Churches. The original English Revised Version, which was led predominantly by the English Committee, made a stipulation on the American Committee that any suggestion they [the Americans] had needed a two thirds majority agreement from the English committee, and any suggestions be placed in the appendix of the RV [Revised Version]. This was further enforced by an agreement made between the parties [committees] that the American scholars would not publish a version of their own for 14 years. The appendix contained approximately 300 suggestions.

With the release of the Revised Version New Testament in 1881, followed by the Revised Version Old Testament in 1885, the English committee began to disband. Oxford and Cambridge Universities published their own Revised

Version edition and did in fact retain the American suggestions, again published in the appendixes.

1901 saw the expiration of the 14 year agreement of the original English and American committees and it was subsequently published by Thomas Nelson & Sons the same year. It was copyrighted as well, to retain not just ownership but the purity of the text. Two decades later the International Council of Religious Education, which eventually merged with the Federal Council of Churches to become the National Council of Churches, purchased the copyright of the American Standard Version from Thomas Nelson & Sons. The Council renewed the copyright in 1929 as a result of several publishers tampering of the original RV text. These publishers alleged they had only done so in the interests of the American reading public. There was no legal precedent as the copyright Thomas Nelson had filed was to protect the ASV text and not the RV text.

Despite all of these efforts the King James Bible retained its prominence as the Bible that many American Protestant Christians would use and refer to. This remained the case until 1952 when the publication called the Revised Standard Version appeared [RSV]. The irony of this new version was the fact that many of the American seminaries favored the use of the American Standard Version over the Revised Standard Version. This can appear somewhat strange in that the general Christian population's preference was the King James Bible. However, this can be explained perhaps in part that the American Standard Version contained [as would be expected] several changes in text to that of the Revised Version. This was due in part to American scholars rendering of the American text in line with their scholarly learning verses that of the schools attended by the English scholars of the RV. The popularity of the American Standard Version perhaps never gained the level of what it should, or could, have accomplished. It did gain much popularity from the Jehovah's Witnesses religion for its repeated reference to the name "Jehovah" versus the same scriptural rendering of "Lord" in the King James Bible.

Then in 1971 the American Standard Version was revised and had the new title New American Standard Version Bible. Today, we often refer to this version by the acronyms NASV, NASB, or simple NAS.

It was this version that is considered to be the most accurate and word for word translation of both the original Greek and Hebrew scriptures into English. According to the New American Standard Bible preface the translators held four aims as its cornerstone for its publication.

The publication had to retain the true rendering of the Hebrew, Greek and Aramaic language. It needed to be grammatically correct. It had to be simple to understand. And the Lord Jesus Christ was to be given His rightful place of prominence in line with the translation of scripture.

The Hebrew text used for the original New American Standard Bible translation was the third edition of Rudolf Kittel's Biblia Hebraica together with the Dead Sea Scrolls.

The 23rd edition of Ebehard Nestle's Novum Testamentum Graece was used for the Greek text.

The translators of the 1971 New American Standard Bible sought to create a literal translation from the original languages into contemporary English while at the same time maintaining a word-for-word translation. Where no literary change could be thought or considered, changes were made to best deliver the idioms of current thought or language to display the meaning as accurately as possible to what the unknown word meant. To reiterate this, footnotes were included by way of explanation.

The greatest strength [as already noted] was the New American Standard Bible's ability to render the original languages reliable via translation. The trade-off, which contributed to its perceived weakness, was that the text did not flow as well as that of the day to day English language which, as a result, caused some confusion to its readers.

Despite this, it continues to hold pride of place among professors, scholars, seminary students and theologians. But some have acknowledged and commented that, because of it being so direct in translation, it does impede the flow of normal English conversation.

As a result, just two years after the New American Standard Bible [or New American Standard Version] appeared, the New International Version or NIV was produced in 1973.

The project to produce the New International Version began in 1965 after a meeting at the Trinity Christian College in Illinois of the Christian Reformed Church, National Association of Evangelicals and a group of international scholars.

The Old Testament manuscript base was from the Biblia Hebraica Stuttgartensia Masoretic Hebrew text along with, again, the Dead Sea Scrolls and the additions of the Samaritan Pentateuch, the Latin Vulgate, the Syriac Pershitta and the Aramaic Targum.

For the New Testament the Greek Koine language editions of the United Bible Societies and Nestle-Aland were used.

Similar to the original English Revised Version and American Standard Version committees, close to 100 scholars were entrusted with the translation. A core group of 15 scholars led these translators and it took a decade to produce what became the New International Version Bible. It truly was a work of International involvement, not only across denominational groups, but countries across the globe.

This Bible was produced as a "dynamic equivalent" translation [more on this subject later]. The New International Version was more of a phrase for phrase translation than a word for word one. It did, in fact, attempt to provide a thought-for-thought frame of speech. Not only did this help the English language to be read more easily it was also suitable for Junior High School reading level.

The New International Version succeeded in its intent to appeal to a broader audience. In December 2012 figures for the Christian Booksellers Association showed the New International Version in top position of the five bestselling Bibles in the USA. In fact, at the time of writing, the New International Version has sold over 450 million copies worldwide.

The old faithful King James Version was updated in 1982 by Thomas Nelson Publishers into what became the New King James Version (NKJV). The attempt was to remove obscure words and Elizabethan pronouns, i.e. 'thee', 'thy', 'thine' and 'thou', as well as verb forms such as 'speaks' rather than 'speaketh'. Fierce debates continue by proponents on both sides of the fence as to whether the New King James Version faithfully preserves the message written in the original King James Version.

Many scholars and laypeople alike have not taken the New King James Version [NKJV] seriously but it has gained much popularity by the general public and was listed 4th in the top five table mentioned earlier in the USA.

Then in 2002 a significant attempt was made to bridge the gap between the simplicity of the New International Version and the precise accuracy of the New American Standard Version. This version is known as the English Standard Version or ESV. This version has gained rapid popularity for its readability and accuracy. (A small note I make to the testament of this version is that I used this version primarily in my first book, "Front and Center".)

The advance of the Bible being translated, not just in English but other tongues, is nothing short of miraculous.

The Bible continues to be the most translated book the world over. The internet site Wikipedia references figures as of 2005 that at least one book of the Bible has been translated into 2400 of the 6900 languages listed by SIL [Sil International, formerly known as Summer Institute of Linguistics].

The Bible is available in whole, or in part, to approximately 98% of the world's population in a language in which they are fluent.

In December 2007 the United Bible Society stated that the Bible was available in 438 languages while the Wycliffe Bible Translators announced Vision 2025, which aims to have translation available in every language community that needs it by that year.

We could go on with more startling statistics like these but what is the point here?

The point is that God has seen to it that His word will not go out and return empty. All across the world people are being taught the gift of God's Grace and the salvation we all can attain through His precious son Jesus Christ.

We mentioned earlier that the New International Version is a "dynamic equivalent" translation. There are two other types of translation used, namely, "Formal equivalence" and "Idiomatic, or Paraphrastic translation" [also known as Functional Equivalence].

All odd phrases and words for many of us but let me explain with examples.

Dynamic Equivalent Translation

This is known as a free translation which clearly conveys the thoughts and ideas of the original text. Unlike just a literal translation, a dynamic equivalent translation attempts to convey the subtleties of the context and its subtext so that when read, the reader sees the translation and the context. An example of this is the New Living Translation (NLT). The New International Version (NIV) attempts to strike a balance both of dynamic and formal equivalence.

Formal Equivalent Translation

This is a literal translation where it tries to stay as close to the original source text as possible. We noted earlier the New American Standard Version is extremely accurate but it lacks the natural flow of the English language. However, a point in favor of formal equivalence is the less the translation departs from the literal word the more it assumes its accuracy. If you own or have access to a Young's Literal Translation [YLT] look at John 3:16 as an example of what I am talking about. You will note the degree of difficulty of translating this into proper conversational English. If you have neither ownership nor access of the YLT, here is the text, *"for God did so love the world, that His Son -- the only begotten -- He gave, that every one who is believing in him may not perish, but may have life age-during" (YLT).*

Here is the same verse in the NIV. *"For God so loved the world that he gave his one and only Son, that whoever believes in him shall not perish but have eternal life" (NIV).*

And here finally is the same verse in the ESV. *"For God so loved the world, that he gave his only Son, that whoever believes in him should not perish but have eternal life" (ESV).*

In the above three examples of the same scripture notice the difficulty when reading the YLT version. It grammatically does not flow with the English we speak.

The next two scripture examples differ only very slightly. In fact, the only difference is the addition of a comma and the removal of the words 'one and'. Nevertheless they both read the way we speak.

Functional Equivalent Translation

This is a thought for thought translation and goes further than a dynamic equivalent translation. It attempts to give meaning of entire phrases, sentences or even passages instead of a single word. Even though it may be less precise than its relatives, functional equivalence can assist in explaining and therefore be considered more accurate for passages that have difficult ancient idioms [combination of words with a figurative meaning]. The Message Bible is a great example of functional equivalence. To illustrate, here is the way the Message Bible renders John 3:16, *"This is how much God loved the world: He gave his Son, his one and only Son. And this is why: so that no one need be destroyed; by believing in him, anyone can have a whole and lasting life" (MSG).*

What can we glean from all the choices we now have from our preferred Bible translation?

Those entrusted or who decide to translate the Bible must ensure that they provide an accurate rendering of the scriptures. It is also incumbent upon each and every one of us to make intelligent and informed decisions as to what translations we choose to read. One thing is certain, translations of the Bible will continue without letup. While writing this book two new translations have been launched as example. We have the last century of translations for further proof, if we needed it. Undoubtedly we will see more appearing in this century.

But we also need to be careful of translations that may divert off to a position that is not scriptural. One could consider some more modern translations which, for the sake of not wanting to highlight or advertise them, I will not mention their specific names. These attempt to change God's word to make it more politically, religiously or denominationally correct. One example is where a translation removes all gender-specific references wherever possible.

But equally dangerous is if we close our minds and reject any translation that has ever been produced since the King James Version. I can personally testify to the rhetoric and un-Christian stance made by such which I will cover in a later chapter.

In closing, we should remember and be grateful to those who blazed a trail before us to ensure a person not only possessed a Bible, but was able to read it in their tongue. They also wrote their translations in a way that was understandable with regard to the current language, speech or grammar of their day.

William Tyndale was strangled and burnt for his desire to provide a Bible for the people. When he was criticized by a papal official for his work in publishing an English Bible it is believed he replied with these words,

"If God spare my life, I will see to it that the boy who drives the plowshare knows more of the scripture than you, Sir!" [Anglicized]

"There came a time in my life when I doubted the divinity of the Scriptures, and I resolved as a lawyer and a judge I would try the Book as I would try anything in the courtroom, taking evidence for and against. It was a long, serious and profound study and using the same principles of evidence in this religious matter as I always do in secular matters, I have come to the decision that the BIBLE is a supernatural Book, that it has come from God, and that the only safety for the human race is to follow its teachings"

Salmon P. Chase (1808-1873)

CHAPTER 9

History of American Bible Translations

We already read in a previous chapter that the Pilgrim Fathers coming from England to America had with them copies of the Geneva Bible.

However, if anyone at the time of their crossing the Atlantic Ocean thought of producing an 'American Bible' it certainly was not on the minds of the early settlers.

In any event, they were, to all intents and purposes, still subjects to the crown, that being either a King or Queen of England and, as such, they were still under the laws of England. This was to prove somewhat of a problem later when Americans wanted to print their own Bibles as the English crown had a monopoly via copyright to prevent anyone printing the King James Bible by anyone other than whom the royal court chose.

John Eliot (1604-1690) was a Puritan missionary and preached to the American Indians. Born in the tiny village of Widford in East Hertfordshire, England, he later attended Jesus College, Cambridge. After his college education he became the assistant to Thomas Hooker (1586-1647) who was a prominent Puritan leader. Hooker was later forced to flee to Holland and, when he did, Eliot emigrated to Boston, Massachusetts arriving in 1631. He eventually became a minister and the teaching elder at the First Church in Roxbury, Massachusetts. Later in 1637-1638 he participated in both the civil and church trials of the Puritan spiritual advisor Anne Hutchinson (1591-1643) who was accused of creating a theological schism that threatened to destroy the Puritans' religious experiment in New England. Eliot, along with another minister representing Roxbury, disapproved of Huchinson and she was eventually excommunicated and exiled.

Along with two other ministers, Thomas Weld (c.1595-1661) of Roxbury and Richard Mather (1596-1669) of Dorchester, Eliot is credited with editing the Bay Psalm Book which was the first book to be published in the colonies in 1640.

Five years later in 1645 Eliot founded the Roxbury Latin School. During 1649 to 1674 he was assisted in his ministry by Samuel Danforth (1626-1674).

Part of John Eliot's ministry that was very important to him was to convert the Massachusett Indians. As a result of this missionary work he translated what became known as the Algonquin Bible into the Massachusett Indian dialect which was published in 1663. Eliot hoped of integrating the Native Americans into planned towns to create a Christian society and at one point he had succeeded in establishing 14 towns of "Praying Indians". Sadly, boundary disputes began to emerge between the colonists and the Indians and many praying Indian towns suffered disruption which resulted in the Indians being offered money to relocate.

Eliot eventually went on to write 'The Christian Commonwealth', also known as 'The Civil Policy of the Rising Kingdom of Jesus Christ', which is considered to be the first book on politics by an American. Unfortunately, it was also the first book to be banned by a North American government due to its call for an elected theocracy in England and throughout the world. This angered England and embarrassed the Massachusetts colony and led to the General Court in 1661 to force Eliot to issue both a retraction and apology. The book was banned and all copies destroyed, which is eerily similar to that of others trying to translate the Bible into the English language.

John Eliot went on to father 6 children and subsequent generations also followed him into ministry.

Eliot's Bible was the only Bible printed for the next 80 years on an American printing press. The next one, although printed in America, was in the German language.

Christopher Sower (1693-1758), born Christophe Saur in Laasphe, Germany, originally studied medicine at the University of Halle, but later moved to Germantown, Pennsylvania. He obtained Bibles and other German publications from Germany to help his fellow Germans continue their education, especially in theology. By 1738 he had a printing press and published a 24 page almanac in German. He followed this a year later with a religious and secular journal which almost reached a circulation of 10,000 and influenced many of his countrymen.

In 1743 he produced a quarto edition of the Bible in German from Martin Luther's translation.

He went on to publish many more publications in both English and German. He established the first type foundry in the colonies and the manufacture of ink. Saur [he signed his name with the original German spelling in his Bible productions] was the classic entrepreneur going on to make his own paper, bind his own books and invented several other items outside of printing.

Despite his wife being a member of the Seventh Day Baptists, Saur never proclaimed any affiliation with any religious organization.

America had to wait until 1782 to have an English Bible printed in their homeland. Leading up to the American Revolution, Bible's became harder to obtain, due in part to the English ordering an import-export embargo against the rebellion.

A new entry in American history regarding the Bible was Robert Aitkin (1734-1802) born in Dalkieth, Scotland.

By the time Aitkin was 35 he was living in Philadelphia and working as a bookseller. In 1775 he began publishing 'The Pennsylvania Magazine' and the next consecutive years he also printed copies of the New Testament.

With the American War of Independence in full swing against Britain, the supply of Bibles was cut off. The result was that on September 11, 1777 the Continental Congress passed a motion to instruct its committee of commerce to import 20,000 Bibles from other parts of Europe. A second motion was made to pass a resolution for the same requirement but was postponed and never brought before Congress again.

A little over 3 years later on January 21, 1781 Aitkin, the now fierce Patriot to the American cause, petitioned Congress to certify his version of the Bible which he had printed already. Although Congress endorsed Aitkin's Bible as textually accurate [Congressional Chaplains White and Duffield reported on its accuracy], they denied his request that the Bible be published under the authority of Congress.

They did however approve and recommend its publication by Aitkin and authorized him to publish it in "the manner he shall think proper". [1]

This is the only time in US history where the US Congress authorized the printing of a Bible. The record of this authorization stated, "Resolved. That the United States in Congress assembled highly approve the pious and laudable undertaking of Mr. Aitkin, as subservient to the interest of religion as well as an influence of the progress of arts in this country and being satisfied from the above report (by the congressional chaplains), they recommend this edition of the Bible to the inhabitants of the United States and hereby authorize him to publish this recommendation" [Modernized spelling]. [1]

By 1782 Aitkin had in fact incurred severe personal expenses in producing the Bible for the American people. Even though he faced no competition from imports for over a year, he did not profit from his publication. On the contrary, he lost over £3,000 [about $4500] on the 10,000 Bibles he printed.

During distribution of Aitkin's Bible in 1783, Dr. John Rodgers of the First Presbyterian Church of New York made the suggestion to George Washington that every soldier who had been discharged be given a copy of Aitkin's publication. With the war coming to a close two thirds of the army had already been discharged prior to Dr. Rodgers suggestion and Congress did not take up the suggestion. George Washington though was not remiss in making his own comments regarding the suggestion saying, "It would have pleased me well, if Congress had been pleased to make such an important present to the brave fellows who have done so much for the security of their country's rights and establishment". [2]

Matthew Carey (1760-1839) was an Irish born American and economist who lived in Philadelphia, Pennsylvania. He had originally entered the bookselling and printing business in his birth town of Dublin, Ireland. At the young age of 17 he published a pamphlet that was critical of dueling. Dueling, although technically illegal, was conducted on a regular basis to settle a man's honor or reputation. Despite the fact that if one involved in a duel was killed the other was charged with murder, it seems that Carey evidently aroused distain from those who chose to settle personal scores in this manner. Carey followed his criticism of dueling with a document criticizing the Irish penal code with the result that the government threatened him with prosecution. In 1781 he moved to Paris, France, where he met Benjamin Franklin who subsequently employed Carey to work in his printing office. After only a year he returned to Ireland and edited two Irish nationalist newspapers. This time the British government took steps to imprison him. As a result he fled to the newly independent United States in 1784.

Again he met another famous character of American history, the Frenchman, the Marquis de Lafayette, who gave Carey $400 to help him. Carey used the money to start a new publishing business as well as a book shop. His work included The Pennsylvania Herald, Columbian Magazine and The American Museum. Despite all of these three enterprises he was unable to secure any profit from these ventures.

Carey is remembered for printing the first Douay-Rheims Bible in 1790, more widely known as the Carey Bible, which was the first Roman Catholic version printed in the United States. Perhaps due to the new colonial America there was very little demand for a Catholic Bible and as a result very few were printed.

Matthew Carey retired in 1825 leaving his business to his son and son-in-law. They went on to make the business a success and for a period of time it held prominence as one of the publishers in the country. The company published The Encyclopedia Americana, and a dictionary of German lexicon.

February 16, 1746 saw the birth of Isaac Collins (1746-1817) in Centerville, Delaware. By age 14 both his parents had died and the young Isaac, along with his sister Elizabeth, became wards of John Hammond [their mother's brother]. Not long after Isaac was apprenticed to a printing shop run by Master printer James Adams. Isaac's indenture was not merely to learn printing but also to serve the needs of the household. Nevertheless, he learned his trade well. After finishing his apprenticeship at the age of 21 he left for Philadelphia where he became a journeyman printer [this was a term for one who had finished an apprenticeship but was yet to become a master in their trade or craft] with William Goddard (1740-1817). Collins remained with Goddard for the next 4 years.

He eventually set up a print shop in Burlington, New Jersey. He realized two benefits from this choice. At the time of his print shop, no other print shop existed in the area. The other benefit was the area of Burlington had a huge Quaker population. One interesting story is that the shop Collins set up is said to have been the same printing shop that Benjamin Franklin had once used.

Yet another stroke of fortune came Collins way with the recent passing of the local official governmental printer James Parker. Collins was in the right place at the right time. Despite Parker's son Samuel wanting the position, Collins had the better political connections, which he had recently secured via the influential Smith family and other Quakers in the area.

Collins was awarded the position which ensured a regular source of work and a guaranteed income of around 250 pounds sterling per year [approx. $400].

During the Revolutionary war, Collins and his skilled employees were given special dispensation of not having to join the continental army in order that his printing shop could continue to produce the New Jersey Gazette and other propaganda that supported the Colonial's endeavors. This exemption extended to Collins paper supplier William Shaffer and his two employees also.

To take advantage of both geographical and industrial benefits in distributing his paper which was supported by subscriptions, Collins moved his business to Trenton, Pennsylvania.

However, not everything went Collins way. He began to experience competition and worse, the Quaker faith disowned him due to his support of the Revolution. This disownment did not extend to his family members who were still allowed to worship. For Collins himself it meant separation from his church for almost a decade.

In 1789 Collins began to set the stage of what would become his finest work. He announced he was going to print, by means of obtaining subscriptions, a new copy of the King James Bible called the Collins Bible. It is interesting to note that Collins decided on subscriptions to finance this work with some degree of financial safety in mind. He was a business acquaintance of Robert Aitkin and would have no doubt known of the financial loss that Aitkin suffered. Collins subsequently produced an attractive four page pamphlet advertising his proposal and request for orders. He set a price and requested a down payment of $1 at the time of placing a subscription, followed by full payment at the time of delivery.

His target, before he commenced printing, was to receive 3000 subscriptions, but at the time, this number fell way short of his expectations. Undaunted, he offered to include a concordance by the English clergyman and theologian John Downame (1571-1652) without increasing the original cost.

Collins' hope of securing 3000 orders was perhaps ambitious. After all, in the mid 1800's most printers did not average more than 300 to 500 copies. The one exception to this was Benjamin Franklin's Poor Richard's Almanack, which produced a staggering print run of 10000 copies per year during its time in print.

Despite the lack of reaching the required 3000 subscriptions, Collins continued on and received substantial help from several religious groups.

The first to show support was the Society of Friends, followed by the Presbyterians, Episcopalians and Baptists. The Quakers also appeared to have accepted Collins back into favor by announcing special committees to help Collins obtain more subscriptions. The Presbyterians also announced in their general assembly the appointment of a number of delegates to assist with obtaining subscriptions, as did both the Episcopalians and Baptists at their respective conventions in 1789. The Presbyterians also set up a three man committee to help Collins revise and correct proof sheets. On this subject, one story of note is that Collins presumably employed the services of his own children in proof reading his work a total of eleven times! He is said to have paid them for each error they detected. After the printing in 1791 the entire work had just one broken letter and a missed punctuation mark!

For this degree of accuracy the Collins Bible is said to be one of the most textually accurate publications to have been produced. It became known as the first "Family Bible" printed in America and eventually exceeded 5000 copies. It was the standard of excellence and, indeed, the prototype for future American Bibles for the next 110 years.

Being the ever faithful Patriot to his country Collins published an address, or essay in place of the traditional dedication to King James written by Dr. John Witherspoon. It read: "As the Dedication of the English translation of the BIBLE to King James the first of England seems to be wholly unnecessary for the purposes of edification, and perhaps on some accounts improper to be continued in an American edition, the editor has been advised by some judicious friends to omit it, and to prefix to this edition a short account of the translations of the Old and New Testaments from the original Hebrew and Greek in which they were written." [3]

Isaac Collins left this earthly life on March 21, 1817 after suffering a stroke. His legacy continued with his children operating the business he had built for the next three decades.

Isaiah Thomas (1749-1831) actually competed with Isaac Collins and produced his Bible about a month before Collins. Curiously we could ask why his did not figure as prominently as Collins. The simple answer was Thomas concentrated on producing illustrated Bibles of beauty. The engravings that were produced required approximately 50 large copperplates which literally doubled the cost of purchasing the Bible. For the most part, people could only afford the version without the engravings. Thomas eventually founded the American Antiquarian Society to which he bequeathed his entire library collection and personal papers.

In 1796 Jacob Berriman produced a large (16 inch tall) folio Bible. The features of this Bible include several examples of American engravers of the 18th century and is considered a work of exceptional beauty.

Two years later in 1798, John Thompson produced the first ever American Bible to be "hot-pressed" in America. This printing technique allowed the ink to be seared clearly into the paper with heat. Thompson, along with Abraham Small advertised the Bible in the Gazette of the United States in April 1796 proudly stating it was the first American Bible produced by the method of hot press and on the finest quality American paper.

Charles Thomson (1729-1824) was a Patriot leader in Philadelphia during the American Revolution and the secretary of the Continental Congress (1774-1789) throughout its existence.

The son of Scots-Irish Parents he was born in Gorteade Townland, Maghera Parish, County Londonderry, Ireland [County Londonderry is now part of Northern Ireland, a province of the United Kingdom]. Upon the death of his mother, his father emigrated to America along with Charles and his siblings. Sadly, his father died at sea and the boys were all separated upon arriving in America.

Charles evidently ended up in the care of a blacksmith in New Castle, Delaware, and educated in New London, Pennsylvania. At the age of 21 he became a tutor in Latin at the Philadelphia Academy.

He later became a leader of the Sons of Liberty in Philadelphia and eventually married the sister of Benjamin Harrison V (1726-1791) who is remembered in history as one of the signatories of the Declaration of Independence.

Thomson served as secretary of the Continental Congress through its entirety which was 15 years of his life. He faithfully recorded the debates and decisions that serve to show us today the faithful dedication to his work. Alongside John Hancock, president of the Congress, Thomson's name [as secretary] appears on the first published version of Declaration of Independence in July 1776.

Thomson, along with William Barton (1754-1817) is noted for designing the Great Seal of the United States which played an important role at the ratification of the Treaty of Paris in 1784.

After he retired as Secretary of the Continental Congress in 1789, Thomson spent almost twenty years perfecting his translation of the Bible from Greek into English. He had long been fascinated with Greek manuscripts of the New Testament and the Septuagint. After finally being satisfied with his translation he sought a publisher for his work and that was none other than a woman by the name of Jane Aitkin.

If you're already wondering if the name Aitkin was familiar you would be correct. Jane Aitkin was the daughter of Robert Aitkin who had produced the first English Bible printed in America in 1782.

Jane Aitkin became the first woman publisher ever to print a Bible and the first modern English Bible publisher since the King James Version two centuries before. Charles Thomson's Bible was finally published by Jane Aitkin on September 12, 1808, in Philadelphia.

Thomson died sometime prior to his ninety fifth birthday in 1824 of a life well lived.

It could probably be said that more than any American, Noah Webster (1758-1843) contributed to the American 'language' and by default to the Bible [although he did in fact translate a Bible of his own which we will read about in a little while].

As a born Englishman [now a proud US citizen] I had never heard of Noah Webster until I undertook the research for this book. In fact, during the course of this research I have 'met' many characters in this historical journey for the first time. I would not be surprised if many home grown Americans had not heard of Noah Webster either, but his history will become apparent shortly.

Born in New Hartford, Connecticut, to family descended from Connecticut Governor John Webster (1590-1661), Noah's father was primarily a farmer and deacon of his local church as well as the town's captain of militia and the founder of a local book society. Despite the lack of any formal college training, Noah's father had an inquiring intellect and a desire for education. His wife taught their children how to spell and trained them in mathematics and music.

By the age of six, Noah Webster was attending a run down one room school which, in later years, he did not have a kind word for. But his negative experience charged him like a lightning bolt to embark on a career and journey that would improve both the experience and the education of future generations of Americans. By age fourteen Webster was learning Greek and Latin from his church pastor in order that he might gain a place at Yale College. Almost two years later he enrolled at Yale but his four years of study there was interrupted by the Revolutionary war.

Webster's father had in fact mortgaged his farm in order for Webster to attend Yale, but it appears later Webster had little or nothing to do with his family further. I'm often reminded of modern events in our own lives, and wonder when I read this, if a wrong word or a disagreement had ensued that caused Webster to disown his family after all they had done for him.

After his graduation from Yale and, possibly due to the Revolutionary war still waging, Webster struggled to find work. He did secure several positions during this period in teaching but none evidently that lasted any great length of time. He turned to studying law and eventually passed the bar examination in 1781 but still struggled to find work which eventually led to bouts of depression. That same year he opened a small school in western Connecticut. Despite this being successful he suddenly closed it and left town, some think due to a broken romance.

It was soon after these events that he turned his attention to literature and embarked on a series of articles he wrote for a prominent newspaper in New England. He again opened a school, this time in Goshen, New York. This time it was a private school catering to children of wealthy parents. By 1785 Webster had written what was to become his famous 'speller', which was a grammar book for elementary schools.

So why do I mention Noah Webster in this chapter?

I mention him for several reasons that will become apparent. By his very nature, Webster was a revolutionary and desired to create a utopic America - clean and pure, devoid of English interference.

Webster dedicated his 'speller' (and what became his dictionary) to provide an intellectual foundation for American nationalism. For decades he became one of America's foremost authors in the new Republic, publishing textbooks, political essays and articles for newspapers for his Federalist party and even a report on infectious diseases. He is even attributed with lobbying individual States to pass a law that protected one's right that is now known as "Copyright".

But his teaching roots would not leave him, which is not unusual given his desire to create a nation of utopia, at least in his own mind. It is not surprising that his dislike of his original elementary school spilled over in witness thereof of the elementary schools that were now evident in his adult years. Many classrooms were overcrowded with upwards of seventy children, and not all of them were simply elementary age children but included many age groups. Coupled with poor underpaid staff, no desks in order for children or teachers to sit, and the most sacrilegious point in Webster's view, textbooks from England no less!

Webster believed with all his heart that Americans should be taught by American textbooks which launched him on to writing a three volume compendium. This consisted of a 'speller', a 'grammar', and a 'reader'. Webster wanted to rescue the native tongue of Americans and remove the pedantry [excessive concern with minor details and rules] which he saw evident in the English language past down from Great Britain. This then, is what Webster believed surrounded English grammar and pronunciation. He believed strongly that the English language had been corrupted by the British aristocracy. He rejected the idea that Greek (or Latin) had to be studied before English. On this point I could not agree more with Webster's reasoning. I, for one, can clearly see where Webster was coming from. One only has to remember in our earlier reading that very few Englishmen spoke the English language in the Middle Ages and even that was a poor example of the English language that we know today. Rather, the gentry, which included practically every scholar of that time, was taught Latin as their first language for communication both by the written and verbal word.

Webster's 'speller', which became known as the 'Blue-Backed Speller' [and is still available today], became an instant success and dominated education and thinking for hundreds of years. By 1837 it had sold 15 million copies which increased to a staggering 60 million by 1890.

Gradually, over a period of time Webster began to introduce changes in spelling making them "Americanized". He substituted "c" for "s" in words like offense and changed "re" to "er" for words like center. He began to drop one of the "L's" as in the example of traveler, and eventually removed the "u" from words like color and favor.

Later in life Webster had an intense interest in religion and one could hardly be excused to wonder if his 'new' Americanized spelling came to the fore, which we all know it did. One only has to look at a Bible's concordance to see the reflection of Webster's influence on American society with regard to spelling, grammar and pronunciation.

Webster's influence extended to include his dictionary. Not satisfied with his first publication in 1806, which he called *A Compendious Dictionary of the English Language*, the following year 1807 saw him compiling his work *An American Dictionary of the English Language*. This work was an expanded and a fully comprehensive dictionary but it would take him twenty eight years to complete it. In order to understand the etymology of words [the study of the origin of words and the way in which their meanings have changed throughout history] Webster embarked on the mammoth task of learning twenty six languages that he hoped would enable him to be able to standardize the American speech. His dictionary entitled An American

Dictionary of the English Language was finally completed in Paris, France, in 1825 while Webster was abroad. It contained seventy thousand words which included twelve thousand words never before seen in a published dictionary. At the age of seventy his dictionary was finally published in 1827. Despite this work of unsurmountable historical and literary significance, only 2500 copies were sold. When Webster decided to work on a second edition he was forced to mortgage his home and from then on never really rescued himself from debt. One can almost identify Webster with say, van Gogh, both never realizing either their fame or legacy during their lifetime.

Webster's religious views were clearly Calvinistic and he became a devout Congregationalist who voiced that America needed to be Christianized. He also felt language should control thoughts. His 1828 American Dictionary had the largest number of definitions regarding Biblical words in any reference of its time. He considered education "useless without the Bible" and in 1833 he released his own edition of the Bible called the Common Bible.

Despite using the King James Version, Webster poured over several Greek and Hebrew works and commentaries and in his version corrected grammar, replaced archaic words that were no longer used in normal vocabulary and removed words that could be construed offensive.

Finally, at the ripe old age of 85, and a life full of literary works that changed the English language as we know it today, Noah Webster died and was buried in New Haven's Grove Cemetery in 1843.

Before I end this chapter it is only fitting to mention the only known woman to have translated the Bible.

Julia Evalina Smith (1792-1886) was born in Glastonbury, Connecticut to parents, Zephaniah Hollister

Smith (1758-1836) and Hannah Hadassah Hicklok (1767-1850). The fourth daughter of five sisters, Julia had a working knowledge of Latin, Greek and Hebrew.

Her father was originally a Congregationalist minister but after only four years he resigned his position and became a successful lawyer. Zephaniah had originally studied theology at Yale but his sectarian opinions led to his separation from the formal church. This was as due in part to Zephaniah's association with Robert Sandeman (1718-1771) whose belief was that established churches and hence the clergy were actually a hindrance to Christianity. Sandeman was a member of the Glasites or Glassites which were a Christian sect founded in about 1730 in Scotland by Sandeman's father-in-law, John Glas (1695-1773). Glas promoted, as part of his faith, the First Great Awakening, which in turn was spread by Sandeman upon his arrival in America. Members who followed Robert Sandeman were called Sandemanians.

The First Awakening was a movement that swept Protestant Europe and British America with the intent to revitalize Christianity. In the colonies in the 1730s and 1740s it left a permanent impact on American religion. This was due to powerful sermons that left church members with a deep personal feeling and revelation of Jesus Christ.

There was a shift to pulling away from rituals and ceremony which led to a person having a deep sense of conviction, spiritually and of the blessing of redemption. The movement [which was also known as the Great Awakening] challenged the established churches authority and incited divisions between old traditionalists and new revivalists. Some of those affected by such change which reshaped their respective Congregational churches were the small Baptist and Methodist Anglican church, the Dutch Reformed church, the German Reformed church, and the Presbyterian church denominations. As far as mainstream Anglican or Quaker churches were concerned, it had little or no impact. However, one good thing is that in certain places it brought Christianity to African slaves.

Although Glas only dissented in his views as to the spiritual nature of the church as well as the functions of the civil magistrate, Sandeman added a distinct doctrine as to the nature of faith. This can be seen on his tombstone which reads [in part], 'That the bare work of Jesus Christ without a deed, or thought on the part of man, is sufficient to present the chief of sinners spotless before God'.

Members of the Sandemanian sect gathered in homes rather than churches for Bible study and worship. This then was what formed the religious teaching of the Smith family household. They may in turn have been regarded with suspicion and mistrust. The Sandemanian sect were Royalists which possibly did nothing to enamor the family to the local town during the era of the American Revolution. Evidently Zephaniah would have been the spiritual leader and patriarch of the family, but his wife Hannah was perhaps the patron of her daughter's education and ongoing teaching. Hannah herself was a linguist as well as an amateur poet. She was also an accomplished astronomer and mathematician and wrote her own almanac. It is said she could wake up at any given time in the night and would know the time by the position of the stars. These factors [regarding both parents] is what drove the Smith sisters to excel in their education and religious activities. Despite their lack of formal education, their home education was incredibly active and informative. They were exposed to languages [no doubt by Hannah] and the constant closeness of Christian fellowship within the home setting.

Zephaniah died in 1836, followed by his wife Hannah in 1850. Whether during Zephaniah's lifetime or preceding Hannah's death (the records are unsure) the Smith family became convinced of the predictions made by William Miller (1782-1849) on Bible prophecy we cannot say. But evidently the family were sufficiently interested in Miller's religious philosophy and beliefs.

Miller, who was a Baptist, is credited with the start of Adventism. Several major religious denominations, such as the Seventh-day Adventists and Advent Christians are among those who formed as a result of Miller's teachings. His own followers were known as Millerites. Miller predicted the second coming of Christ to occur in 1843. Pressed by his followers for a specific date he narrowed his calculation down to March 1843 – March 1844. History already tells us Miller was wrong in his calculations and he still believed that Christ would return before his death in 1849.

The shock of Miller's predictions not coming true was perhaps felt more by Julia Smith than her siblings. Up until Miller's prediction not occurring Julia had kept a daily journal for 32 years which she wrote in French. Her last entry was December 31 1842 and she never wrote in it again.

This may have in fact been the catalyst that launched Julia into translating the Bible. Her thirst for Bible knowledge, perhaps wanting to search for herself if predictions were a reliable source, catapulted her on a 9 year journey of translation from 1847-1856. It would be another 20 years before the world would see The Holy Bible: Containing the Old and New Testaments;

Translated Literally from the Original Tongues by Julia E. Smith.

In several respects, Julia's translation is unique. First and foremost, it is the only one ever made by a woman. It is also the only one, or so it appears, to be made either by a man or woman without help.

In Julia's case she translated the whole Bible completely alone, without consulting anyone. More remarkable is that she did this not once, but five times!!

She translated the Bible twice from Hebrew, twice from Greek, and once from the Latin Vulgate.

One thing that was preeminent in her mind was to translate the words literally. Even though this does not work well with the Hebrew tense [In grammatical terms, tense is a category that locates a situation in time, to indicate when the situation takes place] she acknowledged this fully. Many scholars are highly critical of her translation for this reason, in that they comment that the Hebrew tense translated literally does not equate to a correct sentence in English. Some also argued that because she lacked formal theological training that her interpretation was in some way incorrect.

Without banging the drum for Julia Smith I find myself somewhat in awe of the lady. We have already mentioned her accomplishment in translating the Bible five times. Once would be beyond the scope of the majority. Also of note is the emergence of her translation. Julia never intended to publish her translation. It was originally created for her own private study. After the disappointing predictions of William Miller it is likely she wanted to research scripture herself, which I would suggest is the entitlement of everyone, no matter what their position or station in life is. Twenty years after she had translated her work, she and her surviving sibling

Abby were faced with crippling tax demands from the local tax collector. You may think what was wrong with this? Nothing in terms of paying tax where it is due. But the sisters were ordered to pay higher taxes for their property while properties owned by men had lower tax demands. Ultimately, after litigation, a Republican politician and the rising Suffragists, the sisters won their case, but not before Julia decided they had to raise funds to pay for the taxes and litigation proceedings.

Another point to indicate is that the sisters were not interested in publishing Julia's works for profit, despite the fact that it had cost them $4000 to have the translation published. When they arranged for 1000 copies to be printed they only charged $2.50 per copy.

But let us go back for a moment to read more of this woman's desire for translation and her commitment to the task. We already learned earlier that she devoted some nine years to the translations [remember it was five, not one, translation]. She also taught herself Hebrew. One of her friends, Samuel Farmer Jarvis, apparently had an extensive library and in a letter wrote and advised Julia to learn Hebrew. Jarvis wrote, "Why not study Hebrew, and make a translation from the first of all the texts? It is a very simple language, and soon learned. The Bible is the only pure ancient Hebrew extant, and that is all you need study in the language. You would then be able to see with your own eyes, and not with the glasses of your neighbors". [4]

Her literalness stood out like a beacon of light, and in many ways testified to her producing a work that was, quite simply, literal. Her translation, made almost forty years before the Revised Version, rendered the word "charity" as "love" in reference to 1 Corinthians 8:1 and as an example of agreement to that of the Revised Version. Tyndale translated the same word for this scripture over three hundred centuries before Julia Smith' translation and also used the same word, 'love'. Smith did not know that and never saw Tyndale's translation. Other examples testify to her accuracy of literal translation.

Her work received the endorsements of many learned men of her day. One such man was a Hebrew Professor of Harvard College referred to as Prof. Young. It appears the professor called on Julia sometime after her translation became available. As he examined it he was astonished in the accuracy of her work. Smith asked him, "You acknowledge that I have translated according to the Hebrew idiom?" Young replied, "O yes, you have translated literally". [5]

There is one final thought before closing on this particular translator that perhaps I should say in defense, and indeed, in recognition of her achievement. When King James I commissioned the King James Bible we know he chose fifty-four men. We also know only forty seven of that number fulfilled the work. But what is significant, irrespective whether the translators of the King James Bible numbered fifty four or forty seven, is that their translation took four years [1604-1608]. An additional three years ensued before the King James Bible appeared in 1611.

Compared to these learned theological scholars, one humble woman performed this great work alone without any advice or consultation. That is perhaps the lasting legacy of Julia E. Smith.

During my research it was not my intention to write this chapter, but as the researcher will tell you, like the branches of a tree, or the lines of a person's ancestry much more information is laid bare, which would be remiss of an author not to include.

Indeed, being born in Derby, England, and subsequently becoming an American citizen, I can personally testify to the pleasure of being called an American.

As soon as my research of Bible translations suddenly propelled me to the fact that America had a rich history of Bibles in Colonial America I was hooked. I am more blessed than before in learning of the men and women who lived before us who decided to devote their lives or a portion thereof, in dedication to providing God's word to the masses.

I hope you have also been touched by the stories you have read. A common thread in all of these historical stories is the desire of the individual to realize their dreams. When we accept and know that God gives each and every one of us different gifts [abilities] we can acknowledge that we can all have a part in God's service.

"We the undersigned, students of the Natural Sciences, desire to express our sincere regret that researchers into scientific truth are perverted by some in our own times into occasion for casting doubt upon the truth and authenticity of the Holy Scriptures. We conceive that it is impossible for the Word of God written in the book of nature, and God's Word written in Holy Scripture, to contradict one another ... physical science is not complete, but is only in a condition of progress"

Students of Natural Sciences
[Signed by 800 scientists of Great Britain,
recorded in Bodelian Library, Oxford].

CHAPTER 10

Why do we need New Translations?

So the logical question we all could ask is, why do we need new translations?

And, if we do, do we need so many?

These questions are legitimate and worthy of discussion. Isn't it amazing that in the space of 600 years or so, since John Wycliffe first wrote an English Bible, that we have amassed a considerable amount of translations across so many different denominational groups?

But did you know or ever consider that we can trace partial translations of the Bible into English as early as the end of the 7th century. More impressive than that is that those translations number some 450. The thirst for God's holy written word, as always, has captured the attention and the imagination of man, ever since it was written. Despite these partial translations, the Bible isn't a series of 66 books but is a full testimony from front to back, from cover to cover, of God's plan of redemption for mankind and you can avail yourself of that Grace, which is the free gift of God. It is a life story of Jesus Christ and God's plan for mankind. It is, unquestionably, our blueprint for life.

In our own day, given the explosion of Christian denominations, it is no wonder that we have so many translations. But then we could ask, are they all accurate or correct?

It is ironic that from 66 books Almighty God inspired we now have a proliferation of choices in hundreds, if not thousands, of languages or dialects.

With regard to Christian denominations, there is now an estimated 41,000 different denominational groups of one kind or another.

With this kind of number is it surprising that we would have such a large amount of translations to pool from?

Hardly.

So, how do we answer the question of whether or not we need new translations?

And if we do, why?

A simple answer could suffice in that languages, as we have already noted, have changed tremendously over the centuries of man's existence on the earth. Barriers in translation are also a result of language barriers, due to our country or ethnicity as to where we were born or grew up. Our schooling also factors into this equation in relation to the written and spoken word we are taught from kindergarten upward.

When we factor in all of these variables it can appear justified as to the requirement of new translations. One must remember that the word of God tells us that God wrote the words by inspiring man to write what He wanted contained in His holy word.

HERE IS OUR COMPASS POINT.

God inspired the writers of the Holy Bible so that they wrote what He directed [or dictated] them to write.

None of the translations written since are works of divine authorship.

We could perhaps argue that translators are not authors but copyists. Think back to what we read as to the Masoretes scribes. They were paid copyists whose degree of accuracy was such that they counted every letter. If a change occurred due to the copyist, it was noted in the codex [manuscript]. The scrolls, remember, did not contain all of the Bible as a complete work. Each synagogue would have a series of scrolls to make up the entire work of the Bible and regarding these it was forbidden to write upon or alter any of the text. In fact, once the scroll had become too damaged to use it had to be buried as it was against the Jews law to destroy any of God's sacred documents. Hence, over time, they were copied or translated to retain the accuracy of text.

This would have perhaps been a simple process of continual copying of Hebrew [as in the Old Testament] but as the Greek and then the Roman Empire expanded, more countries, and therefore languages, existed and were adopted by the Jews who were eventually scattered across a wide area of the ancient world.

This should be considered no different in my opinion when we reflect upon new translations. Indeed, as a result of many translations, we have seen a rapid spread of Christianity throughout the whole world, not just a particular geographical area as in the time of the early Christians and Hellenistic Jews. Translations do differ, it is true, some as a result of denominational positions of faith, for example. Theological emphasis can also play a part, with text, style etc. becoming the basis of certain translation works.

It is worth a few moments to review what we have learned so far.

As the King James has been regarded as the 'mainstay' of Bibles during the period of recent generations, we will start here.

Remember, the King James Version was written in 1611 and subsequently saw sporadic alterations until 1769. However, not until 1885 was the King James Version thoroughly updated when the Revised Version or, more accurately, the English Revised Version appeared. Then in 1952 a rival to the 350 year old King James Version appeared in the form of the Revised Standard Version which was known more accurately as the American Standard Version.

In the later part of the 1900's Bibles appeared with less literal meaning in terms of their translation. This comment is not meant to suggest any inaccuracies. We have already commented on such terms as dynamic equivalence etc. which can explain a scripture without taking away any of its value or thought. An example of this could be the Message Bible, which predominantly is a Bible which paraphrases a scripture but at the same time can, and does, give the reader more meaning and explanation.

At this juncture, let me ask you this.

If God thought by allowing these translations it would corrupt His word, do you think He would just stand idly by and not do anything about it?

A person may counter by saying why are there some translations that may be contrary to an accurate rendering of scripture, as in the translations that remove any gender references.

My answer is, for what it is worth, common sense. A true Christian would never accept a translation that had any degree of man-made thoughts that tried to alter or fabricate God's word to no more than something to promote say, a political or denominational agenda. That does not mean Satan would not try to author such a work. In this case he [Satan] would be an author rather than a copyist. He isn't going to copy God's word. If someone wrote in a book that you were the worst ever created person and that you were responsible for all the sickness, evil and death of mankind and that those that followed you would be destroyed along with you would you faithfully copy such a work? Of course not!

But you would be expected to 'author' a book that made you out to be the one being wronged and one who only had the better good for everyone. Satan is no different. While he may not actively pursue altering the Bible as his primary activity we should expect him to attempt to infiltrate men who for their own selfish designs, will reap what they sow by altering God's word.

1946 saw the initiation in the United Kingdom of the New English Bible. This work was an attempt to help people understand the King James Version.

J.B. Phillips (1906-1982) produced an edition of the New Testament letters in 1958. This was a paraphratic work of Letters to Young Churches. His intention of this work was so that his young [youth] group of worshippers could better understand the New Testament and what the authors wrote. In 1966 a similar work appeared called The Good News for Modern Man.

The author Kenneth N. Taylor (1917-2005) published The Living Bible in 1971. This was based upon a literal translation of the American Standard Version of 1901. One can appreciate Taylor's intent of this work. He began his translation so that his children could grasp and understand the scriptures. This work was later positioned to appeal to wider audiences and was eventually marketed to high schools and colleges. Both Phillips' and Taylor's work were a far cry from the King James Version.

The Living Bible [which is really a paraphrastic work] received much criticism, but its popularity grew as a result of people being able to understand God's word easier. This in itself created a need to develop new approaches in Bible translation which in turn gave birth to the likes of dynamic equivalence which, as we have seen, attempts to retain the scriptures original meaning in ways that are easily readable and understood.

To promote the benefits of more people reading scripture, the American Bible Society launched the Good News Bible in 1976. This translation has become one of the widest selling Bibles in modern history.

Taylor's Living Bible saw a revision in 1996 called the New Living Bible. It differs from its predecessor in that it is a full translation from the original languages rather than paraphrasing.

One only has to search via the internet for Bible translations and be met with a plethora of translations that to list here could easily become an entire subject of another book of its own.

In November 2012 the Wycliffe Bible Translators, which was formed in 1942 by the missionary William Cameron Townsend (1896-1982), stated that scripture [in one form or another] existed in 2798 languages out of the 6877 languages known to exist. 518 languages have a complete Bible translation with over 70% of the world's population having access to a complete Bible in their first language.

It is also true that some Bible translations are derived from specific theological issues. Case in point is that of the Jehovah's Witnesses who produce their own Bible to fit into, and within, their own doctrine of faith. I personally do not support this type of Bible despite the fact that I was a Jehovah's Witness for over twenty years. Many key words of the original language have been changed to alter the meaning of scripture or to promote a belief. One such erroneous alteration is to belittle Christ and to place Him as a mere angel created by God. The refusal of the divine deity is another. Even when scripture is cited correctly, wrong interpretation is defended as the correct view, with any attempt to disagree meeting with condemnation and [in the case of members of their own church] excommunication from their faith. A future book will cover this and other dangerous cults in more detail.

Another key component to translating the Bible is the selection of the source text. This in itself has, and perhaps will, continue to be a heavily debated subject.

The original texts of the Bible were written long before printing had been established. As a result we as Christians and scholars alike rely entirely on copies of the sacred work. Every copy has the potential for error [more of that later]. One primary consideration to ensure errors are not contained within the Bible is to consult the extant copies of the original text. Comparing these documents is known as textual criticism.

As far as the Hebrew Bible or Old Testament is concerned we rely upon comparisons of the Masoretic text to that of the Septuagint, the Vulgate, the Samaritan Pentateuch and various Syriac texts along with the Dead Sea Scrolls.

The New Testament, for the obvious reasons of being a later work, has many more manuscripts to glean from. This can present a problem in comparing texts and performing an accurate comparison.

Take for example the King James Version again. This translation was based on the Textus Receptus which, in itself, was an ecletic [a broad and diverse range of sources] Greek text which was collated by Erasmus. He had based this work on Byzantine text Greek manuscripts which make up the majority of existing copies of the New Testament. This was, in effect, a manuscript of several sources made up into one and used as a basis of textual thought.

Over the centuries, the discoveries of other extant documents have caused many New Testament textual critics to favor a text that is derived from manuscripts such as the Alexandrinus Codex and, I believe, that is correct. Ancient translators did not have such documents as the Great Codices and the Dead Sea Scrolls. Bibliographic history has proven not only that God's word has not changed but, in many cases, such documents backed this fact up and proved man-made errors [purposeful or not] needed to be corrected in future translations, which is what has indeed happened.

Over time, the majority of Bible scholars believe that the theological base and knowledge of the original Hebrew and Greek has improved over the centuries, since it was first translated by the trailblazers we have identified in this book. I am not trying to dilute the importance of, or indeed the gratitude to, such men. I simply agree and suggest our modern day education affords us a better opportunity to be able to translate the scriptures into an accurate form.

Coupled with textual criticism technique, archaeological discoveries [some not known at the original time of writing of some ancient works] and linguistics all contribute to a good sound base for translation of the Bible in our modern age.

An excellent example of this was what we read regarding the Dead Sea Scrolls in chapter two with regard to the technology now available from NASA. If you recall, In 1993 NASA staff in their Jet Propulsion Laboratory used digital infrared imaging technology to produce photographs. While using this technology they were able to read a previously unreadable fragment which they noted read, "he wrote the words of Noah". This is significant. When we consider the translations such as Erasmus, Wycliffe, Tyndale, Luther, The King James Committee's etc. none of them had the Dead Sea Scrolls. Even if they had been fortunate enough to have seen them they would not have seen all of the text as is evident by the NASA technology being able to discover previously unreadable text. This, in itself, should provide a strong argument why new translations do indeed deserve a place in society.

Many of those devoted to discovering extant copies and translating them have devoted their entire lives in the study of God's word. Decades of learning have produced much in the way of understanding the scriptures. To question their dedication and loyalty is bordering on the obscene. From their study and belief [for some] in the scriptures they know only too well the responsibility that has been entrusted upon them.

I find it an archaic thought that if we take, for example, the King James Bible of 1611 and its historical success [albeit engineered somewhat by the banning of the Geneva Bible] of over 400 years, many are happy to readily accept that the translators faithfully completed their work. I personally believe that they believed they did. I would not include Archbishop Bancroft in faithfully executing his duties. He blatantly tried to infiltrate and insert his personal twists contrary to scripture, which we know he was successful at doing at least once. But if we can believe an event that took place over 400 years ago, why is it so hard to believe God's infinite ability. Anything other is suggesting that man is better than God. For those that do think they are higher than God, I'm sure God is looking down at them right now knowing what their end will be.

Isn't it a fact that if it wasn't the Bible, some so-called expert would be picking on something else as un-authoritive or inconsistent, at least with their thinking. As a Christian we should not be surprised to see those that will attempt to disenfranchise the Bible as not being the authentic and divine word of God.

For such people I leave them with this thought.

Suppose you assume for a moment there is a force mightier than your own. The choice the mightier force makes is whether you believe the Bible was written by God or not.

If your answer is no, then perhaps you need to identify what mightier force is telling you that. If you're saying the Bible is not the word of God then you're on the opposite side of God and siding with His enemy who already knows his fate.

**If you're still not convinced
I would urge you to read
2 Corinthians 4:3-6
NOW**

"... then, since God wrote it, mark its truthfulness. If I had written it there would be worms of critics who would at once swarm on it, and would cover it with their evil spawn; had I written it, there would be men who would pull it to pieces at once, and perhaps quite right to. But this is the Word of God. Come, search, ye critics, and find a flaw; examine it from its Genesis to its Revelation and find error. This is a vein of pure gold, unalloyed by quartz or any earthly substance. This is a star without a speck; a sun without a blot; a light without darkness; a moon without paleness; a glory without dimness. O BIBLE! It cannot be said of any other book that it is perfect and pure; but of Thee we can declare all wisdom is gathered up in Thee, without a particle of folly. This is the Judge that ends the strife, where wit and reason fail. This is the Book untainted by error, but is pure, unalloyed, perfect truth. Why? Because God wrote it. Ah! Charge God with error if you please, tell Him that His Book is not what it ought to be ... Blessed BIBLE, Thou art all truth."

Charles Haddon Spurgeon (1834-1892)

CHAPTER 11

In Defense of the Bible

Almost a year ago the idea of this book formulized in my mind as a result of a not so friendly encounter I had with a person who claims to represent God.

I don't use the word "claim" loosely, but decidedly. This man I interacted with had, on several occasions, printed information on the internet and had the audacity to call himself a 'watchmen' of God. He refers to the watchmen mentioned in Ezekiel 3:17 which says, ***"Son of man, I have made you a watchman for the people of Israel; so hear the word I speak and give them warning from me" (NIV).***

I had signed up for his newsletter but several times I took issue with what he was saying. Something just didn't fit right with me and being a person who cannot help but speak up, especially if I think or believe God's word is being misinterpreted or wrongly proclaimed, I wrote to ask him why he was saying what he said.

On another occasion this same person made a very pointed attack on several people and Bible translations.

Before I go on to relate the story further, let me say this. I hold no affiliation to any of the individuals this person chose to vilify, but I felt it was wrong that a person professing to be a Christian would speak the way he did. I was also concerned that what he was saying would, or could, influence other individuals. As he chose to copy our correspondence with each other to other members on his blog, I evidently did see his influence by replies that openly criticized my stance.

His first tirade was against Cyrus Ingerson Schofield, known simply as C.I. Schofield (1843-1921). Schofield was an American minister and theologian and writer. In fact he wrote the bestselling annotated Schofield Bible.

Now, did Schofield err and sin? Yes he did. Depending on who you believe you can read and search by means of the internet or books all about Schofield and see the misgiving's and sins he committed. But you will also read the great good Schofield accomplished in the form of the Bible Conference Movement and the creation and support of Bible Schools and Missions. Rather than make this chapter a case of defense for Schofield I leave that for the reader to investigate and decide for themselves. You will find writers on both sides of the argument. But the one thing on the side of those who purport to serve God and condemn and vilify this man that is missing is Forgiveness. It is replaced with Judgment. Here lies my point of this comment on Schofield. Whether we believe in his teachings or doctrines or not is not the point here.

The point here is we should adhere to Christ's command in Matthew 7:1-5 saying, ***"Judge not, that you be not judged. For with the judgment you pronounce you will be judged, and with the measure you use it will be measured to you. Why do you see the speck that is in your brother's eye, but do not notice the*** *log that is in your own eye? Or how can you say to your brother, 'Let me take the speck out of your eye,' when there is the log in your own eye? You hypocrite, first take the log out of your own eye, and then you will see clearly to take the speck out of your brother's eye" (ESV).*

In the confrontation with the Pharisees they tried to trick Jesus with questions. One of those questions, again recorded in Matthew, asked Jesus what the greatest commandment was. In Matthew 22:37-40 Jesus answered far more regarding what we should obey with regard to the Pharisees question. *"Jesus replied: 'Love the Lord your God with all your heart and with all your soul and with all your mind.' This is the first and greatest commandment. And the second is like it: 'Love your neighbor as yourself.' All the Law and the Prophets hang on these two commandments"* *(NIV).*

Not only was Jesus commanding us to first *"Love the Lord your God"* but he went further to tell us to *"Love your neighbor as yourself"*. Remember scripture was written down for Christians not just living then, but for our instruction now.

Jesus was telling us to concern ourselves with what we needed to change in our own lives first, and even after that, commanded us not to judge.

Every one of us have sinned and continue to do so on a daily basis because that is our nature. We do well not to be accused of throwing the first stone, another admonition of Jesus.

I personally own the 2006 English Standard Version [ESV] edition of the Schofield Bible and I have found it to be an excellent resource among the thirty or so other Bible translations that I own [at the time of writing].

This brings me to the next portion of defense for those who follow God. I do not intend to mention the individuals that were next on this 'hit list' by this so called 'watchman' but all of them would be, and are, instantly recognizable by most, if not, all Christians. They are seen daily on our TV screens and despite the fact they have pastoral positions in their own church they are branded with the title "TV evangelists" which I personally think can be sometimes very unfair. The reason I say this is that any pastor, if told they could affect the lives of thousands, perhaps millions, of people with their message by broadcasting their sermons via the technology of TV, would instantly jump at the opportunity. Why on earth wouldn't they? If any one of us were, or are, chosen by God to minister to one person or one million people what would be our choice? Mine would certainly be one million.

Part of the vilification of these ministers is due in part to several reasons, but I will cover just three aspects.

One is the money these ministers make. Now, does God say it is wrong to have money? Absolutely not. I haven't seen a scripture that says that and neither have you. To be a lover of money is most certainly wrong and unscriptural and the scriptures definitely speak directly on this point. But let me submit to you that many, if not all, of these ministers started with nothing but the will of God set upon their hearts. They gave of their time, their commitment, their finances, their tithing, their giving and what was their reward?

Turn with me to Malachi 3:10 which says, *"**Bring the whole tithe into the storehouse, that there may be food in my house. Test me in this, says the Lord Almighty, and see if I will not throw open the floodgates of heaven and pour out so much***

blessing that there will not be room enough to store it" (NIV).

Many of these ministers have increased their ministry by writing Christian books of inspiration and devotion. One minister who wrote the bestselling Christian devotional book of all time did not just give the first of his finances to God where a Christian is commanded to give 10% of their finances. No, this minister reversed it and gave 90% to the Lord and kept just 10% for the finances of his family. Does that sound like someone who doesn't have God's interest at heart?

Does that sound like he is in it for the money? Of course not!

The second aspect our 'watchman' complained about was these same evangelists preach 'warm fuzzy Christianity'.

Are we to assume the God we serve is a cold unfeeling God?

Hardly. If we thought of Him as such then why would He have offered the free gift of Grace in the first place?

Should those that shout and thump the podium in preaching condemnation to their congregation rather than pronouncing the free Grace of God to people be taken seriously? Do not misunderstand me. Sometimes we need the admonishment of scripture to ensure we stay on the right path. But when a preacher is red faced, spitting his words out in fury, should that be the acceptable form of serving God? Only you can answer that question for yourself. My personal view is I do not believe God directs a person to act in that way while they represent his word and teaching.

It is true that if a person rejects the redemption given through the sacrifice of Jesus Christ they certainly risk their eternal future in God's kingdom. But the very nature of God's Grace is one of a loving request that God asks a person to accept. If that is considered warm and fuzzy Christianity then I'll take that medicine any day of the week to be acceptable to God.

Equally, I don't know of many people with all the stresses of today's life, either want, or are open to, the rhetorical shouting of a preacher demanding a person to repent with emphatic repeating of how bad a person is. Hebrews 8:12 tells us, ***"For I will be merciful toward their iniquities, and I will remember their sins no more" (ESV).*** Through God's Grace we have a free gift from Him who saves us. He knows, and a true follower of Christ knows, that only through His Grace can we ever be in unity with Him again.

If you're faced with this argument of the type of preaching you should listen to I would simply say this. Take a look at how many empty seats are in a church with a Bible thumping preacher. Then look at a church who preaches the fundamental belief of God's Grace and goodness. I can tell you first-hand the latter are enjoying increases in church attendance and in many cases have to provide two or three Sunday services to accommodate all that come to listen to the pastor preaching God's word as it should be preached.

The third aspect of our discussion is the comment that became the most shocking to me. I was very quickly vilified myself by this person for my comments and questioning. I was, I admit, somewhat defensive to his vehement rhetoric toward Schofield and his Bible translation and the evangelists. But it was his next sentence that really shocked me. As I read what he wrote, especially since he claimed not just to be a watchman of God but more importantly, a Christian, I could not believe it. After my reply to his email as to why I thought it wrong of him to conduct himself in this manner he wrote, "you need to read a real Bible [referencing the King James Version] instead of the drivel [any Bible other than the King James Version evidently] you read" [paraphrased].

My reply was to immediately discount his comments and have no further communication with him. But it troubled me for several days what this man said.

My immediate frustration, rather than anger, was how could a fellow Christian call the word of God 'drivel'?

Words to define drivel include, nonsense, twaddle, claptrap, balderdash, gibberish, rubbish, mumbo jumbo, garbage, to name a few.

Upon more research (I cannot categorically say this man is a member) I discovered an organization that supports only the use of the King James Version for use of scripture. Some people who believe this have formed what is known as a King James Only movement. Others who do not speak English as their native tongue but accept the King James fully, based on the translation being translated from the Textus Receptus, also insist on using this translation only.

There are several flaws to this belief and argument that is worth investigation and discussion, some of which we have already mentioned.

You will recall the King James Version was produced in 1611. This was long before the Dead Sea Scrolls were found which allowed a greater degree of theological learning by modern day scholars. Knowledge of ancient Hebrew and Greek has certainly improved over the centuries. With the advances of textual criticism, Biblical archaeology and linguistics have led to even more advances in more accurate translations. One example mentioned earlier is the New American Standard Version.

The Textus Receptus was what was used for translation of Greek for Martin Luther's Bible, The New Testament by William Tyndale and the King James Version. Rather than itself being an extant manuscript it was a series of Greek texts derived from six manuscripts which formed the body of work by the Dutch Catholic scholar Erasmus.

Erasmus desired to clean up the Latin Vulgate by Jerome, but when certain portions of text were not available to Erasmus from the six manuscripts he defaulted to the Vulgate. It is known that Erasmus adjusted the text in quite a few places to correspond with readings found in the Vulgate or as quoted by Church fathers. As a result, the Textus Receptus differs in almost 2000 places from what is known as the "Majority Text" noted by Hodges and Farstad. The Majority Text, by nature of its name, forms a collection of Greek New Testament extant documents which were primarily derived from Byzantine text-type.

Although Erasmus had studied Greek for many years the six manuscripts he had access to in Basel were all dated from the 12th century or even later.

Over the years many other publishers produced their own Greek New Testament and rather than doing their own critical work to prove accuracy they simply relied on Erasmus' text.

Again, I reiterate, please don't misunderstand my points here. I am not in any way trying to discredit the King James Version. But when such challenges to what a Christian chooses as to what Bible translation they freely decide to read is attacked then I believe we have a duty to speak out and/or defend why we choose to accept or reject a certain publication.

When we are made aware of extant manuscripts or specifically render them as the source of translation, then they should always be considered the most accurate document we have available. The Dead Sea Scrolls and the Codex Sinaiticus were written centuries earlier than the texts of the Textus Receptus.

Westcott and Hort published The New Testament in the Original Greek in 1881 and in their case they rejected the Textus Receptus in favor of the Codex Vaticanus, again an example of an extant manuscript written centuries earlier.

Ultimately, the one and only important point we should concern ourselves with is this. If we believe that the Bible is the divine, inspired word of God, then we should defend it based on our Christian faith.

It is true we have heard all the arguments mainly against the Bible being the word of God, but not much as to the firm belief it is.

We should consider this important point here and not base it upon what we say but what God says from the scriptures.

Surely, if a critic says the Bible writers never claimed to be inspired, or that they directly received inspiration from God, what are they saying?

Clearly, they are rejecting God as the author and therefore saying the Bible is not the infallible word of God nor did He inspire its writing.

Some claim that the Bible writers did not write down the words or ideas from God but that perhaps God influenced their thinking and they wrote what they decided to write free of any inspiration.

Still others suggest that the Bible writers may have written great words of wisdom in order to attempt to persuade Christians to follow such truths but when history or science is mentioned the writers got it wrong.

As we read in the early portion of this book, 25,000 archaeological and therefore by default historical findings, have proven beyond doubt the authenticity of the Bible. I could mention hundreds of these examples but one that certainly caught my interest while researching for this book was that of King Sargon II. This Assyrian King is mentioned only once in the Bible in Isaiah 20:1. Prior to 1842 Sargon did not appear in classical sources and as a result scholars concluded that Sargon was not a bona fide King but rather an alias of some other ruler. That all changed when in 1842 and 1844 the French archaeologist Paul-Emile Botta discovered Sargon's huge sculptured palace in Khorsabad, Northern Iraq. This vast palace consisted of more than 200 rooms and 30 courtyards. The find also revealed reliefs and inscriptions to King Sargon II. Amazingly, God saw to it that Sargon was mentioned in His word albeit once and because mere man ignored the one scripture the Bible was thought to have it recorded wrongly. The arrogance of mankind is sometimes beyond what a Christian can bear. Calling into question God's holy word? Because it doesn't quite fit with their thinking? Just as the book of Isaiah went into describing those who opposed God, men in this and other generations who have dared call His name into question will receive their reward for their blasphemy.

To suggest the claims that God's word is not by His divine inspiration is to say that the Bible contains errors. Some go as far as to suggest rejecting portions of the Bible, including some who profess to preach the word of God. This is what we know of today as liberalism in our culture. More importantly, who would you say is the real villain behind these pronouncements?

Notice what the Apostle John was inspired to write in Revelation 19:9b, ***"And he said to me [further], These are the true words (the genuine and exact declarations) of God" (AMP).*** Several translations of the Bible render this verse as ***"These are the true words of God".***

The Bible is scattered from cover to cover with God speaking. The Old Testament Prophets declared that ***"the Lord has spoken",*** or the ***"word of the Lord came"*** (See Isaiah 1:2; Jeremiah 10:1-2; Ezekiel 1:3; Hosea 1:1-2; Jonah 1:1; Micah 1:1)

The Apostle Paul left us in no doubt who the author of the Bible was. He tells us in 1 Corinthians 14:37-38, ***"If anyone thinks he is a prophet or spiritual, let him recognize that the things which I write to you are the Lord's commandment. But if anyone does not recognize this, he is not recognized" (NASB).***

I especially like the way the Amplified Bible paraphrased this same scripture. Here it reads, ***"If anyone thinks and claims that he is a prophet [filled with and governed by the Holy Spirit of God and inspired to interpret the divine will and purpose in preaching or teaching] or has any other spiritual endowment, let him understand (recognize and acknowledge) that what I am writing to you is a command of the Lord. But if anyone disregards or does not recognize [that it is a command of the Lord], he is disregarded and not recognized [he is one whom God knows not]" (AMP).***

Paul goes on to say that he received 'direct Revelation'. He tells us in Ephesians 3:2-5, ***"Surely you have heard about the administration of God's grace that was*** *given to me for you, that is, the mystery made known to me by revelation, as I have already written briefly. In reading this, then, you will be able to understand my insight into the mystery of Christ, which was not made known to people in other generations as it has now been revealed by the Spirit to God's holy apostles and prophets" (NIV).*

In 1 Thessalonians 4:15 we see the reference of *"We say by the word of God".*

1 Timothy 4:1 clearly states *"the Spirit [of God] says...."* again showing additional proof of divine authorship.

In John 12:48-50 Jesus issues a warning to those who reject the word of God. He identifies the author directly and issues the proclamation saying, *"He who rejects Me, and does not receive My words, has that which judges him—the word that I have spoken will judge him in the last day. For I have not spoken on My own authority; but the Father who sent Me gave Me a command, what I should say and what I should speak. And I know that His command is everlasting life. Therefore, whatever I speak, just as the Father has told Me, so I speak" (NKJV).*

Then in 1 Thessalonians 1:5 we see the all-encompassing proof and "conviction" of who directs the words of scripture, *"for our gospel did not come to you in word only, but also in power and in the Holy Spirit and with full conviction; just as you know what kind of men we proved to be among you for your sake" (NASB).*

The New Testament writers also made reference to the Old Testament prophet's writings as spoken to them by God. (See Matthew 1:22, 2:15; Acts 1:16, 28:25; Hebrews 1:1-2).

Jesus also testified separately to the Bible being the word of God, that it was inspired, and the Holy Spirit would guide a person to all truth. (See Matthew 15:4, 22:29-32; Luke 10:16; John 16:13).

Multiple scriptures can be cited to refute any notion or possibility that the word of God is not inspired or directly God's word.

The Bible even warns that if a man spoke as if he received a message from God and it was not, then the man was to be punished. The prophet Jeremiah tells us in Jeremiah 14:14, ***"Then the Lord said to me, The [false] prophets prophesy lies in My name. I sent them not, neither have I commanded them, nor have I spoken to them. They prophesy to you a false or pretended vision, a worthless divination [conjuring or practicing magic, trying to call forth the responses supposed to be given by idols], and the deceit of their own minds" (AMP)***. The culmination of such falsehood we read in the next verse resulted in such men being put to death.

God tells us in Ezekiel 3:26-27 that a prophet could not speak until God opened his mouth. He told Ezekiel, ***"I will make your tongue stick to the roof of your mouth so that you will be silent and unable to rebuke them, for they are a rebellious people. But when I speak to you, I will open your mouth and you shall say to them, 'This is what the Sovereign Lord says.' Whoever will listen let them listen, and whoever will refuse let them refuse..." (NIV)***.

Jesus also issued a promise to those who faithfully serve Him. In Matthew 10:19-20 he said, ***"When they deliver you over, do not be anxious how you are to speak or what you are to say, for you are to***

271

say will be given to you in that hour. For it is not you who speak, but the Spirit of your Father speaking through you" (ESV).

Paul tells us that his message was not his but God's when he wrote to the church in Corinth in 1 Corinthians 2: 4-5 saying, *"My message and my preaching were not with wise and persuasive words, but with a demonstration of the Spirit's power, so that your faith might not rest on human wisdom, but on God's power" (NIV).*

Paul follows this last scripture up with a warning in Galatians 1:8-9 saying, *"But even if we or an angel from heaven should preach to you a gospel contrary to the one we preached to you, let him be accursed. As we have said before, so now I say again: If anyone is preaching to you a gospel contrary to the one you received, let him be accursed" (ESV).*

More proof, if we needed more, are the words in 1 Thessalonians 2:13 where we read *"For this reason we also constantly thank God that when you received the word of God which you heard from us, you accepted it not as the word of men, but for what it really is, the word of God, which also performs its work in you who believe" (NASB).*

Paul's fellow Apostle, Peter, was not absent in his own confirmation and was emphatic in his words in 2 Peter 1:20-21, *"But know this first of all, that no prophecy of Scripture is a matter of one's own interpretation, for no prophecy was ever made by an act of human will, but men moved by the Holy Spirit spoke from God" (NASB).*

The Apostle John was also instructed to write in Revelation 22:18-19 the warning, *"I [personally solemnly] warn everyone who listens to the statements of the prophecy [the predictions and the consolations and admonitions pertaining to them] in this book: If anyone shall add anything to them, God will add and lay upon him the plagues (the afflictions and the calamities) that are recorded and described in this book. And if anyone cancels or takes away from the statements of the book of this prophecy [these predictions relating to Christ's kingdom and its speedy triumph, together with the consolations and admonitions or warnings pertaining to them], God will cancel and take away from him his share in the tree of life and in the city of holiness (purity and hallowedness), which are described and promised in this book" (AMP).* Clearly if anyone adds or takes away the words God had commanded they will forfeit their very lives.

So with all of the scriptures quoted, what can we deduce?

It is clear the writers of the Bible never once said they wrote of their own will but that which God dictated to them. For decades many company executive officers [CEO's] have employed the use of secretaries to dictate their letters by shorthand. The secretary faithfully writes the contents in the form of a document so that it is, in effect, the executive's words being spoken. Many surgeons after performing operations speak into a voice recorder to relay how the operation went, what occurred and what they performed during the surgery. They do this so that they can record the information in the 'case notes' for their personal secretaries to transcribe and faithfully record with 100% accuracy what needs to be written and placed into the patients notes or file. Why then, is it so difficult to believe God is far more capable of directing man to write [dictate] His word?

Like the examples of the secretaries we have just mentioned, the writers of the Bible were prohibited from writing anything that was their words, just like the secretary to the CEO or the Surgeon would not be allowed to add or take away anything their boss had instructed.

In the Mosaic Law covenant, God insisted that everything he commanded was to be written down. In Exodus 24:3-4,7-8 we read, *"When Moses went and told the people all the Lord's words and laws, they responded with one voice, "Everything the Lord has said we will do." Moses then wrote down everything the Lord had said....... Then he took the Book of the Covenant and read it to the people. They responded, "We will do everything the Lord has said; we will obey." Moses then took the blood, sprinkled it on the people and said, "This is the blood of the covenant that the Lord has made with you in accordance with all these words" (NIV).*

When Israel began to have a king as its earthly ruler, he was to copy the Law and keep all of its commandments. Deuteronomy 17:18-20 tells us, *"This is what must be done: When he sits down on the throne of his kingdom, the first thing he must do is make himself a copy of this Revelation on a scroll, copied under the supervision of the Levitical priests. That scroll is to remain at his side at all times; he is to study it every day so that he may learn what it means to fear his God, living in reverent obedience before these rules and regulations by following them. He must not become proud and arrogant, changing the commands at whim to suit himself or making up his own versions. If he reads and learns, he will have a long reign as king in Israel, he and his sons"* **(MSG).**

Joshua was told to observe all that was written in the book in Joshua 1:7-8, **"Only you be strong and very courageous, that you may do according to all the law which Moses My servant commanded you. Turn not from it to the right hand or to the left, that you may prosper wherever you go. This Book of the Law shall not depart out of your mouth, but you shall meditate on it day and night, that you may observe and do according to all that is written in it. For then you shall make your way prosperous, and then you shall deal wisely and have good success"** *(AMP).*

And in Matthew 4:4 Jesus said, **"It is written, 'Man shall not live by bread alone, but by every word that proceeds from the mouth of God'"** *(NKJV).*

Peter summarizes nicely the patience we should employ and explains that some people will not believe the Bible to be God's word, and what their result is if they take this position. He writes in 2 Peter 3:15-18, **"And count the patience of our Lord as salvation, just as our beloved brother Paul also wrote to you according to the wisdom given him, as he does in all his letters when he speaks in them of these matters. There are some things in them that are hard to understand, which the ignorant and unstable twist to their own destruction, as they do the other Scriptures. You therefore, beloved, knowing this beforehand, take care that you are not carried away with the error of lawless people and lose your own stability. But grow in the grace and knowledge of our Lord and Savior Jesus Christ. To him be the glory both now and to the day of eternity. Amen"** *(ESV).*

These scriptures are just a small example of why we should defend the Bible. It is and always will be what "God breathed" to us. It is His Holy written word by those inspired by Him under Divine Providence.

The fact that those who claim to be Christian argue over translations shows how subtle Satan can be in attacking us where we least expect.

I leave you to ponder this hypothetical question. If God was being physically attacked by Satan, wouldn't you, as a true Christian, immediately put on your armor and fight for God?

Why then, would you do nothing less than to defend His word?

Why would you not question those who claim to represent Him yet call his word 'drivel'.

His promise, His statement, is worth remembering as we close this chapter. I've purposely repeated the same verse several times from different translations from different time periods of man's history. Some of the scriptures are in the original grammar and spelling in order for you to get a feel for how language has changed and why new translations are useful.

2 Timothy 3:16-17

"For all scripture geven by inspirascion of god, is proffitable to teache, to improve, to informe, and to instruct i rightewesnes, that the man of god maye be perfet, and prepared vnto all good workes" (The New Testament of Our Lord and Saviour Jesus Christ : published in 1526, being the first translation from the Greek

into English (1836) Author Tyndale, William.
d. 1536; Offor, George. 1787-1864) published
by London, S. Bagster – Not_in_Copyright.

"For all fcripture geven by infpiracyon of God
is proffitable to teache to improue to amede
and to inftruct in ryghtewefnes that the man
of God maye be perfecte and prepared vnto all
good works" (Matthew's Bible – 1537 Edition).

"For the whole Scripture is giuen by
infpiration of God, and is profitable to teache,
to improue, to correct and to inftructe in
righteoufnes, That the man of God may be
abfolute, being made perfite vnto all good
works" (The Geneva Bible – 1560 Edition).

"All scripture is given by inspiration of
God, and is profitable for doctrine, for
reproof, for correction, for instruction in
righteousness: That the man of God may
be perfect, thoroughly furnished unto all
good works" (King James Verson).

"All Scripture is inspired by God and
profitable for teaching, for reproof, for
correction, for training in righteousness;
so that the man of God may be adequate,
equipped for every good work" (New
American Standard Bible).

"All Scripture is God-breathed and is useful for teaching, rebuking, correcting and training in righteousness, so that the servant of God may be thoroughly equipped for every good work" *(New International Version).*

"All Scripture is breathed out by God and profitable for teaching, for reproof, for correction, and for training in righteousness, that the man of God may be complete, equipped for every good work" *(English Standard Version).*

"Every part of Scripture is God-breathed and useful one way or another—showing us truth, exposing our rebellion, correcting our mistakes, training us to live God's way. Through the Word we are put together and shaped up for the tasks God has for us" *(The Message Bible).*

"Every Scripture is God-breathed (given by His inspiration) and profitable for instruction, for reproof and conviction of sin, for correction of error and discipline in obedience, [and] for training in righteousness (in holy living, in conformity to God's will in thought, purpose, and action), So that the man of God may be complete and proficient, well fitted and thoroughly equipped for every good work" *(The Amplified Bible).*

Whatever translation you choose to read, read it in the full knowledge that God is talking to you directly as if sitting opposite you in a chair. Not only can we benefit by making it a priority in our lives to read God's word daily but also, take the time to 'Listen' to what God speaks to you.

"The books of men have their day and grow obsolete. God's Word is like Himself, "The same yesterday, today and forever"

Robert Payne Smith (1818-1895)

CHAPTER 12

What does God think?

Far from what anyone may believe or suggest, I for one would certainly not attempt to, nor try to suggest, in anyway shape or form, that I know what God thinks. He tells us in Isaiah 55:8-9, *"For my thoughts are not your thoughts, neither are your ways my ways, declares the Lord. For as the heavens are higher than the earth, so are my ways higher than your ways and my thoughts than your thoughts" (ESV).*
This scripture is interesting in several ways which is worth a few moments of discussion. There are really two parts to this scripture that man can easily miss yet are glaringly obvious. First, we are the created, God is the Creator. Therefore how could we possibly know what God can do? Yet many people think they know better than God, that they do not need Him in their lives. They completely ignore Him, reject Him, vilify Him, curse Him, and utter some of the most heinous things about Him. But the well-known fact of the matter is this. The last time I checked I don't recall any man creating a human being. But many think they know better than God!
The second part I refer to in the scripture is His ways and thoughts are higher than our ways and thoughts. Therefore, how can we even question that He is capable

of inspiring someone to write His word? Could He have written the Bible Himself in a physical sense? Of course. But even that would have been far more supernatural than what we can even begin to comprehend.

Naturally, the naysayers and the scoffers along with the atheists will all say that that is all rubbish. They prefer to spew their thoughts of the 'big bang theory' or that we evolved from an ape or even a fish! They fail to accept common sense of a creative and superior mind. Even scientists acknowledge that to understand the mechanisms of the human brain it would take 500 Encyclopedias to record the information, if, they could even work it out, which they admit they cannot. Sir Isaac Newton is famous for his mechanical working model of the universe that when an atheist friend saw the model himself would not believe Newton when asked who made it and Newton replied "no one, it just appeared". Yet even today, mankind still rejects the majesty of God in preference to things that are neither logical nor believable. All of these suggestions as an alternative to God I would suggest or, rather insist, give the Holiest Almighty God the greatest insult we could ever imagine.

So, how do we reconcile this dilemma that continues to push people towards their eternal destruction if they refuse to accept Christ as their Savior and of the Almighty?

HOLY SCRIPTURE

In Chapter 11 we quoted many scriptures to support our defense of the Bible. It is incumbent upon us to continue that thought and consult additional scriptures in this chapter to bring this subject to a satisfactory conclusion.

For those who accept His word as true and divine we can rest in the assurance of our hope through Jesus Christ. For those who do not, I would suggest they be thankful that God, despite their outright rebellion, has given them a choice. Oh, I know they don't believe that. But for those who refuse to accept God, it is of no consequence to either a believer or myself, for we have faithfully discharged the commandment and duty, as one of Christ's disciples, in declaring Him to those who still reject Him or do not wish to know Him. Jesus never promised us that we would win everyone over to Him. In fact, Jesus gave the command in Matthew 10:12-15 saying, ***"When you knock on a door, be courteous in your greeting. If they welcome you, be gentle in your conversation. If they don't welcome you, quietly withdraw. Don't make a scene. Shrug your shoulders and be on your way. You can be sure that on Judgment Day they'll be mighty sorry—but it's no concern of yours now"*** *(MSG)*.

We read in Chapter 11 the scripture in Revelation 19:9 which said ***"These are true sayings of God"***. Put another way. ***"These are true words of God"***. This we saw was corroborated by the Apostle Peter in 2 Peter 1:20-21.

To illustrate further how God has used man to write and/or speak His words we can look to the example of Moses and Aaron.

We read in the book of Exodus after God has instructed Moses to be His spokesman that Moses was fearful and requested that God choose someone else. He asked this because, as the Bible tells us, ***"he*** *was slow of speech and not eloquent with words"* *(Exodus 4:10).* He pleaded with God to choose another and we read the account of God's decision in Exodus 4:14-16, *"Then the Lord's anger burned against Moses and he said, "What about your brother, Aaron the Levite? I know he can speak well. He is already on his way to meet you, and he will be glad to see you. You shall speak to him and put words in his mouth; I will help both of you speak and will teach you what to do. He will speak to the people for you, and it will be as if he were your mouth and as if you were God to him" (NIV).* Here we clearly see the scripture explaining that God would speak first to Moses and then Moses would utter the words to Aaron. When Moses spoke the words to Aaron it was as if God Himself were talking directly through him.

We then see in Exodus 7:1-2 another example how God was to communicate, *"Then the Lord said to Moses, "See, I make you as God to Pharaoh, and your brother Aaron shall be your prophet. You shall speak all that I command you, and your brother Aaron shall speak to Pharaoh" (NASB).* Notice the point here that God was saying that the words he was to say to Pharaoh via Aaron was as if God Himself was doing the talking. He also tells Moses that Aaron will be his [Moses'] prophet.

One of the many terms for prophet is defined as:

An effective or leading spokesman for a cause, doctrine, or group' (Merriam-Webster).

If we bring this example to its logical conclusion, God was appointing Moses as His messenger and in turn, for Aaron [Moses' spokesman] to tell Pharaoh what God had commanded.

Even though Moses claimed he could not speak well, God did not allow this to be a stumbling block for Himself to speak through Moses and Aaron.

There are numerous examples of scripture we can read that speak of God putting His word into the mouth(s) of those He chose to deliver His word. (See Exodus 24:3-4,8; Deuteronomy 18:18-22; 2 Samuel 23:2; Isaiah 51:16, 59:21; Jeremiah 1:4-9, 30:1-4, 36:1-4; Ezekiel 3:4; Zechariah 7:12; Matthew 10:19-20).

Paul wrote in 1 Corinthians 2:4-5, *"And my speech and my preaching were not with persuasive words of human wisdom, but in demonstration of the Spirit and of power, that your faith should not be in the wisdom of men but in the power of God" (NKJV).*

This scripture is a powerful message in that Paul was acknowledging that his speech and his words were not from his own wisdom, but by the power of the Holy Spirit. In order for that verse to be true, Paul's word had to be from the Holy Spirit or he was lying.

We are compelled as true Christians to not just believe the Bible is the word of God, but to categorically and undeniably believe every single word in the Bible is what God is saying.

That does not mean however that there is no human element within the words in scripture. That would be like saying I have not written this book you are reading now. But just like the writing of this book, God allowed the writers of the Bible to use human expression, their language and vocabulary.

To illustrate this point let us read Luke 1:1-4, *"Since [as is well known] many have undertaken to put in order and draw up a [thorough] narrative of the surely established deeds which have been accomplished and fulfilled in and among us, Exactly as they were handed down to us by those who from the [official] beginning [of Jesus' ministry] were eyewitnesses and ministers of the Word [that is, of the doctrine concerning the attainment through Christ of salvation in the kingdom of God], It seemed good and desirable to me, [and so I have determined] also after having searched out diligently and followed all things closely and traced accurately the course from the highest to the minutest detail from the very first, to write an orderly account for you, most excellent Theophilus, [My purpose is] that you may know the full truth and understand with certainty and security against error the accounts (histories) and doctrines of the faith of which you have been informed and in which you have been orally instructed" (AMP).* Here Luke was explaining the accuracy of events that he had written down and reported to Theophilus. We see here that separate from inspiration, God allowed Luke all of the nuances of vocabulary and speech, as well as documented historical evidence, to show that the scriptures were accurate. Consider this for a moment, had Luke not been allowed to write the way he did then that would apply to the other three gospel accounts. Had that been the case then the books of Matthew, Mark, Luke and John would have had to have read exactly the same. In 1 Corinthians 15:1-8 we read, *"Now, brothers and sisters, I want to remind you of the gospel I preached to you, which you received and on which you have taken your stand. By this gospel you are saved, if you hold firmly to the word I preached to you. Otherwise, you have believed in vain. For what I received I passed on to you as of first importance: that Christ died for our sins according to the Scriptures, that he was buried, that he was raised on the third day according to the Scriptures, and that he appeared to Cephas, and then to the Twelve. After that, he appeared to more than five hundred of the brothers and sisters at the same time, most of whom are still living, though some have fallen asleep. Then he appeared to James, then to all the apostles, and last of all he appeared to me also, as to one abnormally born" (NET).* Here Paul was detailing the events of Jesus appearing to over 500 people. Paul was not just confirming the accuracy of scripture but he was backing the scripture up by citing actual first hand experiences of the events which included his own.

The Psalmist writes in Psalm 19:7-9, *"The law of the Lord is perfect, reviving the soul; the testimony of the Lord is sure, making wise the simple; the precepts of the Lord are right, rejoicing the heart; the commandment of the Lord is pure, enlightening the eyes; the fear of the Lord is clean, enduring forever; the rules of the Lord are true, and righteous altogether" (ESV).*

See how this scripture is paraphrased in the Message Bible.

"The revelation of God is whole and pulls our lives together. The signposts of God are clear and point out the right road. The life-maps of God are right, showing the way to joy. The directions of God are plain and easy on the eyes. God's reputation is twenty-four-carat gold, with a lifetime guarantee. The decisions of God are accurate down to the nth degree" (MSG).

Psalm 33:4 says *"For the word of the Lord is right and true; he is faithful in all he does"* (NIV).

Similarly, Psalms 119:160 proclaims *"All your words are true; all your righteous laws are eternal"* (NIV).

John glorifies God's word in John 17:17 saying, *"Sanctify them in the truth; Your word is truth"* (NASB).

Paul's words ring true in Romans 3:2-5, *"First, there's the matter of being put in charge of writing down and caring for God's revelation, these Holy Scriptures. So, what if, in the course of doing that, some of those Jews abandoned their post? God didn't abandon them. Do you think their faithlessness cancels out his faithfulness? Not on your life! Depend on it: God keeps his word even when the whole world is lying through its teeth. Scripture says the same: Your words stand fast and true; Rejection doesn't faze you"* (MSG). Paul explains that even if the Jews abandoned their task of faithfully writing down the scriptures it would make no difference. While man is unfaithful, God is always faithful and carries out His word. As Paul states, we can depend on it!

Paul goes on to tell us that God cannot lie in Titus 1:1-3, *"Paul, a bondservant of God and an apostle of Jesus Christ, according to the faith of God's elect and the acknowledgment of the truth which accords with godliness, in hope of eternal life which God, who cannot lie, promised before time began, but has in due time manifested His word through preaching, which was committed to me according to the commandment of God our Savior"* (NKJV).

Paul eloquently puts God's thoughts before us in Hebrews 6:16-18 saying, *"Because God wanted to make the unchanging nature of his purpose very clear to the heirs of what was promised, he confirmed it with an oath. God did this so that, by two unchangeable things in which it is impossible for God to lie, we who have fled to take hold of the hope set before us may be greatly encouraged" (NIV).* Here we see two points of particular note. God cannot lie and He gives us His oath of His unchanging nature. Amen!

The conclusion we are faced with, with such overwhelming evidence of God being the author of the Bible, is that we can be assured the Bible is truly the word of God. Anything less, then a person is saying the Bible errs. If that is so, then the person is faced with rejecting the Bible as the written word of God and they are saying God is fallible.

By historically recording and copying the sacred text we cannot argue that there have been those who have attempted to alter God's holy written word. But every time, they have been found out and the error corrected. Psalm 33:8-15 says, *"Let the whole earth fear the Lord! Let all who live in the world stand in awe of him! For he spoke, and it came into existence, he issued the decree, and it stood firm. The Lord frustrates the decisions of the nations; he nullifies the plans of the peoples. The Lord's decisions stand forever; his plans abide throughout the ages. How blessed is the nation whose God is the Lord, the people whom he has chosen to be his special possession. The Lord watches from heaven; he sees all people. From the place where he lives he looks carefully at all the earth's inhabitants. He is the one who forms every human heart, and takes note of all their actions" (NET).* Let us never be fooled. Man cannot fool God and those who try will reap what they sow.

The Bible clearly insists its words are from God. To believe that, a person has to accept the writers did not write down anything that was incorrect. In fact they could not, otherwise God's word would be fallible.

Psalm 147:4-5 tells us God, ***"determines the number of the stars and calls them each by name. Great is our Lord and mighty in power; his understanding has no limit" (NIV).***

We cannot even imagine in our tiny human minds how great God is. His Glory alone could instantly vaporize us. His understanding, not ours, has no limit. And man has the audacity to say that God didn't inspire the writers of the Bible?

Look what the book of Job tells us of God in Job 37:16. The writer asks, ***"Do you know how the clouds are balanced [and poised in the heavens], the wonderful works of Him who is perfect in knowledge?" (AMP).*** God's ways are higher than our ways, and His thoughts are higher than our thoughts. We cannot come close to the almightiness of God. Yet sinful man, who refuse to know Him, think they know better. It would be almost laughable if the reality were not tragic.

We could go on and on with many more scriptures proving the perfection of God, the limitless knowledge and understanding He has.

What we truly have to consider is this: if we say to ourselves that we know what the Bible teaches but we don't believe this part, or that verse, then we are walking on very dangerous ground. Acting or believing in this manner opens the door for more thoughts of questioning the Bible. Let's remind ourselves, that who questioned God's sovereignty in the first place is recorded in the Bible for our benefit and warning – Satan.

Other points to consider is the Bible writers did not take the middle ground. Their choices or decisions had to be black or white, right or wrong, good or evil.

Additional to this is the fact that many of the prophets and even their companions were willing to die for what they believed or preached. Although we do not have the full accounts, based some on historical writings and the scriptures it is generally understood eleven out of the twelve Apostles were martyred for their allegiance to Christ. I'm sure we can recall accounts in history of people dying for a cause. But if someone wrote a Bible book of their own volition without any basis of truth or revelation I seriously doubt they would be prepared to die [in some cases horrifically] for such. Many Christians in the Roman era were torn to pieces by wild beasts in the arena. Others were sawn in two. When we read of the persecutions of Christians, which may I remind you are recorded, not just in the Bible but in a plethora of historical writings, then we are forced to conclude that such factual events occurred. How absurd would it be to suggest those who were willing to die would make up such stories.

Jesus said in John 5:44-47, *"How is it possible for you to believe [how can you learn to believe], you who [are content to seek and] receive praise and honor and glory from one another, and yet do not seek the praise and honor and glory which come from Him Who alone is God? Put out of your minds the thought and do not suppose [as some of you are supposing] that I will accuse you before the Father. There is one who accuses you—it is Moses, the very one on whom you have built your hopes [in whom you trust]. For if you believed and relied on Moses, you would believe and rely on Me, for he wrote about*

Me [personally]. But if you do not believe and trust his writings, how then will you believe and trust My teachings? [How shall you cleave to and rely on My words?]" (AMP).

One thing that amazes me in scripture and personally gives testimony to what Jesus did, is the scripture found in John 20:30-31. It reads, *"And truly Jesus did many other signs in the presence of His disciples, which are not written in this book; but these are written that you may believe that Jesus is the Christ, the Son of God, and that believing you may have life in His name" (NKJV).*
If you haven't captured the thought of this scripture and its meaning fully, re-read it. Read other Bible translations. The Amplified Bible gives a nice paraphrase description. What John is telling us here is that Jesus performed many more things [such as signs, parables, miracles etc.] that are not even contained in the Bible, but the ones that are in God's word stand as a witness to the truth. The Bible also says that the things that are not recorded, had they been, could not have been contained in enough books to write all the information down.
Sadly, for some, if the Bible did contain much more, even if it were four times the thickness that we have today, some would still not believe.
Jesus warned us in Luke 10:16, *"Whoever listens to you listens to me; whoever rejects you rejects me; but whoever rejects me rejects him who sent me" (NIV).*
Paul said in Galatians 1:8-9, *"But even if we or an angel from heaven should preach a gospel other than the one we preached to you, let them be under God's curse! As we have already said, so now I say again:*

If anybody is preaching to you a gospel other than what you accepted, let them be under God's curse!" *(NIV).* Jesus clearly and irrefutable warns anyone that if they believe what a man or angel has said or written they would be cursed along with the man or angel doing the writing. Jesus states unequivocally here that the word of God contained in the Bible is the written word of God and no one else.

1 Thessalonians 4:8 says,*"Therefore whoever disregards this, disregards not man but God, who gives his Holy Spirit to you" (ESV).*

So, what does God think?

I repeat what I said at the beginning of this chapter that neither you nor I can know what God thinks for His thoughts are higher than our thoughts.

But I do know this, and would suggest that a careful study of the scriptures will convince you too. That God is Supreme. His plan was set from the beginning of time and His purpose to redeem mankind was fulfilled in the sacrifice of His dear son Jesus Christ. That through the Holy Spirit, the Great Helper, who Jesus said He would send, provides the person the opportunity to be:

Born Again by the Holy Spirit
Filled with the Holy Spirit
Trains us how to be led by the Holy Spirit
And ultimately forms us with the
qualities of the Holy Spirit.

**That my friend, God does not think
He Knows.**

"God's Word is as good as He is. There is an old saying that a man is as good as his word. Well, God is as good as His Word. His character is behind what He has said."

J. Vernon McGee (1904-1988)

CHAPTER 13

Conclusions

When all is said and done, what are we to conclude with everything we have read? Certainly we can take comfort that there is a significant amount of proof that the Bible has been reliably passed down from the time God ordained and inspired it, to that which we have in our present form today.

We are always going to have those who disagree and sadly, some of the dissenting voices may in fact be those who profess and carry the name Christian, albeit in name only.

I reiterate what I said earlier in the book. How can a Christian call another translation that has been studiously translated by dozens of scholars and theologians, who apply the same degree of responsibility of ensuring the accuracy of the sacred text, drivel? It is beyond my comprehension of thought that one professing to follow and be a representative of Christ would pick up the word of God and say such a thing. To say it is anything but the word of God a person can only be interested in division rather than unity.

I said in my introduction that I am not, nor do I profess to be, a learned theologian of many years standing but, like John Bunyan, I do know the scriptures. I believe and declare God's word is my text book, my exam paper, and my answer page. What God breathed into the Scriptures is what God says as if we were face to face with Him.

I do not know to this day if the person who called God's word drivel is a member of the 'King James Movement' nor is it of any relevance. I could perhaps even thank him in some strange way. For although this book became far more than his comment, it did launch me on this journey and I am more blessed because of it. By default, I would suggest if this person is a member of such a group then he is following man, not God. Through this book we have shown that the King James was not the most accurate version in terms of translation and there were outside influences right at the end with the Bishop of Canterbury attempting to insist on fourteen new writings to be included. We showed that at least one of them was entered and we cannot be sure if several more were added or not. But the entry that did make it proves beyond any measure of doubt that it was contrary to Scripture and was an attempt to justify the use of vestal garments and the like. This was no better than what the Catholic Church also did during the time it attempted to seal shut the Scriptures and embark on a program to corrupt the Bible. Erasmus himself said that the Vulgate was so corrupted it could not be confirmed what was true and what was a lie. For his well-meaning attempt of cleaning up the wrongdoing, he was ostracized by the Catholic Church, despite ironically dedicating his translation to the Pope.

Nevertheless, the word of God could not and was not going to be muffled by men intent with their own position and heresy. Little did these men, who claimed to worship God but proved otherwise by their debauchery, know that they were and are identified in scripture.

I repeat Paul's words to the Galatians in Galatians 1:8-9 saying, ***"But even if we or an angel from heaven should preach to you a gospel contrary to and different from that which we preached to you, let him be accursed (anathema, devoted to destruction, doomed to eternal punishment)! As we said before, so I now say again: If anyone is preaching to you a gospel different from or contrary to that which you received [from us], let him be accursed (anathema, devoted to destruction, doomed to eternal punishment)!" (AMP).***

When I reflect on this verse, not only do I see the clear warning in these scriptures, but I find it irreprehensible that men claiming to serve God knew in complete and full knowledge that they were acting against God's word. There is much discussion that over history during the middle to late ages the Catholic Church was responsible for 50 million people being put to death for speaking against the church. If that is the case this testifies to their wrongdoing.

I am careful to note, other church leaders, many of whom belonged to the Protestant Reformation, also acted in such erroneous ways. Their actions too will be judged by God. I am also careful to point out that the arguments for and against this figure argue not that people were put to death, but the colossal number. The majority of the arguments are related to pointing blame on the deaths from wars and disease for example in an attempt to reduce the figures. The several points of reference in scholars who wrote various calculations did not argue that deaths occurred, only the total number. Even if we were to say 90% of the figure was wrong we would still have a figure of 5 million. History can prove more deaths than this number in the name of religion. But the point here is if one death occurred because of religious falsehood it was one too many. This in all actuality should not shock or deter us. Jesus said in Matthew 5:11-12, *""Blessed are you when people insult you and persecute you, and falsely say all kinds of evil against you because of Me. Rejoice and be glad, for your reward in heaven is great; for in the same way they persecuted the prophets who were before you" (NASB)*.

Jesus further declared in Matthew 24:9 saying, *"Then they will hand you over to suffer affliction and tribulation and put you to death, and you will be hated by all nations for My name's sake" (NASB)*.

This book was written to defend the reasons for translation into the English language. Now that we have the Bible in so many languages, in so many countries, we could perhaps believe everything is now just as it should be.

But is it?

Could we as Christians who reside in the Western Hemisphere actually be complacent and not even know it? Many would answer yes. But in what way?

The battle facing Christians now in many parts of the world isn't having a Bible written in their language. The real battle now is actually being allowed to own one, and to preach the good news of Christ's Kingdom. What is more, many of our fellow Christian brothers and sisters cannot meet freely and when they do meet in secret they exchange single sheets of paper. Those single sheets of paper are single sheets of the Bible! At the time of writing there has been an upsurge in Christians in India and Pakistan as well as many Arab nations being attacked for their faith. Churches have been destroyed or set on fire. Many have paid the ultimate price by giving up their lives in obedience to God.

A recent report noted that approximately 200 million Christians in at least 60 countries are denied their fundamental human rights solely on the basis of their faith.

Wars, battles, 'political' murders and terrorism have all been conducted in the name of religion. We have only to look at our Lord Jesus Christ who was Himself the victim to such false men of God. We can cry, "Many were acting in faith that they were right in what they did in the name of God or religion". That is a person's right if they wish to take that position. But factual evidence of the scriptures and the commands given by God prove beyond doubt that such events were orchestrated by man not God.

What is important is this. Through new translations we have benefited from any errors or erroneous statements made by man in earlier times being identified and corrected. Sinful man, or more correctly, Satan [through such men] will attempt to infiltrate and alter God's word. But the very nature of seeing new translations shows, in part, that God will not stand idly by without such wrongs being corrected.

God's word is the blueprint he provided for mankind to both see and grasp the opportunity of accepting the free gift of Grace provided by His son Jesus Christ. The blueprint drawn or written for an important structure is never altered. Therefore God will ensure no one will meddle with His word.

From the first book of the Bible to the last one, God lays out His divine plan.

It never ceases to amaze me that whatever item of substance we purchase, we have an instruction booklet - an 'IFU' [instructions for use] manual. Much of what we use we could not operate unless we had an 'IFU'.

God's Holy written word, The Bible, is God's 'IFU' for you and me. It's our manual of life. When we need direction, He provides it. When we're broken, He gives comfort. When we don't know which way to turn, He leads a path for us. The Psalmist declared in Psalm 119:105, **"Your word is a lamp to my feet and a light to my path" (NASB).**

When I mentioned the example of an item we have, including an IFU, all of these items are purchased.

God isn't asking anything for His IFU in order for us to get His instructions. In fact He tells us if we accept His word then His IFU is His free gift to us.

I hope by reading this book you have a renewed confidence that the Bible is the irrefutable word of God. If you're learning or believing this fact for the very first time I encourage you to spend each day reading the scriptures. Bask in the Glory of God's presence by immersing yourself in His instructions. In Psalm 139:7-12 we read, **"Is there any place I can go to avoid your Spirit, to be out of your sight? If I climb to the sky, you're there! If I go underground, you're there! If I flew on morning's wings to the far western horizon, you'd find me in a minute — you're already there waiting! Then I said to myself, "Oh, he even sees me in the dark! At night I'm immersed in the light!" It's a fact: darkness isn't dark to you; night and day, darkness and light, they're all the same to you.**

The Almighty God is with you wherever you are. He is Omnipotent [All-Powerful], Omniscient [All-Knowing], Omnipresent [All-Present / All-Seeing]. Proverbs 3:5-6 tells us, **"Trust in the Lord with all your heart, and do not lean on your own understanding. In all your** *ways acknowledge him, and he will make straight your paths" (ESV).*

In conclusion, God does not need anyone to defend what He declares for by the previous scriptures we see He is all-powerful. He knows everything. He sees everything.

Rather, what God desires is our acceptance of Him. He could have easily decided to have forgotten this world we live on and created a new one, somewhere else in the far flung galaxy. When I think of this I'm reminded that man has stubbornly refused to accept God as the Supreme Being of the Universe. When an ant scurrying across a kitchen table to reach a grain of sugar is crushed in an instant by a single finger, God could have eradicated the human race in an instant. With how man in general has treated God, I for one would not, could not, have blamed Him, if He had chosen to have done so.

But He tells us He is a God of love. He has repaired the position we all faced of forever being cut off from a relationship with Him. He did this by offering His son as a sacrifice for our sins. Why?

So we could be given the free gift of Grace and dwell with Him forever in a relationship that no one born to this home we call earth has ever experienced. He gave us His instructions, His words, His IFU of what we need to do in order to have that relationship with Him.

**He gave us HIS infallible word
THE HOLY BIBLE**

A Simple Prayer

Jesus said, "I am the way, the truth and the life. No one gets to the Father but by me" (John 14:6).

If you have never asked Jesus to be your Savior, you can do this right now by praying the following prayer.

Father God, I come to You now, in Jesus' Name, Jesus who loves me, and gave Himself for me. Lord, I love You, and I give myself to You. I ask You right now, come into my heart, come into my life, be my Savior and be my Lord. And by the blood of Jesus, that was shed for me, forgive me right now of every sin, cleanse me from all unrighteousness, make me brand new. And now, fill me with Your peace, with Your joy, with the Holy Spirit, and with the assurance that You'll never leave me, and You'll never forsake me.

And I thank You now in, Jesus' Name. Amen.

Whether you are making this decision for the first time, or recommitting, get into a Bible based church to fulfill and help you on your spiritual journey.

Bibliography

Chapter 1
1. English Historical Review (1904) XIX (LXXIII): 98-121
2. Donald J. Wiseman, "Archaeological Confirmation of the Old Testament," Carl F.H. Henry, ed., Revelation and the Bible. Contemporary Evangelical Thought. Grand Rapids: Baker, 1958 / London: The Tyndale Press, 1959. pp.301-316
3. See   http://www.earlychristianwritings.com/ index.html

Chapter 2
1. VanderKam, James C. & Flint, Peter (2002). The Meaning of the Dead Sea Scrolls. New York: HarperSanFrancisco. p. 32.

Chapter 3
1. Scrivener, Frederick Henry Ambrose (1861). A Plain Introduction to the Criticism of the New Testament 1 (1 ed.). Cambridge: Deighton, Bell, & Co. p. 95.
2. Scrivener, Frederick Henry Ambrose (1875). Six Lectures on the Text of the New Testament and the Ancient Manuscripts. Cambridge. p. 26.

3. T.L. Montefiore, Catechesis Evangelica; bring Questions and Answers based on the "Textus Receptus", (London, 1862), p. 272.

Chapter 4
1. [Adversus Haereses] Irenaeus, Against Heresies Book 5 Chapter 33.4
2. [Adversus Haereses] Irenaeus, Against Heresies Book III Chapter 3.4
3. Jerome, Preface to the Gospels, Translated by Kevin P. Edgecomb, 27 July 1999, Berkeley, California.
4. Jerome's Commentary on Isaiah (Nn. 1.2: CCL 73, 1-3)
5. (Innocent III (1855), Vol. 216).
6. De Hæretico Comburendo (1401) Statutes of the Realm, 2:12S-28: 2 Henry IV.
7. Hus the Heretic by Poggius The Papist, Paul Tice, Page 112.

Chapter 5
1. Encylopaedia Britannica 1972, viii, page 668
2. Life and Letters of Erasmus: Lectures Delivered at Oxford 1893-4, Page 359. By James Anthony Froude.
3. http://www.theopedia.com/95 Theses
4. John Foxe, Actes and Monuments (1570), VIII. 1229.
5. http://en.wikipedia.org/wiki/Edmund_Bonner

Chapter 6
1. Durant, Story of Civilization, 2.
2. Institutes of the Christian Religion by John Calvin.
3. Reid 1974, p. 283; Ridley 1968, p. 518.
4. MacGregor 1957, p. 226.

Chapter 7
1. Historic Origin, p. 78 by Edwin Bissell

Chapter 8
1. The Greatest English Classic by Cleland Boyd McAfee, Page 41.

Chapter 9
1. Journals of Congress for September 1782, page 469.
2. In God We Trust: George Washington and the Spiritual Destiny of the United States of America, Page 196, By Michael A. Shea.
3. Early Bibles of America: Being a Descriptive Account of Bibles Published in the United States, Mexico and Canada by Rev. John Wright. D. D., Third Edition, Revised and Enlarged Thomas Whittaker, 1894 Page 95.
4. The Unitarian Review and Religious Magazine, Volume 5 edited by Charles Lowe, Henry Wilder Foote, James De Normandie, John Hopkins Morison, Henry H. Barber, January 1 1876, Publisher Leonard C. Bowles. A Woman's Translation of the Bible Editors' Note-Book Page 322-4
5. The Woman's Bible – January 1, 1895, Page 150.

About the Author
Martin Roberts

 From around the age of five, Martin Roberts was exposed to religion and over the next twenty years became acquainted with the word of God. At the age of thirteen he was baptized in recognition of accepting Jesus Christ as his Savior.

In 1982 an experience he had with the denomination he was involved with caused him to question all that he had believed.

Instead of seeking God, he led a life for the next twenty years away from God and this led to his life unraveling to a point where he finally questioned what he was doing with it. For more than three decades he had risen in the ranks of his chosen career in medical sales, but still felt an emptiness in his life.

In 2009 he experienced a life changing event that culminated in him losing the sight of his right eye.

After questioning what was missing in his life, he realized it was God. From that point on he and his wife Deborah embarked on their search for a place of worship.

It was at Meadowbrook Church where Martin experienced his "light bulb" moment of finally following his Lord and Savior Jesus Christ. He firmly declares that God's promise is true, that He will never leave you, and He will never forsake you. He insists this is what God promises to those who are willing to openly receive God's Grace and turn around and repent.

His Ministry is now to write Christian related books of inspiration and devotion that he hopes will assist primarily readers who may not currently worship our Lord and Savior but are themselves lost as he once was. He also hopes fellow believers in Christ will benefit from these readings also.

His first book in this genre, Front and Center (ISBN 9781628390162) was published in August 2013 by Xulon Press. This was followed quickly with his second book, Defending the Bible against "Christians" published by Westbow Press (ISBN 978-1-4908-2408-6).

He continues to write and is currently writing his third book and has several more in the stages of development.

The youngest of four siblings, he lost both brothers within a year of one another (2008-9) and has an elder sister who still lives in England today.

After relocating to the United States in 2005, Martin was proud to become a US Citizen in September 2009.

He is a father of 5 children and has 3 grandchildren.

Martin is currently enrolled in the Berean Bible and Theology School with Global University.

He and Deborah attend Meadowbrook Church (www.mbcocala.com) in Ocala FL and live close by with their two Labradors Rose and Rusty.

Contact Details

For further information for this and other books by Martin Roberts please refer to the following Contact information below.

Website: MDRMinistries.com
Email: Deborah@MDRMinistries.com